Praise for Tony Aspler and his previous books ...

Witty and engaging – [*Wine Lover's Companion*] provides
most everything you need to know to get started in wine.
WINE & SPIRITS

Tony Aspler has compiled some of his most memorable wine experiences, places
and people in *Travels With My Corkscrew*. It's random, engaging and funny, setting
a mood that's all too rare in wine books.
THE GLOBE AND MAIL

Tony Aspler, who is one of the most respected and knowledgeable wine educators
around ... has authored *Aligoté to Zinfandel* ... It's all done in Aspler's easy, flow-
ing, crystal-clear style, geared to answering consumers' simplest questions in
straightforward, concise terms.
THE HAMILTON SPECTATOR

Only a handful of writers ... combine authoritative knowledge ... with an easy-
reading, fluid style. Tony Aspler is one of them. The *Wine Lover's Companion* makes
for delightful reading, and yet is an authentic wine reference. Well-done!"
Ed McCarthy, WINE FOR DUMMIES

Travels With My Corkscrew is an entertaining, anecdotal account of [Tony Aspler's]
"drinking life" from the early 1960s to the present ...
QUILL & QUIRE

[Tony Aspler's] *Guide to New World Wines* points you to the better producers, and
the front section has useful tips on food matching, cellaring and service.
It's good to see Canadian wineries getting their share of
coverage in this kind of internationally focused book.
THE GLOBE AND MAIL

Wine Lover's Companion is full of information that presupposes nothing, and
explains simply, without pretension."
THE GLOBE AND MAIL

Tony Aspler's *Aligoté to Zinfandel* is one of the best straight-forward, basic guides
to wine I've ever seen ... Practical, common sense, loads of information and a light
reassuring touch make this a very useful book.
TODAY'S SENIORS

THIRD EDITION
vintage
CANADA

**The
Complete
Reference
to Canadian
Wines**

TONY ASPLER

THIRD EDITION

vintage CANADA

The
Complete
Reference
to Canadian
Wines

McGraw-Hill
Ryerson

Toronto Montréal New York Burr Ridge Bangkok Bogotá Caracas
Lisbon London Madrid Mexico City Milan New Delhi Seoul
Singapore Sydney Taipei

McGraw-Hill
Ryerson Limited
A Subsidiary of The **McGraw·Hill** Companies

ISBN: 0-07-086043-2

1234567890 GTC 99
Printed and bound in Canada.

Canadian Cataloguing in Publication Data

Aspler, Tony, 1939 -
       Vintage Canada: the complete guide to Canadian wines

3rd ed.
Previous eds. published under title: Tony Aspler's vintage Canada
ISBN 0-07-086043-2

1. Wine industry – Canada – History. 2. Wineries – Canada. 3. Wine and wine making – Canada. I. Title. II. Title: Tony Aspler's vintage Canada.

TP559.C3A857   1999   338.4'76632'00971   C99-932104-8

Publisher: **Joan Homewood**
Editorial Co-ordinator: **Catherine Leek**
Production Co-ordinator: **Susanne Penny**
Editor: **Risa Vandersluis**
Interior Design: **Dianna Little**
Electronic Page Composition: **Pages Design Ltd.**
Cover Design: **Sharon Matthews**
Cover Photo Prop: **Wine Establishment Ltd.**

For Peter Gamble

TABLE OF CONTENTS

British Columbia *99*

Québec 169

Nova Scotia   209

Prince Edward Island   217

Newfoundland   218

Acknowledgements

Sharing is second nature to wine lovers. Show interest and a winemaker will lead you into the cellar and introduce you to all his "children". Over the past twenty-five years, I have been privileged to meet virtually all of Canada's winemakers and through their generosity I have tasted an unprecedented number of Canadian wines. I thank them for the opportunity and for their continuing dedication. And I would like to pay a special tribute here to all those people who are not winemakers but whose efforts behind the scenes to turn Canada into a globally recognized wine-producing country have made this book and its previous editions possible. I refer specifically to such institutions are The Wine Council of Ontario, The British Columbia Wine Institute, The Vintners Quality Alliance, The Ontario Grape Growers Marketing Board, The Association of British Columbia Grape Growers, The Grape Growers Association of Nova Scotia and the Association of Winemakers of Quebec.

I would also like to thank some special individuals who have made my research much easier and more pleasurable: Peter Gamble, director of Canada's VQA; Dave Gamble (no relation), editor of *B.C. Wine Trails* and *Ontario Wine Trails,* Thomas Bachelder (who did much of the research for me in Quebec); fellow wine writer Linda Bramble; and last, but not least, my wife Deborah Benoit, who assisted me in researching and collating all the new material for this edition.

INTRODUCTION

ighteen years ago I began writing a book called *Vintage Canada*. It was a history of winemaking in Canada, complete with profiles of the thirty-four wineries in five provinces that existed then (including Andrew Wolf of Alberta who makes wine from frozen California grapes).

While researching that book, I travelled across the country, visiting wineries, grape growers, liquor boards and government research stations, and I sampled over 600 products. Only a handful impressed me then as being of international standard and my critical assessments, I admit now, leaned towards the charitable — rather like the statements you make after sitting through a school concert in which your kids are performing. I really wanted Canadian wines to be good and I did everything I could in that book and through subsequent wine columns and magazine articles to encourage our wineries to make wines Canadians could take pride in.

Fifteen years later, I came back to the subject to document how the industry had changed. Pressures of the free trade agreement and GATT had radically altered the oenological landscape — geographically, financially and psychologically. Over that decade, major wineries with long histories disappeared while many others had sprung up to take their place. Not one of the 22 Ontario wineries that existed in 1947 operate today under the same label. The success of Canadian wines at home and in overseas competitions has been unprecedented, so much so that many growers have been encouraged to take the plunge and start up wineries of their own. There is no shortage of entrepreneurs, it seems, who believe that Canada is a wine-growing country. At the time of writing there are close to 150 wineries in seven provinces making wine from locally grown grapes or fruit (which is the focus of this book, not those operations in Quebec that bottle imported wines or other producers who bottle off-shore wines).

No excuses have to be made for Canadian wines today. They stand on their merits in the global wine world. They win prizes in international competitions. They are exported to Europe, the Far East and the United States. They appear on the wine lists of fine dining rooms — and, more importantly, Canadian consumers now realise that wines of quality are being produced in their own backyards.

Permit me to quote myself. Fifteen years ago, I wrote in the first edition of *Vintage Canada*:

> *Today, the Canadian wine industry is on the verge of producing products in the blended table wine range that can stand up against those from any wine-producing country in the world. Canada may never produce a Château Lafite, a Richebourg or a Hermitage, but a fine Chardonnay or Johannisberg Riesling is certainly within reach — as well as wines that have nothing to do with a European tradition, like Seyval Blanc, Vidal, Baco Noir and Maréchal Foch. Given our climate and the delicacy of the vines which produce the noble wines of Europe we can only hope that through clonal selection the wineries can find varieties sturdy enough to withstand winter cold and fungal diseases and, equally important, to find the right soil and microclimate in which to plant them.... It*

must not be forgotten that the Canadian wine industry — in terms of the produc-
tion of table wines — really only began after World War II. It took the French and
the Germans 2,000 years of trial and error to achieve their Lafites and
Bernkasteler Doktors. With modern technology and European know-how the
Californians, blessed with a better climate than Niagara or the Okanagan Valley,
took 200 years to produce their excellent Cabernets and Chardonnays. Today, the
Canadian wine industry is where California was in the late 1960s. We have
nowhere to go but up. As long as it remembers it is a wine industry and not a com-
modities market where the bottom line is all that counts, it can win the respect and
admiration of wine lovers across Canada.

Perhaps I was a little optimistic in my time frame. In fifteen years, we have not developed the way the Californians have. Our wineries have moved cautiously, even timidly. The second generation of small boutique operations (after Inniskillin and Château des Charmes in Ontario and the now defunct Claremont in B.C.) have become the engine, dragging the old established firms reluctantly behind them into a bright new dawn.

From tastings I have done, I am now convinced that we can make good red wines as well from the noble European varieties but only in great vintages such as 1991 1995, 1997 and 1998 or by seriously reducing yields in the vineyard in average to good years.

Ironically, what has awakened the consumers' interest in Canadian wines both at home and abroad is not Chardonnay or Riesling, Cabernet or Pinot Noir, but a luxury product as rare as it is expensive — Icewine. Icewine made in Ontario and B.C. from frozen grapes is the one wine that no winelover can resist, and we make it as well as the Germans who invented it. Overseas buyers are clamouring for our Icewine.

But the industry cannot sustain itself on Icewine alone. It needs a solid consumer base for its inexpensive table wines, white and red, as well as its single vineyard, vintage-dated bottlings. And, more importantly, our wineries cannot rely on an export market for their financial health. Canadians have to drink Canadian wine and have all wineries represented in all provinces. Right now we experience the ludicrous situation of having free trade with the United States but inter-provincial tariffs on our own wines. Surely, it is not beyond the wit of our politicians to allow us to have B.C. and Quebec wines in Ontario and vice versa.

And what of the future? The optimism of our young winemakers is infectious. Taste their wines blind against comparable bottles from Europe and you will be amazed by the result. There is no question now that Canada is a wine-growing country, even if the rest of the world has not woken up to that fact.

Then again, perhaps it is not a bad thing that Canadian wines have yet to be discovered. That means the best that we produce still remains within our borders for our own delectation and delight.

IN THE BEGINNING . . .

"A bunch of grapes is beautiful, static and innocent. It is merely a fruit. But when it is crushed it becomes an animal, for the crushed grapes become wine and wine has an animal life."

William Younger, *Gods, Men and Wine*

Winemaking is the world's second-oldest profession. According to a Persian legend, it was a woman who first discovered the delights of the fermented grape. This unnamed heroine was a concubine in the harem of King Jamsheed. Her royal master had a weakness for grapes and ordered bunches to be stored in jars so that he could enjoy them at his table all year round (presumably as raisins).

One of the jars began to ferment and the raisins lost their sweetness. The king supposed that the juice was poisonous and had the container labelled as such. One day, our unknown benefactress, who suffered from constant migraines, decided to put herself out of her misery. Finding the jar marked "poison," she drank deeply and immediately fell asleep. She awoke feeling on top of the world and returned to the jar to finish it off. Summoned before the king to explain her odd, euphoric behaviour, she confessed her misdemeanour. Intrigued, King Jamsheed ordered a quantity of wine to be made for the pleasure of his entire court. The fabled king is said to have lived for 700 years — the earliest testimonial we have to the salutary effects of the fermented grape.

William Younger, in *Gods, Men and Wine*, argues that winemaking may date back 10,000 years or more to the Magdalenian rock painters of southern France. "During the Upper Palaeolithic Age which marks the emergence of 'modern man,' some of the conditions existed for the deliberate making of wine, although they did not exist for the deliberate growing of grapes."

It is a pleasing thought that those primordial artists working in the bowels of the earth with their charcoal and vegetable dyes might have stepped back to admire their work by the light of the fire, with a bowl of wine in their hands.

Certainly they would have had grapes to eat, if not to ferment, since wild vines have existed since the Tertiary Period, which dates from a million to 70 million years ago. But the first vigneron, who deliberately cultivated grapes, was Noah. According to the Book of *Genesis* (IX, 20), "Noah began to be an husbandman, and he planted a vineyard; And he drank of the wine, and was drunken. He uncovered himself in his tent." Scholars have placed that first vineyard near Erivan in Armenia, though they have yet to agree on what "uncovered" meant.

The Old Testament is replete with references to vineyards, grapes and wine. Perhaps the best-known has provided the logo for the Israeli Tourist Board — Moses' spies returning from Canaan, the land of milk and honey: "... and they came upon the Brook of Eschol and cut down from thence a branch with one cluster of grapes and they bare it between two upon a staff" (*Numbers* XII, 23). Imagine! One bunch of grapes that required two men to carry it! Grape growers through the ages must share this same sense of hyperbole when it comes to describing the quality of their harvest!

The story of Moses' spies has its echo in the first documented discovery of grapes growing in Canada.

In the summer of 1001 A.D., Leif Ericsson set sail from Norway in a Viking longboat. According to the two sagas handed down from oral sources around 1250, Leif, a newly baptized Christian, was "a big strapping fellow, handsome to look at, thoughtful and temperate in all things." But this did not prevent him from provisioning his crew of 35 with beer and mead to help them survive the rigours of the journey.

The expedition sailed first to Baffin Island, which Leif named "The Country of Flat Stones," and then on to Labrador ("Land of Forests"). Historians still argue where the intrepid explorer made his final landfall on the American continent — the place he was to call "Vinland." As Samuel Eliot Morrison says in *The European Discovery of America*, "There are few local histories of seaport towns between Newfoundland and the Virginia capes which do not open with a chapter asserting 'Leif Ericsson was here!'" In the Latin translation of the sagas published by Thormodus Torfaeus at Copenhagen in 1705, the author was unequivocal in identifying Vinland as Newfoundland.

In 1960, Helga Ingstad, a Norwegian archaeologist, pinpointed Leif's landfall at L'Anse aux Meadows in northern Newfoundland. Morrison is convinced that this is the spot "where Leif Ericsson spent one winter and where members of his family founded a short-lived colony." The exact location is significant because of what the sagas tell us in the narrating of the "history" of the voyage to Vinland. According to a tale in the *Greenlanders Saga*, one member of the party — Leif's foster father, a German named Tyrker, emerged triumphantly from the woods "rolling his eyes and babbling, first in a German dialect none of his shipmates understood, then in Norse." The crew gathered round him and the excited old man broke the news: "I found grape vines and grapes!" Leif was incredulous and not a little dubious. "Certainly," replied the German, "I was born where there is no lack of either vines or grapes."

Leif ordered his men to harvest the grapes and load them aboard along with the cargo of timber they had cut. When spring allowed the expedition to sail home again, Leif had already named the unknown country Vinland — the land of the vines.

Adam of Bremen was the first chronicler of Leif Ericsson's original voyage, and around the year 1075 he reported to the King of Denmark that Leif "spoke of an island in that (northern) ocean, discovered by many which is called WINLAND, for the reason that vines yielding the best of wine grows there wild."

Grapes growing in northern Newfoundland? Grapes that produce "the best of wine"? Certainly, today, the finest European grapes as well as hybrids flourish in the Annapolis Valley above the Bay of Fundy and the Northumberland Strait in Nova Scotia. So perhaps there is a microclimate where the hardy wild grapes might have grown around L'Anse aux Meadows in Newfoundland.

Cynics have suggested that what Leif Ericsson actually found were blueberries, wild currants, gooseberries or, possibly, the mountain cranberry. Samuel Eliot Morrison dismisses such speculation: "If it be objected that Leif Ericsson, after whooping it up in the court of King Olaf (of Norway), must have known wine and would not have been put off by a poor substitute made from berries, one may reply that, just as his father Eric (the Red) put the 'Green' in Greenland to attract settlers, so Leif put the 'Vin' in Vinland. And with such success as to throw off all Vinland-seekers for centuries!"

But it was 500 years after Ericsson before we have more evidence of grapes and winemaking in eastern Canada. In 1535, when Jacques Cartier sailed down the St. Lawrence on his second voyage to New France, he anchored off "a great island." Here Cartier found masses of wild grape vines growing up the trees. He named it Ile de Bacchus, but on reflection — thinking that this might be seem too frivolous for his masters in Paris — renamed it Île d'Orléans after the duc d'Orléans, son of his monarch, Francis I.

From this point on, the history of the grape is closely bound with the history of Canada.

The Jesuit missionaries who followed in Cartier's footsteps brought sacramental wine with them, and when they ran out they tried their hands at winemaking using the native wild grape. They recorded that the grapes were plentiful but the wine they produced (probably from *Vitis riparia*) was obviously only tolerable enough to be sipped at Mass, not to be quaffed back to warm the hearts of the settlers during the long winters.

The Jesuits may have been able to supply their own sacramental needs, but their congregation required something a little more palatable. In 1648, a certain Jacques Boisdon in Quebec City applied to the Council of New France for a licence to open the first tavern. The Council agreed and even supplied Boisdon with eight barrels of French wine, free of charge, to help him start his business. But in true bureaucratic style, they set down stringent regulations. "To prevent any unseemliness, drunkenness, blasphemy or games of chance," the inn had to be located in a public square within sight of the church, allowing the priest to be a one-man Liquor Control Board.

But the Church fathers, far from frowning on the practice of winemaking, actively encouraged it. Father Jacques Bruyas wrote in a letter dated 1668: "If one were to take the trouble to plant some vines and trees, they would yield as well as they do in France ... and (properly pruned) the grapes would be as good as those of France" — a sentiment which would be echoed down the years to our own day by every grape grower who put a plant in the ground.

If the new settlers, accustomed to the wines of France, were less than enthusiastic about the possibility of winemaking from wild grapes, the indigenous peoples of Upper Canada were untroubled by such latent wine snobbery. Indian tribes, such as the Seneca, Tuscarora and Cayuga, are believed to have offered tributes of fermented grape juice to the gods who lived at the foot of Niagara Falls. The ceremony, during which the wine was poured into the churning waters to placate the gods, was known as the "Wischgimi." The bands travelled great distances to make their offering, and as Percy Rowe suggests in *The Wines of Canada*, "It is conceivable that the journey would have been a dusty one so that the Indians were sufficiently tempted to slake their throats with a portion of the 'gifts.'"

If wild grapes like *Vitis riparia* and *Vitis labrusca* flourished in eastern Canada, it would not be until the nineteenth century when committed amateurs tried to cultivate vines for the express purpose of producing wines fit to drink. The wild *labrusca* grapes with their small berries would have produced a wine of poor quality — harsh and acidic, with a decidedly "foxy" flavour.

Father Bruyas's suggestion of planting vines had already been tried by British colonists in Virginia and the Carolinas at the instigation of Lord Delaware who, in 1619, imported French cuttings along with French vignerons to oversee their planting. The vines they planted died, unfortunately, before a commercial wine industry based on French *vinifera* grapes could be established in the new colonies. But their presence among the native varieties was enough to create new strains. Through cross-pollination with wild grapes, the first North American hybrids were created.

THE EARLY YEARS

In the years to follow, the nascent Canadian wine industry in the east was to benefit from American grapes which flourished in the more conducive climate of the south. The poor performance of imported vines forced the early American winemakers to reevaluate the native root stock. As early as 1683, William Penn called for better viticultural practices to improve the quality of the vine in the hope that "the consequence will be as good wine as any European countries of the same latitude do yield."

Some ninety years later, during the American revolution, Governor John Penn's gardener, a certain John Alexander, discovered the first accidental hybrid growing by a river near Philadelphia. He had been experimenting unsuccessfully with European varieties, and some of them survived long enough to cross with nearby wild varieties. Alexander planted a cutting and happily it took root in Governor Penn's garden. The Alexander grape became popular around 1800 as the Cape, a name which suggested South African origins.

With the blessing of President Thomas Jefferson, who had vines growing in his garden in Virginia, the Alexander enjoyed a brief moment in the sun before it was eclipsed by two new hybrids — Isabella, introduced in 1816, and Catawba, introduced in 1823.

At the same time in Ontario, a retired German soldier, Corporal Johann Schiller (variously spelled Schuler, Sheler or Sheeler, according to one of his descendants, John Scheeler of Port Lambton, Ontario) was tending his *labrusca* vines on a 20-acre plot by the Credit River. He had built himself a house on North Dundas Street, Cooksville (now Mississauga) on land granted to him by the Crown on October 12, 1811 — Lots 9 and 17 Concession 1 (north of Dundas Street). Schiller had served with the 29th Regiment of Foot at Quebec in 1784. On his discharge from the British army, he lived in Montreal for eight years on a land grant of 400 acres there but eventually moved to Niagara where he reapplied for the same acreage in Ontario.

By 1811, Schiller, who had previous winemaking experience in the Rhine, was fermenting grapes he had grown from cuttings of wild vines and early American hybrids furnished by settlers from Pennsylvania. He made sufficient quantities to be able to service his own needs and sell to his neighbours. Johann Schiller is generally acknowledged to be the father of the Canadian wine industry.

We have no indication as to how long Schiller's winery lasted. He died five years to the day after he received his Ontario land grant. His sons, William and Michael, proceeded to sell Lot 17 in 1824, parcels of which were bought by Thomas Silverthorn who was later associated with the Canada Winegrowers Association. The Schiller property itself was bought in 1864 by Count Justin M. de Courtenay, who formed a company called the Vine Growers Association. He extended the original vineyards to 40 acres of Clinton and Isabella grapes, making his Clair House label the largest in Ontario.

De Courtenay was an aggressive evangelist in the cause of Canadian wine, harrying the government of the day with letters and pamphlets to proselytize its members in support of the infant industry.

The owner of Clair House had begun his wine-producing experiences in Quebec. He was convinced that European grapes could not only grow in Lower Canada, but could outperform their Burgundian cousins in terms of the wine they produced: "It will be easily perceived the importance attached in Burgundy to their wines," wrote de Courtenay, "and there is no reason why we should not produce better ones on the borders of the St. Lawrence."

To prove his point, de Courtenay sent some bottles to the premier of Lower Canada, L.V. Sicotta, on January 15, 1863, with a covering letter:

> I have now the honour to present you with the samples of wine furnished by the cultivated wild grape, and am persuaded that, making allowances for the green taste which it possesses in common with almost all new wines, you will consider it equal to ordinary Burgundy which it resembles not only in flavour but in its qualities and colour ... The fact that a good, sound wine can be produced in this country, I consider has been by me practically demonstrated.

The Honorable L.V. Sicotta was not won over by such confident huckstering, and passed the bottles over to a government consultant, a Mr. McDougall, who pronounced the wine sour.

But de Courtenay would not take this criticism of his wine lying down. He shot back a letter to Quebec City full of righteous indignation: "I deny the wine in question being sour, but admit it to be bitter in consequence of containing too much tannin." The age-old cry of the winemaker: "All it needs is bottle-age."

What Justin de Courtenay could not accomplish in Quebec he tried with more success in Ontario. He considered his Clair House of sufficient quality to be exhibited in Paris in celebration of Canada's nationhood in 1867. On July 8th, the *Toronto Leader* printed the following story:

> The French exposition has established the character of our Canadian wines. The jury on wines, which would naturally be composed of the best judges to be found in Europe, speak in very high terms of the wines sent from the Clair House Vineyards, Cooksville. They find in them a resemblance to the Beaujolais wine, which is known to be the best produced in France. They say of those wines that they resemble more the great French table wines than any other foreign wines they have examined, and that the fact of the wine being so solide as to bear the sea voyage, and the variations of heat and cold without losing anything of either its quality or limpidity, should be a question of great consideration even to our own producers.
>
> This authoritative opinion of the quality of Ontario wine will do more than anything else that could possibly occur, at present, to bring this wine into general use ... The time will come, we hope and verily believe, when grape-growing and winemaking will be one of the principal employments of our population; and when it does come, the cause of temperance will be advanced to a degree that could be reached by no other process.

De Courtenay had been vindicated. His red wine, at an alcoholic strength of 13 per cent, was the talk of Toronto. But the newspaper's predictions failed to come about. In 1878, no longer able to secure a grant from the Parliament of Upper Canada, de Courtenay was forced to close his winery.

Justin de Courtenay, the flamboyant count who dashed off letters of blistering irony to parliamentarians, quoting Pliny and Virgil, overshadowed the efforts of those stolid Ontario farmers of lesser education who laboured quietly in the background. For example, Porter Adams was shipping grapes to the Toronto market from the Queenston area in the same year that de Courtenay was shipping his wines to France. John Kilborn — as early as 1862 — won a prize of $3 at the Provincial Exhibition in Toronto for the "best bottles of wine made from the grape."

Kilborn owned 17 acres of land on Ontario Street in Beamsville. In 1860, he reported to *The Canadian Agriculturist* that his wine was fetching $1.75 a gallon locally "and probably would bring in more if we asked for it. At all events it is worth four times as much as the miserable stuff sold by our merchants under the name of wine."

Winemaking in the late nineteenth century was more of a basement hobby than a business. When it was not sold through the kitchen door, it would have been available at the local drugstore. Farm wineries, such as those owned by John Kilborn and W.W. Kitchen of Grimsby, were, however, large enough to advertise their products.

Kitchen's broadsheet declared that his wines were "in use by some Hundreds of Churches for sacramental services." In addition, "It is sold by most of the principal Chemists in Canada East and West."

The problem for those early winemakers, whether they made wine for their own consumption or for profit, was the alcohol strength. The native hybrids like Catawba and Isabella were low in fructose and high in acidity so sugar had to be added to the fermentation to bring up the alcohol level. The grapes would be pressed a second time after water or sugar syrup had been added to the skins to extract every last ounce of juice.

The first growers along that Niagara Peninsula, like Porter Adams, planted their vines basically to service the fresh fruit trade. One of the best table varieties, as well as an excellent taste in jams and jellies, was the Concord grape whose flavour is unmistakable to us today as the essence of virtually all grape-flavoured products. The grape was named after the Massachusetts town were it was propagated by a man who rejoiced in the splendid name of Ephraim Wales Bull.

As a boy growing up in New York's Hudson River Valley, Bull became interested in grape growing. In 1836, he moved to Concord to pursue his hobby more vigorously — and to make wine. In his quest for a grape that would survive the New England winter better than the Isabella, he planted the seeds of some wild Labrusca grapes. The one that succeeded best he named Concord in honour of the town where it was raised.

In 1854, Bull offered his Concord vines to nurseries at a hefty price of five dollars a vine, but the nurserymen managed to propagate the vine for themselves and Bull saw little remuneration for his gift to the North American wine industry. He died penniless in Concord's Home for the Aged in 1895. His tombstone bears the forlorn legend: "He sowed, but others reaped."

When the Concord grape was exhibited at the Massachusetts Horticultural Society, it was an instant winner. In his book *American Wines and How to Make Them*, Philip Wagner explains why: "It produces so cheaply and abundantly that it makes a dismal joke of all competition: it is virtually indifferent to climate, growing rankly in both hot and cold regions, and flourishes in practically any soil; it is immune to most of the vine diseases and thrives under neglect; it travels well and withstands storage moderately well; it does not winter kill."

The only problem is that Concord grapes make awful wine. As grape juice it can be enjoyable, or when its "foxy" taste is camouflaged as sherry or port, but as wine I'd rather drink the gum they used to stick on the label. Yet the Concord was to become the backbone of the Canadian wine industry up until the 1940s — and as the major constituent in the "Duck" range of pop wines it provided 90 per cent of the company profits until the late 1970s.[1]

Not only did the Americans send their grapes north, they also dispatched their entrepreneurs whose presence would give the youthful industry a nudge toward the twentieth century. In the 1860s, most of the operations in Ontario were small-volume businesses, a sideline for farmers who had crops other than grapes to harvest.

In 1866, "a company of gentlemen from Kentucky," according to a letter in the *Canadian Farmer*, "who have been in the grape business for 14 years, have purchased a farm on Pelee Island and planted 30 acres this spring, and intend to plant 20 acres next spring." Pelee Island — the most southerly part of Canada, on the same latitude as northern California — stands 12 miles to the north of Kelly's Island in Lake Erie. In 1860, Catawba grapes were successfully planted there to supply the wineries at Sandusky, Ohio, one of the oldest winemaking centres in the United States. (In 1893, Brights bought Catawba from Pelee Island to produce a sweet table wine.)

The southern gentlemen were D.J. Williams, Thomas Williams and Thaddeus Smith, who formed a company called Vin Villa to create the first commercial winery on Pelee Island. Before they had built a house on their land, they excavated a wine cellar, 40 feet by 60 feet and 12 feet deep, which showed that this was to be no bathtub operation.

But Vin Villa was not to be without competition. A few months after the Kentuckians acquired land on Pelee Island, two English brothers, Edward and John Wardoper, purchased fifteen acres and planted a rival vineyard. Today, the Pelee Island Vineyards boast the largest *vinifera* planting in Canada — Riesling, Gewürztraminer, Chardonnay and Pinot Noir — planted by Walter Strehn in 1980.

An enterprising grocer in Brantford named Major J.S. Hamilton bought the grapes as well as finished wine from the Pelee vineyards. Hamilton had opened his store in 1871 and in the same year was granted a royal charter to sell wine and liquor. Three years later he met Thaddeus Smith and was impressed by the yield of his vineyards (four to five tonnes per acre of Delaware and Catawba) and the quality of his wine. He asked Smith if he could sell Vin Villa for him in the eastern United States.

---

[1] Ten years after it started its grape-breeding program in 1913, the Horticultural Research Institute of Ontario at Vineland had given up using the Concord as a "parent." In 1942, the Institute stated in its report that the goal of the grape-breeding program was to produce hybrids that no longer had the *labrusca* taste characteristics and resembled more those of the European *viniferas*.

Hamilton also wanted to market these wines in Canada, and to do so he entered into an agreement with the Pelee Island growers to transfer the winemaking operation from the island to the city of Brantford.

The assets of J.S. Hamilton and Company Limited, which absorbed the Pelee Island Wine and Vineyard Company in 1909, would be sold in 1949 to London Winery, giving that company the longest pedigree in the venerable art of Canadian winemaking.

In the same decade that Major Hamilton was shipping casks of wine over from Pelee Island, some 2,000 miles away, the Oblate Fathers' tiny vineyard at their mission seven miles south of Kelowna in British Columbia's Okanagan Valley was reaching maturity. In British Columbia, as in Québec, it was the Church that first fostered and encouraged the cultivation of the grape for winemaking.

If Justin de Courtenay moved from Québec to Ontario to find more favourable microclimates in which to grow vines to produce better Burgundies than those of France, other English-speaking farmers remained to battle the winters. A certain Mr. Menzies of Pointe Claire, Québec, created a vineyard "on a larger scale than usual in the province" which he called the Beaconsfield Vineyard. Two years later, he was joined by a partner but the association was brief. After a few months, Mr. Menzies was forced to publish a pamphlet warning his clients that his former associate had set up a farm a mile from his own from which the rascal had been selling American wines under the name of the Beaconsfield Vineyard.

But the lustiest child in the nation's vinicultural nursery was Ontario. From the 1860s, vineyards flourished in the Beamsville-Vineland-Grimsby area. Grape growers experimented in their own backyards to find new varieties that were disease resistant and winter hardy. The process was long and difficult. It takes at least three years for a vine to produce a commercial crop, let alone the years it takes to develop a successful crossing. So when a new variety was introduced, the effect was rather like a coronation or the arrival of a royal baby.

In 1868, in Lockport, New York, two growers created what they were to call the Niagara grape by crossing the Concord with a relatively little-known variety called the Cassady. It was to be the white wine equivalent of the unkillable purple Concord. The two growers, mindful of what had happened to Ephraim Bull, sold their vines at $1.25 a piece with a written understanding that the purchaser would return all cuttings to them so the vines could not be pirated.

In 1882, the Niagara grape was introduced to Ontario and, like the Concord, it is still with us today.

By 1890, there were 41 commercial wineries across Canada, 35 of which were situated in Ontario. The great majority of these, fully two-thirds, were centred around Essex County, which in 1904 boasted 1,784 acres of vines. The pre-eminence of Essex as Canada's grape-growing centre was to last twenty years. By 1921, the grape vines had been torn out in favour of such cash crops as tobacco and soft fruit. A mere 50 acres remained, but this concentration was still greater than anywhere else in Canada.

In 1873, two years after Major James Hamilton had shaken the hand of the gentlemen from the South to confirm their business arrangement, George Barnes, a relative of grape-grower Porter Adams by marriage, started a winery in St. Catharines.

With the literalness of a German wine label, he embraced every function of the company in its name so there could be no mistaking its purpose: The Ontario Grape Growing and Wine Manufacturing Company, Limited. What it lacked in imagination it made up for in longevity because it operated until 1988 as Barnes Wines.

George Barnes's vines had been in the ground one year when Thomas Bright and his partner, F.A. Shirriff, opened a winery in Toronto. In naming it they must have subconsciously realized they would have to move closer to their grape supply. They called it The Niagara Falls Wine Company and move they did, 16 years later, in 1890, to the outskirts of the town. In 1911, they changed the name to T.G. Bright and Company.

Those years at the end of the nineteenth century showed a remarkable growth for Ontario, and for the grape-growing areas south and southwest of the province. At the turn of the century, there were some 5,000 acres under vine along the Niagara Peninsula.

However, two events were to check the new wine industry and to set it off on a path of incipient self-destruction: World War I and Prohibition.

PROHIBITION

n the early days of this century, a small Canadian wine industry resided in Ontario. And those companies that survived into the 1900s were targets for the growing number of drum-beating temperance societies in the province, particularly in the rural areas. Some farmers refused to sell their grapes to winemakers, and by 1892, the public outcry against alcoholic beverages had reached such a crescendo that even the idea of planting more vineyards in Niagara came under scrutiny.

When World War I broke out, the government's need for industrial alcohol to make explosives synchronized with the popular sentiment for prohibition. Once the Temperance Act had been passed, the distilleries could be converted to the production of industrial alcohol for the war effort.

On September 15, 1916, the government of Sir William F. Hearst, an active Methodist layman and dedicated temperance advocate, passed the legislation known as the Ontario Temperance Act. Under its statutes all bars, clubs and liquor shops would be closed for the duration of the war. No one could sell any intoxicating liquor unless authorized to do so by the province and no one could "have, keep, give, or consume liquor except in a private dwelling house."

In 1916 and 1917, all but one of the provinces went dry. Québec, which marches to a different drum in these matters, held out until 1919 and then proscribed the sale of liquor, but not wine or beer.

The Women's Christian Temperance Union of Ontario, the vanguard of the movement, had triumphed but political realities began to nibble away at their victory. Pressure from the strong grape growers' lobby caused the Conservative government to exempt native wines from the provisions of the act. Section 44 stated that wines made from Ontario-grown grapes could be produced by manufacturers who held permits from the Board of Licence Commissioners. This political sleight of hand was to elicit a raised eyebrow — if somewhat belated — from the editorial page of the *Toronto Telegram* (April 21, 1921): "There may be political reasons for protecting wine and banning beer. But there is no moral or social reason. There is no inherent vice in barley which does not also lodge in grapes."

When the Ontario Temperance Act became law, there were 10 wineries in operation in the provinces. While they were able to vinify legally during Prohibition, the government saw to it that consumers had a difficult time getting hold of their wine. Each winery was allowed one store outlet and that had to be located on its premises. Customers could only buy a five-gallon quantity or its equivalent in bottles — two cases. What an extraordinary piece of double-think by a government dedicated to the proposition that people must be denied alcoholic beverages!

Another bizarre anomaly of Prohibition in Canada was that while it might have been illegal to sell liquor, it was not against the law to manufacture it. Alcohol was readily available for "sacramental, industrial, artistic, mechanical, scientific and medicinal purposes." And it was the medical profession that was to become the barman of the nation. A doctor could prescribe alcohol to a patient if he felt that patient might benefit from such "medicine." Peter Newman writes of those days in *The*

Bronfman Dynasty: "As well as selling straight liquor through the drug stores to patients with doctors sympathetic enough to prescribe it, the booze was sold to processors who concocted a variety of mixtures for the drug trade, including a Dandy Bracer–Liver and Kidney Cure which, when analyzed, was found to contain a mixture of sugar, molasses, bluestone and 36 per cent pure alcohol, plus a spit of tobacco juice."

Stephen Leacock summed up the social situation with the observation that "to get a drink during Prohibition it is necessary to go to the drug store ... and lean up against the counter making a gurgling sigh like apoplexy. One often sees there apoplexy cases lined up four deep."

Nevertheless, during the 11 years of Prohibition in Ontario, the only alcoholic beverage that could be sold legally was wine. The natural consequence was to spark off a mad scramble by European immigrants who had some brush with winemaking in the Old Country to get in on the act, and even those native-born Ontarians who could not tell wine from vinegar jumped on the bandwagon. Wineries were started up in basements, at the back of grocery stores and in garages — and even in the converted pig shed of a Beamsville farm!

The Board of Liquor Commissioners handed out permits with heady abandon to placate the vociferous grape growers' lobby. Between 1917 and October 31, 1927, no fewer than 57 licences for new wineries were issued, in addition to the ten that were already established. The three major centres for these wineries were the Niagara Peninsula (at the source of the grapes); Toronto (as the largest urban population); and Windsor (to take advantage of the great thirst across the Detroit River).

But distance from the vineyards was of little consequence to those early wine producers. There were two successful wineries in the lakehead cities of Fort William and Port Arthur (Twin City Wine Company and Fort William Wine Co.), one in Kitchener (in the basement of Fred J. Kampmann's house), one in Belleville (John Tantardini who started in Guelph, eventually selling out to the Belleville Wine Company in 1926) and yet another in Sudbury (The Sudbury Wine Company). There were even two Toronto rabbis who made kosher wines: Rabbi M.H. Levy of Bathurst Street was granted a licence in 1921. His company was purchased in 1925 by Canada Wine Products Ltd., which in turn was swallowed by Jordan in 1938. The other was Rabbi Jacob Gordon, who manufactured Passover wine in the cellar of his home at 116 Beverly Street. In 1928, the rabbi's winery licence was purchased by the Oporto Wine Company on Danforth Avenue, which sold medicated wine. After a series of takeovers the rabbinical company — originally called the Concord Wine Co. Ltd. in 1923 — ended up as part of Château-Gai in 1978.

Only those companies that made a drinkable product survived this extraordinary era — companies like Brights who introduced the first bottling line in Canada, Jordan Wines (a company formed to take over Canadian Grape Products Ltd. in 1926), London Winery (which purchased a three-year-old licence from Giovanni Paproni in 1925) and the Turner Wine Company. This last enterprise dated back to 1885 when it was founded by a Brantford grocer, no doubt in competition with the enterprising Major J.S. Hamilton. They distributed a product known as "Turner's Tonic Bitters," which was heavy on alcohol and quinine.

As far as most winemakers were concerned there were no quality controls, no government interference and, in many cases, little of the basic knowledge of the craft. American equipment and cooperage, hastily bought by the newly formed companies, was calibrated in U.S. gallons as opposed to Imperial measurements, but this meant nothing to some unscrupulous manufacturers who were simply out to line their pockets at the expense of the public thirst. They squeezed their grapes — literally — till the pips squeaked and with added water they were getting as much as 660 gallons of wine from every tonne of grapes. (Today, the negotiated limit is 818 litres per tonne.)

Sugar was poured into the vats by the sackful during fermentation to bring up the alcohol level. If the colour wasn't right after so much dilution, there was always coal tar or vegetable dyes like cochineal to deepen it. Blocks of sulphur were pitched into the vats to kill bacteria, and one enterprising vintner even used aspirins to control his fermentation.

For all those who made wretched wine under licence, there were many countless others who did so without the bureaucratic blessing of a permissive government. Unlike moonshine whisky, homemade wine was legal and the hobbyist who had a few hundred gallons of wine could always plead that he had made it for the home consumption of his entire family rather than for selling through the back door. Few such cases ever came to court, and the government took a lenient view of new immigrants who wished to make their own wine, as evidenced when the LCBO was created in 1927. All home producers would require was a home winemaking licence, and they could produce up to 100 gallons for their own use. (Today no such permit is required.)

In spite of the abysmal quality of most wines available during the 11-year hiatus, the mere fact of Prohibition had focused the attentions of Canadians on their domestic wine industry, and Prohibition more than anything else turned Canadians into a nation of wine drinkers. During 1920-21, Canadians consumed 221,985 gallons of domestic wine. A decade later the figure was 2,208,807 gallons — for Ontario alone! And 80 per cent of it was a red port-style wine of maximum alcoholic strength made from the Concord grape.

After 11 years of social dislocation, Canada passed through the wilderness of Prohibition. Even those who were loudest in its support saw that Prohibition had failed. Sanity finally prevailed. It was seen by most conservative politicians as a victory for "British values" over "all the evils ... wished on Canada by agitators who took their ideals not from the Motherland but from that hotbed of political experiment, the American Middle West."

If the politicians could not stop the fermented juice of the forbidden fruit from finding its way down the throats of the people, at least they could regulate its use.

Eventually, province after province would adopt a form of government control over the sales and distribution of alcohol — a system which involved a state monopoly, based on the Scandinavian model, and more importantly, control over the quality of the product. The new system meant that each province would decide, individually, which wines of the world they would make available to their consumers and how much they would tax them for that privilege.

With the advent of government liquor stores, consumers now had a focus for their complaints if the wines they purchased were substandard — and they had a lot to complain about. During Prohibition, the mere idea of beating the regulations in acquiring wine made the drinker overlook its dubious quality. However, now it was legal and the government was held responsible for every bottle that tasted of vinegar, was black with sediment or contained such foreign bodies as spiders and flies. Some bottles never reached the consumer as they exploded on the liquor store shelves owing to a secondary fermentation — much to the consternation of employees, who felt as if they were working in a minefield. And the bottles themselves could be any shape. A.N. Knowles, vice-president of London Winery, recalls seeing the same label of his father's company on three or four different types of bottle. "Winery employees used to visit the junk yards," he said, "buy up boxes of old bottles, wash them out and fill them with wine. Bottles were hard to get in those days."

In Ontario, the government acted by bringing in a rudimentary quality control for the products it accepted for sale from the wineries. The new Liquor Control Board under Sir Henry Drayton, a former federal minister of finance, administered the new regulations which set a maximum of 250 gallons per tonne of grapes, limiting the amount of water that could be added to the wine. The new restrictions stressed cleanliness of operations above all and fixed the permissable level of volatile acid at four per cent, which was still enough to make a wine taste of vinegar. (Even this generous limit was beyond the capabilities of most basement vintners.) But the bureaucrats had to move cautiously since the Depression was looming and the vocal farmers' lobby was concerned about the dropping price of grapes. King Concord had fallen as low as 12 dollars a tonne.

In an effort to improve the quality of winemaking, the Board's chief analyst, Bert Bonham, suggested that the provincial Department of Health set up a winemaking school at the laboratory in the east block of Queen's Park. When the more marginal companies found their products were being refused for listing at the liquor stores, their winemakers flocked to attend. Many were new immigrants whose command of English was limited and they decided that winemaking in the New World was not for them. The courses lasted for two years, but they had the desired effect. The bathtub school of winemaking as a commercial proposition quietly died.

Encouraged by the government, viable companies such as Brights and Jordan began buying up the licences of these precarious operations lock, stock and barrel at prices as low as $5,000 to $10,000. Over the years, Brights acquired thirteen such licences, not for the wine which was generally sent to the distillers or for the equipment, but for the privilege of owning another retail store. The wineries still had their own single outlet and the government now allowed them to locate these stores away from the facility in the cities of their choice. Through this expedient, the government eventually reduced the number of Ontario wineries from 51 to eight.

The next problem was to rationalize the sale of tonic wines and patent medicines which were readily available over grocery store counters. Doubtful products such as Dandy Bracer–Liver and Kidney Cure were extraordinarily high in alcohol and of questionable therapeutic value. The Liquor Control Board came up with an elegant solution. The sale of medicated wines could continue, but the makers had to blend in a "certain additive." If the tonic in question were taken without reference to the stated dosage, the additive induced vomiting in the would-be patient. Needless to say, such nostrums quickly disappeared from the shelves for all time.

But the well-intentioned government did not address the fundamental question of what Ontarians were drinking. Wines made from the Catawba and Concord grapes were selling for 30 cents a bottle. They were sweet and highly alcoholic — twice the strength of European table wines. (In 1932, the government established a 20 per cent by volume limit.) In an effort to help the wine industry and the growers, the Ontario government had removed the 50-cent-a-gallon tax on wines in January 1929 to enable the Liquor Board to sell Ontario products at such a low price. These beverages were known as "Block-and-Tackle" wines — you drank a bottle, walked a block and you could tackle anybody!

Further representations from the grape growers and the wine lobby convinced the Department of National Revenue to allow the fortification of domestic wines. By adding pure grape spirit, the producers could now manufacture fortified wines. The new legislation was a godsend for the industry which could now use wine that was badly oxidized. Before, they would have had to pour it into the sewer. Now they could distil it for grape alcohol.

The Ontario grape growers, too, were happy because they could sell more grapes and doubly so when in 1931 the government banned the importation of grapes from outside the province. The Liquor Board also insisted that the wineries pay a minimum of forty dollars a ton for those they bought.

Concerned about the rocketing sales of these new fortified wines — 42 per cent of all wines sold in 1933 — the government appointed a Wines Standards Committee in an attempt to wean Canadians from such heady products towards lighter wines to be drunk with meals. In its report, the committee suggested that it was the industry's responsibility to supply the marketplace with a range of "good quality light wines." It stated that, "the distribution of pamphlets fully describing the merits and low alcoholic content of table wines will unquestionably materially assist in promoting the sale of same."

But the Canadian public was not yet ready for wines of nine to 12 per cent alcohol; their palates had become accustomed to fortified products which were closer to whisky than wine in their alcoholic strength. It would take another 25 years before the industry would suddenly be caught off-guard by the demand for the style of wines consumed by the Europeans. In the meantime, port and sherry would be the mainstays of the Canadian industry, especially during the Depression when disenchantment and despair found solace in cheap alcohol.

The brand leaders at this time were Brights' Catawba sherry, (affectionately known as "Bright's Disease") and Jordan's Bran-Vin.

Without the ability to advertise or promote their products — a legacy of the Prohibition mentality — the Wine Standards Committee loftily reported that "many people in this province associate drinking of any kind of alcoholic beverage with fostering drunkeness." So the wineries struggled through the 1930s to keep their industry alive. No new winery licences were to be granted in Ontario to allow those currently operating to stay afloat.

But in those dismal years between the two world wars, a dedicated group of individuals laboured in their respective vineyards to produce wines of quality, and if this goal proved to be beyond the capabilities of the native grapes, these men were determined to find varieties that could do so.

In the early 1930s, Harry Hatch, the new owner of Brights, brought a young chemist and winemaker from Montreal to his Niagara Falls winery. A French aristocrat by birth, Viscomte Adhemar de Chaunac de Lanzac was working at Brights' Québec plant in Lachine at the time. Nurtured on the wines of his native land, he had little time for the company's sweet "ports" and "sherries" and set about to make experimental batches of dry table wines from Catawba and Delaware grapes he found in Brights' mainly Concord vineyards. Harry Hatch was so impressed by the results that he gave de Chaunac his head to experiment further, setting aside funds for his winemaker to buy vines from New York State to be planted in the company's experimental plot. In 1937, de Chaunac returned to France to find out more about the hybrids being experimented with there.

At the same time, the Horticultural Research Institute at Vineland was conducting similar experiments to provide the wineries with hardy varieties to resist winterkill. Patiently, the scientists at Vineland had been crossing vines to produce the magic grape free of *labrusca* flavour. William Rannie writes in *The Wines of Ontario* that the Institute planted and evaluated 57,000 seedlings between 1913 and 1928, and retained only six as "promising for table grapes and five wine making!"

World War II interrupted this quiet revolution, the fruits of which would eventually change the nation's wine-drinking habits.

Cut off from Europe during the war, the wineries retrenched. All experimentation ceased; it was enough to keep the companies going until the servicemen returned home. As members of a non-essential industry, winemakers found themselves short of bottles and were forced to recycle those they could find.

During the war, wineries were rationed by the government as to how much wine they could sell; the figure varied between 75 and 80 per cent of their production in the base of year 1939. Wine drinkers used to line up for three hours outside the liquor stores until they opened at 10 am.

The Canadian wine industry marked time and waited for the peace that would signal its renaissance.

POST-WORLD WAR II

When the war ended, Adhemar de Chaunac of Brights was determined to upgrade the quality of his company's table wines. In 1946, he visited France again and ordered forty European vine varieties — hybrids and such noble *viniferas* as Chardonnay (the grape of white Burgundy) and Pinot Noir (red Burgundy). The vines were planted in the spring of that year, some on their own roots, while others grafted onto a European root-stock known as Couderc 3309.

Ten varieties, including the two *viniferas*, adapted reasonably well to their new surroundings. In 1952, Harry Hatch ordered 600 acres of Concord and Niagara vines torn out between Lake Ontario and the Niagara Escarpment to make way for the new varieties. Among them was a hybrid called Seibel 9549 which would be rechristened de Chaunac in 1972 as an accolade to the Frenchman for his contribution to the Canadian wine industry.

De Chaunac also selected a list of varieties for the Horticultural Research Institute at Vineland after discussion with J.R. Van Haarlem, who was in charge of grape development at the time. These vines were planted in the spring of 1947. HRI's initial experiments suggested that a hybrid called Chelois would be the grape of the future. It took ten years before they found that Chelois was susceptible to a disease called "dead arm."

Other commercial concerns were also experimenting. Parkdale Winery, based in Toronto, brought in vines from Hungary in 1947. Although they proved to be a "dead loss," they did have some success with Gamay Beaujolais on their test farm as well as Johannisberg Riesling and a Muscat-flavoured Couderc, which de Chaunac had brought in as well. (A young nurseryman in Niagara-on-the-Lake, Donald Ziraldo, would eventually propagate these vines for cuttings and starting in 1971 would sell them to other wineries.)

Of all the hybrids planted at Vineland, it was the Seibel 9549 — or as we know it today, de Chaunac — which would prove to be the leading commercial variety for red wines in Ontario during the 1960s and 1970s.

If Brights thought back in the 1950s that their Pinot Noir vines would give them wine to rival the best of Burgundy — as Justin de Courtenay had dreamed about — they were disappointed. The vines produced a mere tonne per acre, well below commercial viability; in fact, in winemaker's parlance, "a nuisance volume."

But the initial step to plant better grapes had been taken and Brights' former director of Viticultural Research, George Hostetter (the first vintner to be awarded the Order of Canada), could justifiably claim that their 1946 experiment predated the introduction of the finest French grapes to the Eastern United States by that outspoken champion of *vinifera*, the late Dr. Constantin Frank of the Finger Lakes in New York State.

In 1955, Brights produced the first 100 per cent Canadian Chardonnay from the vines de Chaunac brought back from France. Now, every Canadian winery worth its salt has a Chardonnay among its premium varietal wines.

De Chaunac also brought to Canada 88 vines of a red hybrid called Maréchal Foch (a cross between Pinot Noir and Gamay). Nine years later, in 1958, having propagated them and allowing them to reach maturity, Brights put on the market a wine called Canadian Burgundy, much to the disgust of the French who were unhappy that their finest wines should be impugned with such a soubriquet.

Brights shared their research willingly with the rest of the industry, and when de Chaunac retired in 1961 the wineries were nudging their growers to replant their vineyards with more acceptable hybrid varieties such as Seibel, Foch and Verdelet and, where possible, *vinifera*. They were now in a position to produce the style of products the Wine Standards Committee had called for back in 1933, only this time it was the consumers' voice they heard demanding drier wines that resembled those of France and Germany — if not in complexity and finesse, at least in alcoholic strength and without the overriding "foxy" *labrusca* taste. But old Mr. Fox would be a long time a-dying and a new craze would give him a breath of life again.

Social behaviour is governed by the law of the pendulum and wine drinking like everything else has its cycles, its fads and its fashions. In the affluent 1960s, young people became a formidable force in the marketplace and the wine companies began to take notice of this new section of society. In the late 1960s, at the request of a Detroit tavern owner, a German winemaker in Michigan created a blended sparkling wine named "Cold Duck" which immediately took off.[2] Everyone started making Cold Ducks — a 12 per cent alcohol sparkling wine made from *labrusca* grapes with sugar and water added.

In 1952, when Brights purchased the Fred Marsh Wine Company, one of the products Marsh was working on was a seven per cent sparkling wine. Adehmar de Chaunac overcame the problems of instability and developed Brights' Winette which was originally sold in a 13-ounce pop bottle. Since it was a sparkling product, the champagne tax of $2.50 per gallon was applied. M.F. Jones of Brights argued successfully with the LCBO to lower the tax and the markup because of the product's low alcohol level. The tax per gallon was fixed at 25 cents.

The seven per cent "wine" was an inspiration: not only did it score Brownie points with those pressure groups who wanted to see less alcohol consumed, but it saved the company vatfuls of money. The *labrusca* grapes which were — and still are — used are the cheapest on the market. The crush is stretched with water and the excise tax is half that of table wines.

For several years, Brights had the market to themselves with Winette and Du Barry Sparkling Vin Rosé. However, out in British Columbia, Andrew Peller at Andrés was looking for a new product line and, realizing that there were high profits to be made from this style of beverage, he and his company took the plunge.

Andrés created a range of Chanté wines (as in *enchanté*) and one of these evolved as the "wine" that would create a revolution in Canadian taste — Baby Duck. At its peak, two years after its 1971 launch, one out of every 24 bottles of wine sold in

---

[2] There is a European tradition, convivial though unsanitary, which calls for the guests to pour their glasses into a common bowl at the end of the party. The mixture of wines of whatever hue are then sampled. This is called, in German, *Das Caulde Ende* — the cold end. The German word *Ente*, meaning "duck," very similar in sound, is a pun which gave the winemaker his name.

Canada was Andrés Baby Duck.[3] The rest of the trade — and by now it was corporate business run by marketing men and Harvard-trained MBAs — scrambled to make a light sparkling wine. In consequence, a whole menagerie of pop wines descended on liquor board shelves. Their names suggested Noah's ark rather than a wine shop; Little White Duck, Luv-A-Duck, Fuddle Duck, Baby Bear, Baby Deer, Pink Flamingo, Gimli Goose and Pussycat were just some of them.

The generation of post-war Canadians may have turned their backs on the whisky-substitutes of the Depression era, but there were few Canadian wines of sufficient quality to fill the gap between the ports and sherries and the Ducks. The provincial liquor boards, seeing there were hefty profits to be made by catering to the growing demand for wine, began to increase their imports of European products until, in 1975, 3,315 imports were listed across the country as opposed to 1,875 domestic products. This posed a new problem for the indigenous wineries that had to contend with a public that knew what it didn't want from Canadian wineries and went elsewhere for what it thought it ought to be drinking — the wines of France, Italy and Germany.

Alarmed at the influx of inexpensive wines from overseas, the grape growers and the wineries appealed to the Ontario government. In 1976, Queen's Park instituted the Ontario Wine Industry Assistance Program. The LCBO sent around a memo to all its stores saying, "Delist imported wines that are not meeting their sales quotas and thereby make room for Ontario wines.... Urge store managers and wine consultants to mention Ontario wines.... Store managers will rearrange shelf-facings and thereby make room for additional brands of Ontario wines." The government also initiated a program for the growers to help change over from *labrusca* to the more desirable hybrids and *viniferas* so that the wineries could produce European-style wines. The program provided interest-free loans for five years.

The "Big Four" wineries of Ontario — Andrés, Brights, Château-Gai and Jordan — in searching for ways to sell more of their products, began to build bottling plants and blending facilities in nongrape-growing provinces. The initial capital outlay would soon be ameliorated by a grateful province which would now list all that company's products in its stores. Their investment was welcomed because the new facilities provided local jobs. And the companies gained the added benefit of being able to manufacture wines without the regulations that restricted them in Ontario and, to a lesser extent, in British Columbia.

The mid-1970s were a watershed for the Canadian wine industry. The large companies were desperately searching for a table wine that would appeal to the nation's palate to compete with such imported blends as Black Tower, Blue Nun, Colli Albani and Donini.

Indications from south of the border suggested that Americans were drinking white wine instead of red and that the same phenomenon would happen here. The sherry and port market virtually collapsed. Diet- and health-conscious Canadians switched their allegiance from red to white, and there were hardly enough quality white hybrid grapes in the ground to satisfy the demand.

---

[3] As Winston Collins wrote of the Baby Duck phenomenon: "Most Canadian grow up on soft drinks, and prefer to consume their alcoholic beverages flavoured, sweetened, carbonated, chilled, and diluted — rum and Coke, rye and ginger. Baby Duck was an easy transition from soft drinks to not-too-hard alcohol for the baby-boom generation, young people who may have been attracted to wine but were put off by its 'come-alive-for-a-dollar-five' image, or else intimidated by the overly sophisticated aura of something with an unpronounceable foreign name." (*Saturday Night*, June 1982)

The Baby Duck drinkers had graduated to Mateus Rosé and the blended whites of Europe. Imports enjoyed a cachet on the strength of their label alone, irrespective of the quality of the wine in the bottle.

In 1976, Calona Wines in British Columbia entered the field with a wine to compete with the top-selling Black Tower called Schloss Laderheim. It looked suspiciously like a Rhine Riesling in its brown bottle and German gothic scripted label. In 1978, Château-Gai launched Alpenweiss in Ontario, the first of that company's wines to contain California grapes blended with the locally grown Seyval. The success of these two wines sent the other companies off in the direction of brand names and labels which were unashamedly European in appearance and style. The age of the packaged wine had arrived. The way the bottle looked was as important as what was in it.

The "Big Four," with their modern plants strung out across the country, not only had to contend with burgeoning imports but also with the arrival of a new source of competition — the boutique wineries. The last licence issued by the Ontario government was in 1930, but the young nurseryman, Donald Ziraldo, so impressed Major-General George Kitching, chairman of the Liquor Board of Ontario, with his concept of a cottage winery that he and his winemaker-partner Karl Kaiser were given the green light to produce 10,000 gallons of wine from the 1974 vintage. Inniskillin Wines was born that year.

A few months earlier, a Hungarian winemaker named Karl Podamer had been granted a licence to create the Podamer Champagne Company in Beamsville, Ontario (subsequently bought by Magnotta). These two small wineries were the first since the bad old days of Prohibition and paved the way for other such adventuresome entrepreneurs as Alan Eastman at Charal (now defunct), Paul Bosc at Château des Charmes, Joe Pohorly at Newark (subsequently renamed Hillebrand Estates Winery) and Enzo DeLuca and his winemaker Carlo Negri at Collio Wines in Harrow.

In British Columbia, the first estate winery, Claremont, was opened in 1979. This opened the doors for Uniacke Cellars (now Cedar Creek), Sumac Ridge and Gray Monk. And in 1980 the tiny Grand Pré Winery began fermenting grapes grown on its own property near Wolfville in Nova Scotia.

These cottage enterprises were dedicated to producing labour-intensive wines of quality from *vinifera* and hybrid grapes, and would nudge the big wineries in both grape-growing provinces to follow their lead. The public, in the belief that smaller is better, snapped up the wines of Inniskillin and Château des Charmes, and over-enthusiastic nationalists held blind tastings against European products to prove that Canadian wines could hold their own in the international marketplace.

There is no question that since the introduction of the appellation VQA, Canadian wines have improved out of all recognition to what was offered to the consuming public in the past. Tasted blind in competition against wines of similar style and character from Europe or other New World regions, they have more than held their own. Slowly, a style is evolving in Ontario and British Columbia that is unique to these growing regions and has nothing to do with California taste profiles, let alone those of France, Italy or Germany. Canadian white wines, both dry and sweet, have come of age. They have consistently won medals in international competitions. The reds are improving steadily and some Pinot Noirs, Merlots and Cabernets are very fine indeed. If, over the next 10 years, our winemakers can continue to lower yields, perfect their cold fermentation techniques and their use of barrel ageing, we will have a wine industry to rival those whose products currently take up the majority of space on our restaurant wine lists and provincial liquor board racks.

ONTARIO

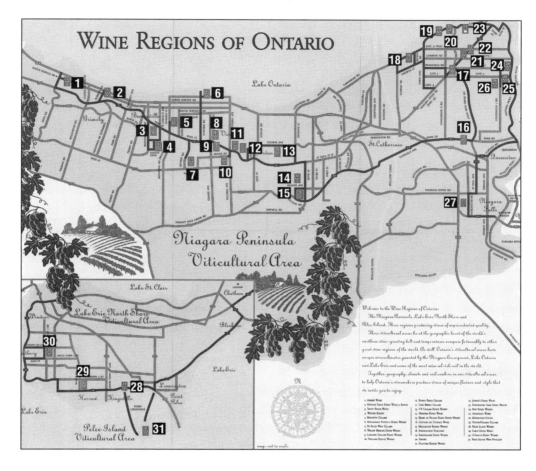

1. Andrés Wines
2. Kittling Ridge Estate Wines & Spirits
3. Thirty Bench Wines
4. Walters Estates
5. Magnotta Cellars
6. Maplegrove Vinoteca Estate Winery
7. DeSousa Wine Cellars
8. Willow Heights Estate Winery
9. Lakeview Cellars Estate Winery
10. Vineland Estates Winery
11. Stoney Ridge Cellars
12. Cave Spring Cellars
13. V.P. Cellars Estate Winery
14. Hernder Estate Wines
15. Henry of Pelham Family Estate Winery
16. Château des Charmes Wines

17. Hillebrand Estates Winery
18. Stonechurch Vineyards
19. Konzelmann Estate Winery
20. Strewn
21. Pillitteri Estates Winery
22. Joseph's Estate Wines
23. Sunnybrook Farm Estate Winery
24. Reif Estate Winery
25. Inniskillin Wines
26. Marynissen Estates
27. Vincor-Niagara Cellars
28. Pelee Island Winery
29. Colio Wines
30. D'Angelo Estate Winery
31. Pelee Island Wine Pavillion

Wine Regions and Wine Routes of Ontario

Ontario's vineyards, which produce over 80 per cent of Canadian wine, lie within the same latitude as Languedoc-Roussillon in Southern France, the Chianti Classico zone of Italy and Spain's Rioja region. From a geographer's perspective, the Niagara Peninsula, the north shore of Lake Erie and Pelee Island are smack in the middle of the Northern Hemisphere's wine belt.

True, cities such as Hamilton and London, Ontario, may not enjoy the same climate as Cannes and Florence, but Lake Erie and Lake Ontario smooth the rough edges of our harsher weather — reflecting sunshine and storing heat in the summer, acting like hot water bottles during the winter — making it possible to grow wine grapes of quality in Ontario.

Today there are some 17,000 acres of vines in the province, down from the 24,000 that existed prior to the Free Trade Agreement with the United States. That political reality, coupled with a GATT (now the World Trade Organisation) ruling in 1988, has radically changed the Ontario wine industry — ironically, for the better. Although at the time, winery executives and farmers joined in a collective "tearing of hair," convinced that the end of the world was at hand.

The pull-out program that resulted eliminated a lot of unwanted varieties and farmers now had the confidence to plant *vinifera* varieties (Chardonnay, Cabernets, etc.) which had hitherto been adjudged too tender to survive the winters.

To see how far the industry has come you have to understand where it has been. Its progress over three decades has moved in waves. In the early 1970s large companies controlled the market and laid down its production values. Remember the era when Baby Duck waddled across every table in the country and that endless series of French and German knock-offs using hybrid and *labrusca* grapes?

The next wave was the advent of the "cottage" enterprises in 1974 — Inniskillin and Podamer followed by Château des Charmes and Newark (now Hillebrand Estates). As these wineries grew and flourished, concentrating more and more on the noble European grapes, other players got into the game. A second wave of estate wineries began to challenge the pioneers in the early 1980s — Cave Spring, Vineland Estates, Pelee Island and Reif. But still the large companies, Andrés, Barnes, Brights, Château-Gai, Jordan and London, kept a tight hold on the industry reins through their voting power on the Wine Council of Ontario.

By the mid-1980s the power began to shift subtly from the large corporate wineries to the small estates as consumers recognised the superior quality of their wines produced from vinifera grapes at low yields. The next wave came in the form of farmgate wineries established between 1989 and 1993 — growers who decided not to sell their grapes to large wineries but to go into business for themselves, like John Marynissen, Ed Gurniskas at Lakeview Cellars, the late Paul Speck, Sr., at Henry of Pelham, Rick Hunse at Stonechurch and Gary Pillitteri. The new kids on the block were healthy competition for the established estate wineries and their combined success in the marketplace, coupled with the introduction of VQA (Vintners Quality Alliance) standards, forced the corporate wineries to improve the quality of their products. Today, of all the major wineries that once dominated the industry, only Andrés remains as a corporate entity.

Vincor (and its estate-sounding label, Jackson-Triggs) and Andrés (Peller Estates) responded to the challenge and broadened the concept of VQA, expanding it from an upscale idea to a mass market product by making wines that conformed to the appellation's standards at affordable prices. And the estate wineries, such as Colio and Magnotta, who started out small are now significant players in the industry and are also playing their part in the "mainstreaming" of quality wines.

The next wave for Ontario is under way now — the Super Premium revolution — small niche wineries dedicated to producing high end wines from low yields. They won't be cheap but they will represent a new level of quality and commitment — wineries such as Thirty Bench, Malivoire, Creekside, Thomas & Vaughan and The Thirteenth Street Winery. All of this would not have come about were it not for the introduction of the VQA whose seal you see on every bottle of wine made from 100 per cent locally grown grapes. The VQA set out minimal standards for wine production and to get the seal the wines must pass a panel of LCBO tasters for quality and typicity.

Two years after its introduction in Ontario the VQA concept was accepted in British Columbia and negotiations are continuing with Québec and Nova Scotia to make it the Canada-wide appellation.

When the VQA is passed into law both provincially and federally it will make life much easier for the wineries in their export endeavours to the European Union. (Currently the EU will not accept Canadian wines until such legislation is in place.)

Once the VQA is in place under federal law (it has recently been passed by the Ontario legislature) it will have a marked effect on how other markets perceive Canada as a wine-growing country and how we ourselves perceive wines from other provinces. Not only will VQA ensure higher winemaking standards but it will also protect such desirable categories as Icewine, Select Late Harvest and Late Harvest wines — as well as estate bottles and single vineyard designated wines — from fraudulent copies and substandard products.

Imagine going into a bistro in Lyon and finding only three Burgundies on the list; or four Chiantis in a Florence trattoria. In no other wine region of the world do you find so little of the locally grown product on restaurant wine lists as you do in Ontario. This will change dramatically in the next year or so in Ontario. Recently enacted legislation allows Ontario wineries to supply restaurants directly with VQA wines without having to go through the Liquor Control Board of Ontario. Since they will not have to pay the LCBO mark-up, the profits could go to the improvement of lower-priced wines which is to the benefit of the consuming public. The net effect will be to raise the profile of Ontario wines across the board.

Eventually, the geographic designations of the Niagara Peninsula and Lake Erie North Shore will be fragmented into smaller sub-zones, just as Bordeaux is broken down into communes such as St. Emilion, Pauillac, Graves, etc. There is a case for wines grown on the bench of the Niagara Escarpment to be differentiated from those grown on the Lakeshore plain since their taste profiles are perceptibly different. And who is to say that only the Niagara Peninsula, Lake Erie's North Shore and Pelee

Island are the only regions of the province that can produce wine? Wine grapes are being cultivated in Prince Edward County, around Lake Scugog and, believe it or not, there's a small but thriving viticultural community around Peterborough. Within 20 miles of that city there are at least 15 tiny vineyards. The driving force behind this minor explosion of ampelographic activity is Larry Patterson, an LCBO employee and the Johnny Appleseed of Ontario wine.

Just think of it — with a degree or two of global warming, who knows, the Canadian Shield might look like Burgundy — a sea of vines right up to Owen Sound! At the time of writing there are 60 wineries operating in Ontario with a further 17 standing by awaiting their licences. The growth of the industry since 1988 has been exponential; there appears to be no end of people willing to invest in it. To service the need for winemakers in the future Brock University created Canada's first oenology school, CCOVI (Cool Climate Oenology and Viticulture Institute) in St. Catherines. The first class will graduate in the year 2000.

And while the industry looks to the future it is not ignoring its past. A wine archive has been set up at Brock University, called the Ontario Wine Library, as Linda Bramble wrote in *Winetidings* magazine, "...to hold in trust selected premium wines of Ontario in order to conduct research, promote Canadian wines and educate."

These are exciting times for lovers of Ontario wines. The winemakers are beginning to understand their terroir, learning what grapes do best in which soils and microclimates. They are lowering their yields to get more concentrated flavours and they are experimenting with wild yeast fermentations. The emphasis has switched from *wine making* to wine *growing*, a distinction no longer lost on the large corporate enterprises.

The Ontario industry has never been healthier. I have written elsewhere — "Vintage of the century is one of those phrases that comes home to haunt journalists once they have committed it to paper. But I have little hesitation in suggesting that 1998 in Ontario will be just that for red wines (unless the last harvest of the 1990s surpasses it!). None of the previous years since Johann Schiller first put his feet in a vat of grapes back in 1812 has shown such early potential. It was not only 1998's perfect growing season but the accumulated experience of Ontario's winemakers that leads me to the extravagant statement: 1998 is Ontario's Vintage of the Millennium."

ONTARIO WINERIES

Andrés Wines

(See under Peller Estates)

Archibald Orchards & Estate Winery

6275 Liberty Street North
RR5
Bowmanville, Ontario
L1C 3K6
Telephone: (905) 263-2396
Fax: (905) 263-4263
e-mail: archibaldorchards@sympatico.ca
web site:
www.archibalds-estatewinery.on.ca

Archibald Orchards was established in 1967 on a farm that has been in the family for four generations. Fred and Sandy Archibald created the fruit winery in 1997 using the apples from their orchard and offering an amazingly wide variety of fruit wine experiences. Pies and preserves are also made from the apples, from recipes passed down to Sandy by her Mennonite grandmother.

Winemaker: Fred Archibald

Acreage: 40

Soil: Clay loam

Varieties planted: 20 types of apple, including McIntosh, Ida Red, Empire, Spy and Golden Russet used in fruit wine making

Production: 5,500 cases

Winemaking philosophy: "Fruit wines should taste like fruit and, to borrow a popular expression — great wines are grown, not made. It is important to be in control of all steps, from the site selection and varietal choices to final blending and balancing."

Wines: (dry) Ida Red, McIntosh, Empire; (off-dry) Ida Red, McIntosh, Apple Raspberry, Sparkling Apple Raspberry, Hard Cider; (sweet) Apple Strawberry,

Apple Peach, Royal Raspberry, Sweet Apple Cherry, Winter Apple, Spiced Winter Apple, Sparkling Sweet Apple Cider, Sparkling Apple Raspberry, Hard Peach

Store hours: *January to April:* Friday to Sunday, 10 am — 6 pm

May to December: Daily, 10 am — 6 pm

Winery tours: Sunday, 2 pm

Public tastings: Free

Bellamere Country Wines

1260 Gainsborough Road
London, Ontario
N6H 5K8
Telephone: (519) 473-2273
Fax: (519) 473-5312
e-mail: farm@Bellamere.ca
web site: www.Bellamere.com

Dan Mader turned his pick-your-own fruit farm into a winery that produces fruit and grape wines. When Vincor bought London Winery he hired London's long-time winemaker, Jim Patience. Jim brought his expertise from grape to fruit and now oak ages McIntosh apples whose flavour, he contends, is similar to Chardonnay. The company's first grape crush was the 1998 vintage.

The winery, next to the Bellamere Market, is an imposing timber-frame building with exposed beams that reach 38 feet. There are also banqueting facilities at the winery and picnic tables for the casual visitor.

Winemaker: Jim Patience

Acreage: 60 (orchards and berry fields)

Soil: Gravel/clay loam

Production: 4,000 cases in first year of production

Average tonnage crushed: grapes — 8 tonnes; fruit — 28 tonnes

Average tonnage purchased: 22 tonnes

Winemaking philosophy: "To make wines that capture fruit character and captivate customers."

Wines: *White*—Vidal, Chardonnay

Red—Merlot, Cabernet Franc, Baco Noir

Fruit—Bosc Pear, Harvest Apple, McIntosh Apple, Blackberry, Raspberry, Strawberry, Cranberry, Cherry

Sparkling—Poire, Fraise, Pomme

Specialty—Pear Ice, Apple Ice, Cranberry Ice, Apple-Raspberry Ice

Store hours: *May to September:* Daily, 10 am — 7 pm

October to April: Daily, 10 am — 6 pm

Winery tours: By appointment. A steam engine tour of the orchards

Public tastings: Free

Cave Spring Cellars

3836 Main Street
Jordan, Ontario
L0R 1S0
Telephone: (905) 562-3581
Fax: (905) 562-3232

Cave Spring is a model for what a medium-sized Ontario winery should be. The company produces a limited number of wines, but each has a style and quality that expresses what the region is capable of growing. The "farm on the bench" is owned by Len Pennachetti, who went into partnership with winemaker Angelo Pavan in 1986. The winery and store are located seven km away in an old stone building in Jordan that used to be an apple warehouse dating back to 1870. In 1978, Len planted the original 12 acres of vines.

Cave Spring is one of the few medium wineries in that it only uses *vinifera* grapes for its products. Most of its grapes are sourced from the Beamsville Bench of the Niagara Escarpment located between Twenty Mile Creek and Thirty Mile Creek. The principals are so dedicated to the Bench as "Ontario's finest growing microclimate" that they have called their newsletter *Benchmark*.

The winery's restaurant, On The Twenty, is certainly worth a detour ((905) 562-7313). Across the street from the restaurant and winery is the Vintner's Inn, a luxury wine country inn, open all year round ((905) 562-5336).

Cave Spring has always stressed its commitment to the terroir of the Beamsville Bench by expanding the estate's vineyard (CVS) and another farm owned by Tom Pennachetti and Anne Weis (45 acres on an escarpment bench above Jordan). The focus here is Riesling (Anne's father Hermann Weis who once owned Vineland Estates has developed his own clone at his nursery in Germany).

Winemaker: Angelo Pavan

Acreage: 105 estate; additional 45 family-owned

Soil: Moderately well-drained clay loam soil of the Benchland. A steep north-facing slope affords good natural water drainage and excellent air drainage. Close proximity to the Escarpment gives a relatively high concentration of mineral deposits from erosion which add complexity as trace elements in the wine.

Grape varieties: Chardonnay, Riesling, Gamay, Pinot Noir, Cabernet Sauvignon, Cabernet Franc, Merlot, Sauvignon Blanc, Chenin Blanc, Semillon

Production: 55,000 cases

Average tonnage crushed: 775 tonnes

Winemaking philosophy: "One hundred per cent *Vitis vinifera* to produce only premium varietal wines. No house wines produced. Minimal intervention in the winemaking process. Filtration is kept to an absolute minimum with diatomaceous earth filtration only prior to bottling. No pad filtration."

Wines: LCBO: *White*—Chardonnay Beamsville Bench, Dry Riesling, Off-Dry Riesling

Red—Gamay, Chardonnay Estate

Own store: *White*—Chardonnay Reserve, Chardonnay Musqué, Riesling Reserve, Indian Summer Riesling, Riesling Icewine, Gewürztraminer, Auxerrois, Sauvignon Blanc

Red—Pinot Noir, Cabernet/Merlot

Rosé—Gamay Rosé

Store hours: *November 1 to April 30:* Monday to Saturday, 10 am — 5 pm; Sunday, 11 am — 5 pm

May 1 to October 31: Monday to Saturday, 10 am — 6 pm; Sunday, 11 am — 6 pm

Winery tours: *November 1 to April 30:* Saturday and Sunday, 11 am, 3 pm

May 1 to October 31: Monday to Friday, 3 pm; Saturday and Sunday, 11 am and 3 pm

Private tours: Call for appointment

Public tastings: During store hours

————

Recommended wines: Chardonnay Reserve, Chardonnay CSV, Chardonnay Musqué, Riesling Reserve, Indian Summer Riesling, Icewine

Château des Charmes Wines

1025 York Road
P.O. Box 280 St. David's
Niagara-on-the-Lake, Ontario
L0S 1P0
Telephone: (905) 262-4219
Fax: (905) 262-5548
e-mail:
pabosc@chateaudescharmes.com
web site: chateaudescharmes.com

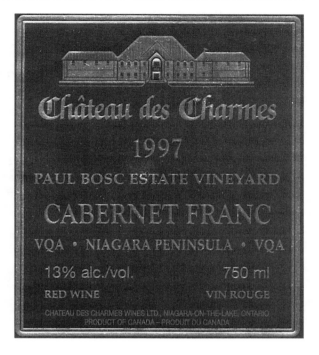

Paul Bosc trained at the University of Burgunday at Dijon and made wine in Algeria before emigrating to Canada. A stint as winemaker with Château-Gai convinced him that there was an opportunity to make fine wines in Niagara, so in 1978 he opened his own winery with its 60-acre vineyard with lawyer Rodger Gordon as a partner. Paul did much to convince the industry that the future lay in *vinifera* varieties and his early Rieslings and Chardonnays were a model for other wineries.

His winemaking style is totally Burgundian, especially in his penchant for the difficult Aligoté grape and his insistence in making a Gamay Nouveau every year (the best in Ontario). He also makes the one of the best traditional method sparkling wines in Canada.

Paul's wife Andree, and his sons, Paul Jr. and Pierre-Jean, are very active in the company. The black-labelled Estate refers to the original farm (now a warehouse) while Paul Bosc Estate refers to the property purchased in 1983 with its dramatic 35,000 sq. ft. French château constructed in the St. David's Bench Vineyard. The Boscs own a 93-acre vineyard on St. David's Bench. He uses Allier oak barrels for his range of Chardonnays and reds.

Winemaker: Paul Bosc, Sr. and Pierre-Jean Bosc

Acreage: Château des Charmes Estate—60 acres (Chardonnay, Riesling, Gamay, Pinot Noir, Aligoté, Auxerrois)

Soil: Four different soil types, 70 per cent sandy loam, some clay. Paul Bosc Estate Vineyard—60 acres (35 planted): Chardonnay, Pinot Noir, Gamay, Riesling, Cabernet Sauvignon, Cabernet Franc, Merlot. Vineyard features extensive under-drainage. St. David's Bench Vineyard—93 acres (84 planted):

Chardonnay, Aligoté, Sauvignon Blanc, Viognier, Savagnin, Cabernet Franc, Merlot. Heavily under-drained

Grape varieties: Aligoté, Cabernet Sauvignon, Cabernet Franc, Merlot

Production: 100,000 cases

Average tonnage crushed: 1,000 tonnes

Annual tonnage purchased: 300 tonnes (approximately)

Winemaking philosophy: "The Boscs produce wines which are the closest to the French style by virtue of their heritage (fifth- and sixth-generation French winegrowers) and education. Paul Bosc's experience in Burgundy has allowed him to enjoy his greatest success with those varieties (Chardonnay, Pinot Noir, Gamay, Aligoté) and he has produced a range of styles (Sparkling, Nouveau dry whites, dry reds) with these varieties."

Wines: LCBO: *White*—Chardonnay, Estate Chardonnay, Aligoté, Sauvignon Blanc, Riesling, Paul Bosc Estate Chardonnay, Auxerrois, Gewürztraminer, Riesling Icewine, Late Harvest Riesling

Sparkling—Sec, Brut

Red—Gamay Noir, Pinot Noir, Cabernet Sauvignon, Estate Pinot Noir, Paul Bosc Estate Merlot, Paul Bosc Estate Cabernet Franc, Paul Bosc Estate Cabernet Sauvignon, Paul Bosc Estate Cabernet, St. David's Bench Vineyard and Cabernet Franc

Stores: (3)—At the winery

Oakville: Lakeshore Rd. Loblaws store

Ottawa: Minto Place, Laurier Ave. at Lyon St.

Toronto: 3329 Yonge St.

Store hours: Monday to Sunday, 10 am—6 pm

Public tastings: During store hours

Winery tours: Seven days a week: 11 am, noon, 1 pm, 2 pm, 3 pm, 4 pm

---

Recommended Wines: Sparkling Sec and Brut,
St. David Bench Vineyard Bottlings, Paul Bosc Estate Bottlings, Riesling Icewine,
Late Harvest Riesling

Cilento Wines

672 Chrislea Road
Woodbridge, Ontario
L4L 8K9
Telephone: (905) 856-3874
Fax: (416) 746-1144
web site: www.cilento.com

Grace Locilento's grand-mother was involved in the wine business in Italy and it had always been the ambition of Grace and her husband Angelo to open a winery in Canada. They built a two storey building in Vaughan with 35,000 square feet to accommodate the winery and retail store. Their first crush was in 1995.

Winemaker: Ann Sperling
    (consulting)
Acreage: 50
Grape varieties: Pinot Noir, Cabernet Sauvignon, Baco Noir, Pinot Gris, Riesling,
    Chardonnay, Sauvignon Blanc
Production: 21,000 cases
Average tonnage crushed: 266 tonnes
Average tonnage purchased: 266 tonnes
Winemaking philosophy: "Strive to grow only the highest quality grapes to pro-
    duce the best VQA wines."
Wines: *Wine*—Riesling, Chardonnay, Vidal, Auxerrois, Chardonnay (No Oak),
    Select Late Harvest Vidal, Late Harvest Riesling, Vidal Icewine
Red—Maréchal Foch, Cabernet, Cabernet Franc, La Vita, Cabernet Sauvignon Reserve
Store hours: Monday to Friday, 9 am — 7 pm; Saturday, 9 am — 6 pm; Sunday,
    11 am — 4 pm
Winery tours: By appointment
Public tastings: Free

Recommended Wines: Chardonnay (No Oak), Riesling, Auxerrois, Select Late
Harvest Riesling, Maréchal Foch

Colio Wines of Canada

1 Colio Drive
P.O. Box 372
Harrow, Ontario
N0R 1G0
Telephone: (519) 738-2241
Fax: (519) 738-3070
e-mail: colio@total.net
web site:www.colio.com

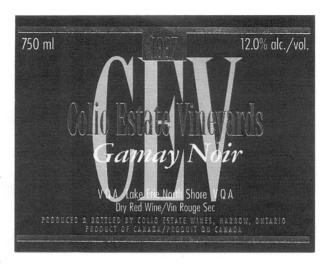

Colio, as its name suggests, was founded by a group of Italian businessmen in 1978. They brought over a winemaker from Trentino Alto-Adige, Carlo Negri, for their first crush in 1980. The style of wines from the beginning was unrepentantly commercial, but Carlo's natural ability has given them a flair generally lacking in competitively priced brand-name wines. The winery is located in the village of Harrow and its exterior belies the extent of the investment in stainless steel within.

In March 1992, Colio purchased the vineyard acreage of the former Kingsville Estate Winery first planted in 1983.

Carlo not only produces Icewine but has gone back to his roots to produce a wine he first called Vin Santo and then Vin de Curé (made from grapes dried in a greenhouse). Colio is the only winery to use grapes from all three of Ontario's designated viticultural areas in its blends. Carlo also uses American oak.

Two of his wines are sold in a British supermarket chain as North Shore White (Vidal) and North Shore Red (Baco Noir, Villard Noir and Maréchal Foch). A new line of premium and ultra-premium wines was launched in spring 1999 under the Colio Estates Vineyard label (CEV).

Winemaker: Carlo Negri

Acreage: Colio Estate—100; Harrow Estate—80

Grape varieties: Riesling-Traminer, Riesling, Cabernet Franc, Gamay Noir, Merlot, Zweigelt, Baco Noir, Pinot Gris, Chardonnay, Gewürztraminer, GM 318, Vidal and other French hybrids

Production: 200,000 cases

Average tonnage crushed: 1,300 tonnes

Annual tonnage purchased: 700 tonnes

Winemaking philosophy: "To produce dry wines which not only are Italian in style but also coincide with all major wine-producing countries. To be proud of the entire production, not only of the small per centage of the production that would be written up from wine tastings. All the wines Colio enters in wine tastings and competitions are produced in quantities available to the public, mostly through general listings."

Wines: *Colio Estate Vineyards—White*—Chardonnay (No Oak), Sauvignon Blanc, Chardonnay Reserve, Select Late Harvest, Late Harvest Vidal, Vidal Icewine

Red—Gamay Noir, Pinot Noir Reserve, Cabernet Franc Reserve, Merlot Reserve

Harrow Estates—White—Gewürztraminer, Riesling, Vidal, Chardonnay (No Oak), Sauvignon Blanc, Blanc de Noir

Red—Maréchal Foch, Cabernet Franc, Cabernet Merlot, Zweigelt

Oak Age Classic—Chardonnay, Sauvignon Blanc, Merlot, Cabernet

House Wine— Extra Dry White, Bianco Secco, Bianco, Bianco Riserva, Rosso Secco, Rosso Riserva

Sparkling— Chardonnay Lily, Chateau d'Or, Spumante

Fortified— Port, Sherry, Dry Sherry

Stores: (13)

> Harrow (inside Winery): 1 Colio Dr., Harrow
> Brampton (inside Fortino's): 55 Mountainash Road, Brampton
> Brampton (inside Fortino's): 60 Quarry Edge Drive, Brampton
> Burlington (inside Fortino's): 1059 Plains Rd. E., Burlington
> London: 1166 Commissioners Rd. E., London
> Scarborough: 16 William Kitchen Road, Scarborough
> Mississauga: 2300 Haines Road, Mississauga
> Nepean: 250 Greenbank Rd., Greenbank Square, Ottawa
> Newmarket: 16655 Yonge St., Newmarket
> St. Clair Beach (inside Zehr's): 400 Manning Rd., St Clair Beach
> Windsor (inside A&P): 6740 Wyandotte St. E., Windsor
> Whitby: (inside Deville's): 3570 Brock Street North, Whitby
> Woodbridge (inside Fortino's): 3940 Highway #7, RR#2, Woodbridge

Store hours: Monday to Saturday, 10 am — 5 pm; *May to October:* Sunday, 12 pm — 5 pm

Winery tours: Daily at 1 pm, 2 pm and 3 pm; Saturday, hourly, 12 pm — 4 pm. Bus tours welcome by appointment. Admission free.

Cost of tour/tasting: $3/person (includes a complimentary wineglass)

Group rates (10 minimum): $2/person (includes tour/tasting/wineglass)

Public tastings: During store hours from 11 am — 5 pm

Recommended wines: CEV Cabernet Franc, Chardonnay (No Oak), Chardonnay Lily; Harrow Estates Cabernet Franc, Cabernet Merlot, Icewine, Late Harvest Vidal

County Cider Company

RR #4
Picton, Ontario
K0K 2T0
Telephone/Fax:
(613) 476-6224
web site:
www.countycider.com

Grant Howes began with fermenting apples for cider in 1995 and has planted grapes on two sloping sites on his orchard property that overlooks Lake Ontario. In the spring of 1999 he put in three acres of Riesling, Zweigelt and Gamay.

Picnic tables are available for visitors to enjoy the view over the lake.

Winemaker: Grant Howes

Acreage: 50 (3 acres of grapes)

Soil: Sandy loam to shallow, well-drained limestone conglomerate

Production: 4,500 cases (cider)

Average tonnage crushed: 48 tonnes

Average tonnage bought in: 8 tonnes

Winemaking philosophy: "To grow exceptional fruit to be used in the making of our Hard Apple Ciders and wines."

Wines: *Still ciders*— Northern Spy, Winter Apple (dessert wine)

Sparkling— County Cider, Waupoos Draft Cider

Store hours: *May to November:* Daily, 10 am — 6 pm

Cox Creek Cellars Estate Winery

RR #5
Guelph, Ontario
N1H 6J2
Telephone: (519) 767-3253
Fax: (519) 824-0808
e-mail: wine@coxcreekcellars.on.ca
web site: www.coxcreekcellars.on.ca

Cox Creek Cellars takes its name from the creek that runs through the northern part of the estate. The Trochta family opened their store in November 1998, offering two styles of Baco Noir (one barrel-aged) and Seyval Blanc, as well as their fruit wines.

Winemaker: Adrian Trochta

Acreage: 5 (2 acres of black currants, 2.5 acres of apple trees)

Wines: Cox Creek White (Seyval), Cox Creek Red (Baco Noir), Cox Creek Red barrel-aged

Fruit wines: *White*—Apple Dream, Evening Romance

Red—Country Sunrise, Back Home, Cherry Mystique, Apple Sunset

Store hours: Closed Monday; Tuesday to Thursday, 1 pm — 7 pm; Friday, 1 pm — 8 pm; Saturday, 11 am — 6 pm; Sunday, 1 pm — 4 pm

Creekside Estate Winery

2170 Fourth Avenue
Jordan Station, Ontario
L0R 1S0
Telephone: (905) 562-0035
Fax: (905) 562-5493
e-mail: ptjensen@aol.com
web site: CreeksideWinery.ca

Under the name The New World Wine Company, Peter Jensen and Laura McCain Jensen operate wineries in Ontario (Creekside Estate) and Nova Scotia (Habitant Vineyards). Peter had been in the business of designing and building wineries for bulk production until 1996. The couple took over the struggling VP Cellars in 1997 and acquired a 50-acre parcel of land near Château des Charmes with the idea of building a winery called Paragon (for Bordeaux red varieties due to open in 2001). They started off in Ontario with a bang, producing 12,000 cases under the watchful eye of consulting oenologist Ann Sperling.

Picnic tables are available on the deck or stroll the grounds beside Sixteen Mile Creek.

Winemaker: Peter Jensen

Acreage: 20

Soil: Limestone, clay

Grape varieties: Chardonnay, Sauvignon Blanc, Riesling, Vidal, Merlot

Production: 12,000 cases

Average tonnage crushed: 50 tonnes

Average tonnage purchased: 80 tonnes

Winemaking philosophy: "Producing Ontario's finest white wines using traditional methods, including barrel fermentation and ageing in European oak and back-blending with higher quality varietal whites."

Wines: *White*—Riesling, Chardonnay, Gewürztraminer, Sauvignon Blanc

Red—Pinot Noir, Merlot, Cabernet Sauvignon, Cabernet Franc, Cabernet/Merlot

Store hours: Monday to Friday, 10 am — 5 pm; Saturday, 10 am — 6 pm; Sunday, noon — 5 pm

Winery tours: By appointment

Public tastings: Free

Recommended wines: Cabernet Sauvignon, Riesling, Chardonnay, Gewürztraminer

D'Angelo Estate Winery

5141 Concession 5, RR #4
Amherstberg, Ontario
N9V 2Y9
Telephone: (519) 736-7959
Fax: (519) 736-1912

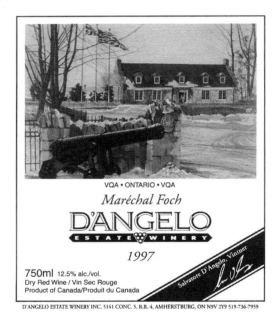

Salvatore (Sal) D'Angelo planted his vineyard in 1983. As an accomplished amateur winemaker, his ambition was to open his own winery — which he did seven years later. Located south of Windsor and just east of Amherstberg in the heart of Essex County, the winery bears the Lake Erie North Shore appellation. Only grapes grown on the estate are used in Sal's wines, which are vinted in his temperature-controlled fermenting room. In the vineyard, he uses several trellising systems to provide the ripeness and exposure to air contact he seeks.

Sal's art labels, historic and contemporary, are some of the most appealing in Ontario.

Winemaker: Salvatore D'Angelo

Acreage: 40 (Amherstberg), 10 (Colchester, lakeside)

Soil: Clay loam; vineyard in Amherstberg at the centre of Essex County, surrounded by Lake St. Clair and Lake Erie. Well-drained, with breezes off Lake Erie six km away. Colchester is sandy gravel, a lake property 50 feet above the lake.

Grape varieties: Chardonnay, Riesling, Pinot Blanc, Seyval Blanc, Vidal, Cabernet Sauvignon, Pinot Noir, Merlot, Gamay, Maréchal Foch, Baco Noir, Cabernet Franc, Chamburcin and experimental Sangiovese, Syrah

Production: 5,000 cases (10,000 in 2000)

Average tonnage crushed: 100 tonnes

Winemaking philosophy: "To produce the best wines from our own vineyards. We make wine the old-fashioned way. We grow it."

Wines: LCBO: Vidal, Vidal Icewine, Vidal Select Late Harvest, Maréchal Foch, Cabernet

Own store: *White*—Riesling, Chardonnay, Pinot Blanc, Select Late Harvest Riesling, Vidal Icewine

Red—Maréchal Foch, Pinot Noir, Merlot, Cabernet Sauvignon, Cabernet-Merlot, Gamay Rosé

Store hours: *April to December:* Daily 10 am— 6 pm; *January to March:* Tuesday to Saturday, 10 am — 5 pm; Sunday, noon — 5 pm

Winery tours: Yes

Public tastings: During store hours

Recommended wines: Maréchal Foch, Vidal Icewine, Select Late Harvest Riesling

De Sousa Wine Cellars

3753 Quarry Road
Beamsville, Ontario
L0R 1B0
Telephone: (905) 563-7269
Fax: (905) 338-9404
e-mail:
desousa@desousawines.com
web site:www.desousawines.com

802A Dundas Street West
Toronto, Ontario
M6J 1V3
Telephone: (416) 603-0202
Fax: (905) 338-9404

In 1987, John and Mary De Sousa decided to turn the grapes they grew high on the bench of the Escarpment into the Portuguese-style wines they drank in their native land. Their Dois Amigos labelled red and white are aimed at the expatriate Portuguese

community, the red being aged in oak in the traditional Portuguese manner. Their son John Jr. has taken over the winemaking and in 1998 the family opened a facility in Toronto. Apart from producing and selling their wines from this outlet, the De Sousas offer a Lisbon-by-night experience in the restaurant on the second floor.

Try tasting their red wines from a traditional Portuguese clay cup that cuts down the perception of tannin.

Winemaker: John De Sousa, Jr.

Acreage: 80

Grape varieties: Chardonnay, Riesling, Vidal, Seyval Blanc, Cabernet Franc, Cabernet Sauvignon, Merlot, Baco Noir, Maréchal Foch, De Chaunac, Geneva Red

Production: 14,000 cases

Average tonnage crushed: 200 tonnes

Average tonnage purchased: 100 tonnes

Winemaking philosophy: "Tradition never compromised."

Wines: *White*—Dois Amigos, Chardonnay, Riesling, Vidal, Vidal Icewine

Red—Dois Amigos, Cabernet Sauvignon, Cabernet Franc, Merlot, Maréchal Foch, Baco Noir

Specialty — Port, Port Reserve

Stores hours: Beamsville winery: May to October: Daily, 10:30 am — 5:30 pm; **November to April:** Weekends only

Toronto winery: Monday to Saturday, 11 am — 7 pm

Winery tours: Beamsville: May to October: Daily, 11 am, 1 pm and 3 pm

Public tastings: Yes (both facilities; Beamsville has picnic sites)

————

Recommended wines: Cabernet Sauvignon Reserve, Maréchal Foch, Riesling Icewine

Domaine Vagners

1973 Four Mile Creek Rd., RR #3
Niagara-on-the-Lake, Ontario
L0S 1J0
Telephone: (905) 468-7296
e-mail: mvagners@netcom.ca

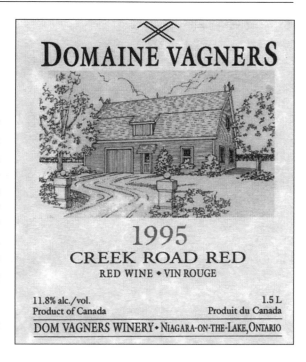

"I may be Canada's smallest winery and may remain so," says Martin Vagners, who started his operation "to make a good red wine" in 1994 in a converted barn. An executive for Scott Laboratories for many years, and an experienced taster and wine judge, he is determined to grow only the top *vinifera* (except Chardonnay, "because everyone else has it").

Martin planted his tiny vineyard in 1990 and made his first crush three years later. He ages his wines in reshaved French oak barrels and uses a minimum of chemicals. Ultimately, he plans to make a champagne-method sparkler.

Winemaker: Martin A. Vagners

Acreage: 5

Soil: Sandy, well drained, about 2 km from the lake

Grape varieties: Merlot, Cabernet Franc, Cabernet Sauvignon, Riesling, Pinot Gris, Gewürztraminer, Pinot Noir

Average tonnage crushed: 6 tonnes

Production: "Max out at about 10,000 litres. I will not increase production until vines mature."

Winemaking philosophy: "Country wines, handcrafted for early enjoyment. Our grapes are 100 per cent handpicked at the correct time, therefore no SO_2 is required. The wines are lightly filtered, slightly bruised. Basically, I realize we cannot make a Bordeaux château-style red wine, but we can make an early drinking, fruity Loire (Chinon) type. I feel that a blend of 60 per cent Merlot, 30 per cent Cabernet Franc and 10 per cent Cabernet Sauvignon for me will work, whereas 60 per cent Cabernet Sauvignon, 30 per cent Cabernet Franc and 10 per cent Merlot will not."

Winery store: *White*—Riesling, Pinot Gris, Pinot Blanc, Gewürztraminer

Red—Cabernet Franc, Merlot, Creek Road Red (Bordeaux blend), Cabernet Sauvignon, Pinot Noir

Winery tours: Saturday 10 am — 3 pm or by appointment

Public tastings: None

***

Recommended wines: Creek Road Red, Pinot Blanc

East Dell Estates

3999 Locust Lane, RR #2
Beamsville, Ontario
L0R 1B2
Telephone:
(905) 563-9463 (WINE)
Fax: (905) 563-4633
e-mail:
SMODell@eastdell.com

Susan O'Dell, sales and marketing consultant and author, purchased the three-year-old Walters Estates Winery in 1999 with her partner, Michael East, a long-time amateur wine-maker. In 1996, they had bought a 15-acre property not far from their winery and have been supplying grapes to local wineries. Their winemaker, Tatjana Cuk, worked with Jim Warren and Ray Cornell at Stoney Ridge.

The property boasts a rustic stone-and-milled wood wine facility with a bistro above the cellar, offering a splendid view of Lake Ontario and the distant Toronto skyline (open Thursday — Sunday all year round). There is also a one-bedroom cabin accommodation by a large duck pond.

Winemaker: Tatjana Cuk

Acreage: 42 planted (63 total)

Soil: Beamsville Bench Cayuga clay

Grape varieties: Cabernet Sauvignon, Cabernet Franc, Merlot, Chardonnay, Riesling, Vidal, Pinot Gris, Pinot Noir (for 2000, Muscat Canelli, Viognier)

Production: 8,000 - 10,000 cases

Average tonnage crushed: 120 tonnes

Annual tonnage purchased: 50 tonnes

Winemaking philosophy: "The Nature of Niagara rules! Selecting grape varieties and clones that are exactly suited to the Escarpment's soil and microclimate allows us to work with Nature, not against it. EastDell's non-invasive viticultural practices and simple, traditional winemaking methods are respectful of both the land and the local wine community's cottage-industry approach. We want to transfer what Nature gives us in the most gentle way into something we can remember and enjoy as part of everyday living."

Wines: *White*—Viognier, Muscat, Riesling, Chardonnay, Riesling-Traminer, Pinot Grigio, Vidal

Red—Cabernet (Sauvignon and Franc blend), Merlot, Pinot Noir

Fortified—Port, Sherry

Specialty—Iced fruit series, including cranberry

Store hours: *Summer:* Monday to Thursday, 11 am — 5 pm; Friday until 7 pm; Saturday to Sunday, 10 am — 6 pm

Winter: Wednesday to Thursday, 11 am — 5 pm; Friday until 7 pm; Saturday to Sunday, 10 am — 6 pm

Winery tours: Self-guided — all year; conducted tours — summer weekends. Groups by appointment

Public tastings: Daily cellar selection — no charge; other wines $0.50 to $3 per tasting

---

Recommended wines: None tasted yet

Harbour Estates Winery

4362 Jordan Road
Jordan Station, Ontario
L0R 1S0
Telephone: 1-877 HEWWINE (439-9463)
Fax: (905) 562-3829
web site: www.hewwine.com

Fraser Mowat, a credit advisor with the Farm Credit Corporation, is the latest Ontario winery operator to be licensed as this book goes to the printer. So new he is still looking for a winemaker. His 30-acre estate is a beautiful wooded setting overlooking Jordan Harbour. He plans a restaurant, patio and wine bar, cigar lounge, banqueting facilities and corporate meeting rooms. There will be picnicking facilities overlooking the harbour and a barrel cellar. Construction will begin in 2000.

Acreage: 30

Soil: Sandy loam with lower clay strata

Grape varieties: Merlot, Cabernet Sauvignon, Cabernet Franc

Production: (1999) projected 10,000 cases (full production, 30,000)

Average tonnage crushed: 120 tonnes (projected 350 tonnes)

Annual tonnage purchased: 120 tonnes

Winemaking philosophy: "Focus on premium *vinifera* reds."

Wines: *White*—Chardonnay, Riesling, Sauvignon Blanc, Late Harvest Vidal, Vidal Icewine, Riesling Icewine

Red—Merlot, Cabernet Sauvignon, Cabernet Franc, Pinot Noir, Syrah

Store hours: Monday to Friday, 10 am —5 pm; Saturday, 10 am —7 pm; Sunday, 10 am — 5 pm

Public tastings: Free

Henry of Pelham

1469 Pelham Road, RR #1
St. Catharines, Ontario
L2R 6P7
Telephone: (905) 684-8423
Fax: (905) 684-8444
web site:www.henryofpelham.com

Empire Loyalist Henry of Pelham, whose lugubrious hand-drawn features grace the winery's labels, is an ancestor of the Speck family, owners of this historic property. Henry's father, Nicholas Smith, was a bugle boy in the Revolutionary War of 1776. The graveyard next to the winery attests to the fact that the property has been in the Smith family in an uninterrupted line.

The modern, well-equipped winery, located on the Bench of the Escarpment, is housed behind the ancient coaching inn (1842) with its atmospheric cellars — now the tasting room — wine shop and cooperage storage. When the late Paul Speck, his wife Bobbi and their three sons took over the property in 1983, there was already a 20-acre vineyard which had been planted 75 years ago. They have planted 110 more acres of vines with a further 75 acres at their disposal.

Winemaker: Ron Giesbrecht

Acreage: 110

Soil: Heavy clay/loam soil called Smithville Till Clay, high in calcerous content which contributes to low yields. Good air drainage and water run off. Lower humidity than the lakeshore below and marginally higher heat accumulation.

Grape varieties: Chardonnay, Riesling, Cabernet Sauvignon, Baco Noir, Gamay Noir, Pinot Noir, Merlot

Production: 50,000 cases

Average tonnage crushed: 600 tonnes

Annual tonnage purchased: 300 tonnes (mainly from the Bench)

Winemaking philosophy: "To provide handcrafted wines which mirror the qualities and potential of our unique conditions in Niagara, and in particular the Niagara Bench. Our philosophy of winemaking embraces innovation, enabling the creation of what tradition and Nature have inspired."

Wines: LCBO: *White*—Vidal, Riesling, Chardonnay, Reserve Chardonnay, Reserve Riesling

Red—Loyalist House Red, Baco Noir, Cabernet Sauvignon Blanc

Own store: *White*—Riesling Icewine, Barrel Fermented Chardonnay, Sauvignon Blanc, Late Harvest Sauvignon Blanc, Late Harvest Vidal

Red—Merlot, Pinot Noir, Cabernet/Merlot, Zweigelt/Gamay

Rosé—Cabernet Franc Rosé

Store hours: Daily 10 am — 6 pm

Winery tours: Yes

Public tastings: During store hours

Recommended wines: Merlot, Cabernet Merlot, Riesling, Chardonnays, Icewine, Baco Noir

---

Hernder Estate Wines

1607 8th Avenue
St. Catharines, Ontario
L2R 6P7
Telephone: (905) 684-3300
Fax: (905) 684-3303
web site: www.hernder.com

In 1987, Fred Hernder purchased the 8th Avenue farm which included a dilapidated Victorian barn. Fully renovated and restored, the barn is now the focal point of the estate housing the winery and three hospitality rooms (which can seat over 500 guests) as well as the wine boutique and retail shop. The first crush in 1991 offered

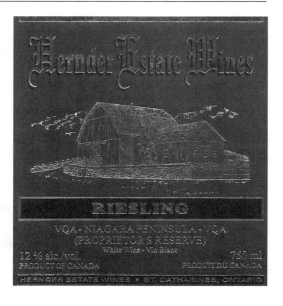

French hybrids but plantings of *vinifera* have now come on stream and Hernder has had much international success with Riesling.

Winemaker: (consulting) Ray Cornell

Grape varieties: Merlot, Cabernet Sauvignon, Cabernet Franc, Gamay, Baco Noir, Sauvignon Blanc, Chardonnay, Chardonnay Musqué, Pinot Gris, Riesling, Vidal

Production: over 10,000 cases

Average tonnage crushed: 3,500 tonnes (for wines and juices)

Winemaking philosophy: "In this family endeavour we are perpetually expanding our horizons … better wines, improved varieties and a more spectacular place to showcase them in, all to share them with new and old friends alike. The clear focus is to keep our products consistently 100 per cent Ontario superior VQA wines and to make them enjoyable to consume."

Wines: LCBO: *Vintages*—Riesling, Vidal, Baco Noir, Cabernet Franc, Select Late Harvest Vidal

Winery Store: *White*—Barrel Fermented Chardonnay, Chardonnay Reserve, Chardonnay Musqué, Riesling, Gewürztraminer, Pinot Gris, Riesling-Traminer, Vidal Icewine Riesling-Vidal Icewine, Select Late Harvest, Vidal

Red—Cabernet-Merlot, Pinot Noir Rosé, Cabernet Franc, Merlot, Cabernet Sauvignon, Baco Noir

Store hours: Monday to Friday, 9 am — 5 pm; Saturdays and Sundays, 10 am — 5 pm

Tours: 1:30 pm — 3:30 pm during summer hours, otherwise by appointment. Group/bus tours by appointment only.

Public tastings: Complimentary (Icewines: $2.50)

Recommended wines: Riesling, Barrel-fermented Chardonnay, Chardonnay, Vidal

---

Hillebrand Estates

RR #2, Highway 55
Niagara-on-the-Lake, Ontario
L0S 1J0
Telephone: (905) 468-7123
Fax: (905) 468-4789
web site: www.hillebrand.com

Joe Pohorly created a winery in 1979 called Newark, but three years later debt problems forced him to sell to Underberg, the giant Swiss bitters company which held a controlling interest in Peter

Mielzynski, the Toronto-based wine and spirit importers. The name was changed to Hillebrand Estates.

The company's winemaking expertise was evident in early brands such as Schloss Hillebrand and the initial Rieslings, and no winery in Canada has grown as quickly as Hillebrand, thanks to the injection of capital from Switzerland. Hillebrand's equipment and facilities are the envy of their colleagues. In 1990, the company built a new building to house the offices above a bottling line which is itself over a new sparkling wine cellar for its Trius sparkler. In July 1994, Underberg sold its 100 per cent interest in Hillebrand Estates to Andrés Wines of Winona. Hillebrand's Vineyard Café is built into the winery and overlooks the barrel-ageing cellar.

Hillebrand, although large, concentrates on quality in its varietals, especially Chardonnay (24,000 cases), Cabernet and Riesling, of which there are a bewildering number of labels.

Heavy emphasis is placed on barrel-fermenting and ageing with oak from Nevers, Vosges, Tronçais and Allier as well as American.

Winemaker: Jean-Laurent Groux (known as "J-L")

Acreage: 30

Soil: Clay

Grape varieties: Chardonnay, Riesling, Pinot Noir, Pinot Gris, Cabernet Franc

Production: 340,000 cases

Average tonnage crushed: 3,000 tonnes

Annual tonnage purchased: 900 tonnes

Winemaking philosophy: "Our philosophy in making wine is to respect the fruit that Mother Nature has given us. We associate art and technology to produce varietal wines with distinctive character from the finest vineyards of the Niagara Peninsula."

Wines: LCBO: *White*—Harvest Chardonnay VQA, Harvest Riesling VQA, Cuvée 1812, Canadian Chablis, Stone Road (Chardonnay, Sauvignon Blanc)

Red—Harvest Cabernet VQA, Harvest Gamay Noir VQA, Cuvée 1812, Stone Road (Cabernet, Merlot, Gamay Noir)

Vintages: *White*—Collector's Choice Chardonnay VQA, Trius Chardonnay VQA, Trius Riesling VQA, Vidal Icewine

Red—Collector's Choice Cabernet-Merlot VQA, Trius Red VQA

Own Stores: *White*—Vineyard Select VQA, Stone Road Reserve

Rosé— Vineyard Select VQA, Stone Road Reserve

Stores: At the winery

Ajax:	Loblaws, 125 Harwood Avenue North
Ancaster:	Sobeys, 977 Golf Links Road
Barrie:	Zehrs, 201 Cundles Road E.
	Zehrs, 11 Byrne Road
Bramalea:	Miracle Ultra, Highway 7 & Dixie Road

Brampton:	Centennial Mall, 227 Vodden Street
	IGA, 930 North Park Drive
	IGA, 29-380 Bovaird Drive
	IGA, 400 Queen Street W.
Burlington:	Fortino's, 2025 Guelph Line
	Marilu's Market, 4025 New Street
	Sobey's, 1250 Brant Street
	Walker's Place, 3305 Upper Middle Road
	Lakeside Shopping Village, 5353 Lakeshore Road
Cambridge:	Zehrs, Highway 8 and 97
	Zehrs, 180 Holiday Inn
Collingwood:	Blue Mountain Mall, 55 Mountain Road
East York:	Loblaws, 11 Redway Road
	IGA, 1015 Broadview Avenue
	Bruno's Fine Foods, 1605 Bayview Avenue
Etobicoke:	Bruno's Fine Foods, 4242 Dundas Street W.
	Loblaws, 245 Dixon Road
Gloucester:	Loblaws, 1224 Place D'Orleans
Hamilton:	2 King Street W.
	Fortino's, 50 Dundurn Street S.
	Fortino's, 75 Centennial Parkway N.
Kitchener:	Highland Hills Mall, 46-875 Higland Road
	Zehrs, 700 Strasburg Road
	Zehrs, 1375 Weber Street
London:	Loblaws, 7 Baseline Road
	Oakridge Mall, 1201 Oxford Street W.
	A&P, 1244 Commissioners Road
	A&P, 1030 Adelaide Street N.
	A&P, 395 Wellington Street
Mississauga:	Clarkson Village, 1865 Lakeshore Road W.
	Loblaws, 250 Lakeshore Road E.
	South Common Mall, 2150 Burnamthorpe Road W.
	Dominion Plus, 2550 Hurontario Street
	Dominion Plus, 1151 Dundas Street W.
	Price Chopper, 4040 Creditview Drive
	IGA, 6040 Glen Erin Drive
	Dominion Plus, 1240 Eglinton Avenue West
	Loblaws, 620 Eglinton West
	Michael Angelos, 4099 Erin Mills Parkway

Nepean:	Loblaws, 1460 Merivale Road
	Loblaws, 59 Robertson Road
Newmarket:	Newmarket Place, 17725 Yonge Street N.
	Dominion Plus, 1111 Davis Drive
	Loblaws, 20 Davis Drive
Oakville:	IGA, 511 Maple Grove Drive
	IGA, 1500 Upper Middle Road
	2431 Trafalgar Road
Oshawa:	Loblaws, 1300 King Street E.
	A&P, 285 Taunton Road E.
Ottawa:	Hunt Club Centre, 2-3320 McCarthy Road
	Southgate Shopping Centre, 2515 Bank Street
Peterborough:	Loblaws, 661 Landsdowne Street
St. Catharines:	Zellers, 366 Buntin Road
	Super Fresh, 126 Welland Avenue
	Commisso's, 318 Ontario Street
	Fairview Mall, 285 Geneva Street
	Zehrs, 221 Gelndale Avenue
	Port Plaza, 600 Ontario Street
Scarborough:	Markington Square, 3227 Eglinton Avenue E.
	Super Centre, 1880 Eglinton Avenue E.
	Maxi & Co., 1455 McCowan Road
	IGA, 2490 Gerrard Street E.
	Ultra Mart, 5085 Sheppard Avenue
Toronto:	1689 Bayview Avenue
	446 Spadina Avenue
	2273 Bloor Street W.
	238 Queen Street W.
	2144 Queen Street E.
	Dominion, 656 Eglinton Avenue E.
Vanier:	Loblaws, 100 McArthur Road
Waterloo:	Zehrs, 450 Erb Street W.
Welland:	Seaway Mall, 800 Niagara Street N.
Whitby:	Loblaws, 3050 Garden Street

Winery tours (one hour): Seven days a week, twelve months a year, on the hour. Additional tours on weekends during the summer and fall harvest. Deluxe private tours for groups. Catering on request.

Public tastings: During store hours, 10 am — 6 pm (Vineyard Concert series in June, July and August)

Recommended wines: Trius series, "Showcase" reds, Harvest Riesling, Vidal Icewine

Inniskillin Wines Inc.

RR #1, Line 3 at the Niagara Parkway
Niagara-on-the-Lake, Ontario
L0S 1J0
Telephone:
Administration: (905) 468-2187
Fax: (905) 468-5355
Tour & Retail: (905) 468-3554, ext. 3
Fax: (905) 468-7501
e-mail: inniskil@inniskillin.com
web site:www.inniskillin.com
          www.icewine.com

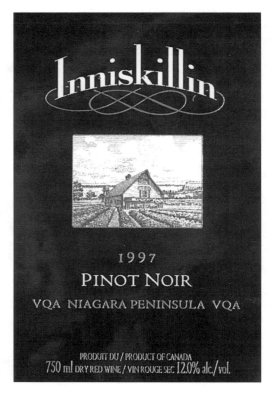

Donald Ziraldo and Karl Kaiser must get the credit for rejuvenating the Canadian wine industry at a time when it could easily have foundered in the swamps of *labrusca*. They received their boutique winery licence — a new concept in 1975 when the industry was dominated by large commercial wineries ferociously competing with Baby Duck-style products and imitation Liebfraumlich — and they determined to make only quality wines. For a decade it was an uphill battle, but they have earned their place in the sun with a range of single vineyard Chardonnays, Pinot Noir, Cabernet Sauvignon and Vidal Icewine. And along the way they have raised the profile of Canadian wines both at home and around the world.

The tireless Donald Ziraldo was the prime mover in setting up the Vintners Quality Alliance, Canada's appellation system, and lobbying the provincial government to create a wine route through the Peninsula. Inniskillin's 1989 Vidal Icewine won a gold award at Vinexpo in 1991, the first such international accolade and one that has drawn global attention to Niagara as a wine region.

Ziraldo was a moving force behind the establishment of the Cool Climate Oenology and Viticulture Institute at Brock University.

The winery itself, beautifully sited just off the Niagara Parkway, has a California look and feel. The Brae Burn barn, which acts as the store and loft, is well worth a visit.

Given Karl Kaiser's Austrian background, you'd expect to find Zweigeltrebe in the vineyard — and you do. Each year he brings in 40 to 80 new barrels from France.

In 1992, Inniskillin merged with Cartier Wines, and a year later that new conglomerate was taken over by Brights and was renamed Vincor International. Inniskillin continues to operate independently and is now making wine in British Columbia at Inniskillin Okanagan Vineyards (see page 138). The partners have an agreement with the Burgundy shipper Jaffelin to create a Pinot Noir and a Chardonnay — a selection of their best barrels — to be marketed under the name Alliance.

Winemaker: Karl Kaiser

Acreage: 120

Soil: Medium light to medium heavy sandy loam with some clay

Grape varieties: Pinot Noir, Gamay, Cabernet Sauvignon, Cabernet Franc, Merlot, Zweigeltrebe, Maréchal Foch, Baco Noir, Chardonnay, Riesling, Vidal, Pinot Grigio, Pinot Blanc, Auxerrois, Viognier, Chenin Blanc

Production: 150,000 - 200,000 cases

Average tonnage purchased: 2,000 tonnes

Winemaking philosophy: "Our basic philosophy of expanding varietal planting in Ontario has not changed since 1974. In winemaking, our goal is to establish a style for whites that will be remembered for their balance and finesse, offering the appropriate flavours for our region's cool autumn climate."

Wines: LCBO: *White*—Auxerrois, Chardonnay, Chardonnay Reserve, Culp Vineyard Chardonnay, Pinot Grigio, Riesling, Late Autumn Riesling

Red—Gamay Noir, Old Vines Foch, Pinot Noir, Cabernet Franc

Sparkling—Sparkling Icewine

Speciality—Icewine

Winery store: *White*—Chardonnay Single Vineyards (Seeger, Klose, Schuele, Montague), Riesling Reserve, Pinot Blanc, Icewine, Alliance Chardonnay, Founders' Chardonnay, Chardonnay, Chardonnay Reserve, Auxerrois, Pinot Grigio, Pinot Blanc, Late Autumn Riesling, Late Autumn Vidal

Red—Pinot Noir, Pinot Noir Reserve, Merlot, Klose Vineyard Cabernet Sauvignon, Cabernet Franc/Merlot, Zweigelt, Gamay Noir, Cabernet Franc, Old Vines Foch, Founders' Reserve Pinot Noir, Alliance Pinot Noir, Cabernet Sauvignon, 3, 6 and 9 litre large format specialty bottlings

Specialty—Icewine, Icewine Sculpture, Rosé de Saignée, Fleur de Niagara

Sparkling—Riesling Millennium, Sparkling Icewine

Stores: At the winery store in Niagara-on-the-Lake and at your neighbourhood Wine Rack Store (160 throughout Ontario)

Winery store hours: Open daily. Winter: *November to April:* 10 am — 5 pm; Summer: *May to October:* 10 am — 6 pm. Closed for major holidays.

Tours: Inniskillin is open year round and boasts a thorough tour program. Guided tours daily — *May to October:* 10:30 am, 11:30 am, 1:30 pm, 2:30 pm, 3:30 pm, and 4:30 pm; *May through October* and *November through April* 10:30 pm and 2:30 pm. To accommodate visitor flexibility, Inniskillin has an unique twenty station self-guided tour which winds throughout the facility.

Tastings: Fifty cents per serving. *November to April:* 11 am — 4:30 pm; *May to October:* 11 am — 5:30 pm. Featured at the tasting bar is the Wine Boutique.

————

Recommended wines: Single Vineyard Chardonnays, Pinot Noir, Alliance wines, Klose Vineyard Cabernet Sauvignon, Icewines

Joseph's Estate Wines

1811 Niagara Stone Road
(Hwy 55) RR#3
Niagara-on-the-Lake, Ontario
L0S 1J0
Telephone: (905) 468-1259
Fax: (905) 468-3103
e-mail:
info@josephsestatewine.com
web site:josephsestatewines.com

Joe Pohorly belongs to the history of Ontario wine. In 1979, he founded Newark Wines which was bought out by a Swiss company and renamed Hillebrand Estate in 1983. Joe left the wine business to concentrate on his hotel enterprise but the itch to make wine was too strong and in 1992 he bought his 20-acre estate down the highway from Hillebrand. Two acres are planted with peaches, pears and strawberries.

Winemaker: Joseph Pohorly and associate Katherine Reid

Acreage: 20

Soil: Sandy loam

Grape varieties: Pinot Gris, Gewürztraminer, Riesling, Chardonnay, Vidal, Muscat Ottonel, Cabernet Franc, Cabernet Sauvignon, Merlot, Petite Sirah, Pinot Noir, Chancellor, Baco Noir

Production: 12,000 - 15,000 cases

Average tonnage crushed: 130 tonnes

Average tonnage purchased: 20 tonnes

Winemaking philosophy: "To produce world class wines at an affordable price."

Wines: *White*—Pinot Gris, Chardonnay, Riesling, Festival Reserve (blend), Gewürztraminer, Winter Harvest (Vidal), Vidal Icewine

Red—Cabernet Franc, Cabernet Sauvignon, Merlot, Trois Rouge (blend), Petite Sirah, Chancellor, Baco Noir

Fruit —Strawberry, Pear, Peach, Iced Peach, Iced Apple

Fortified—(for 2000) Olde Towne Cream Sherry, Old Towne Port

Store hours: *May to October:* Monday to Saturday, 10 am — 6 pm; Sunday, 10 am — 5 pm; *November to April:* 11 am — 5 pm

Winery tours: Daily— 11 am, 1 pm, 3 pm, 5 pm. Bus tours and larger groups by appointment

Public tastings: Minimal charge

Recommended wines: Pinot Gris, Winter Harvest, Vidal Icewine, Strawberry

Kittling Ridge Estate Wines & Spirits

297 South Service Road
Grimsby, Ontario
L3M 4E9
Telephone: (905) 945-9225
(416) 777-6300
Fax: (905) 945-4330
e-mail:
admin@KittlingRidge.com
web sites:
www.KittlingRidge.com
www.InternoVodka.com

Kittling Ridge is the phoenix risen from the ashes of the old Rieder Distillery (founded in 1970 by Otto Rieder). The bird analogy is apt because "kittling" is a term used for migratory birds as they soar on circling updraughts, a sight common on the Niagara Escarpment at Grimsby where the facility is located. John Hall officially opened his winery-distillery in July 1994, although it started operations in 1992 and boasts Ontario's first on-premise spirits store. Apart from grapes brought in for their varietal wines (aged in American and French oak), Kittling Ridge also purchases quantities of Niagara tender fruit — strawberries, cherries, plums, pears and apples — for its distillates. It also created a new category — "fortified Icewine." Kittling Ridge also produces Canadian whisky, rum, vodka, brandy, eaux-de-vie, bitters and liqueurs.

The facility has a buffet-style dining room for private group functions.
Winemaker: John K. Hall

Production: 400,000 cases

Winemaking philosophy: "If you do not like our wines, simply return the unused portion and we will drink it. Taste, Quality and Value."

Wines: LCBO: *White*—Proprietor's Cuvée: Chardonnay, Sauvignon Blanc, Reserve White

VQA—Chardonnay, Riesling, Riesling-Gewürztraminer, Vidal Blanc, Seyval Blanc

Red—Proprietor's Cuvée: Cabernet Sauvignon, Merlot, Shiraz, Reserve Red

VQA—Cabernet, Maréchal Foch

Rosé—White Zinfandel Vidal

Dessert—Icewine, Icewine & Brandy

Winery stores: White—VQA Pinot Gris

Red—VQA Baco Noir

Rosé—VQA Vidal Blush

Dessert—Kingsgate Sherry, Vintage Port, Icewine Eau de Vie

Sparkling—Close Cuvée Brut, Amore Spumante

Also from the grape—Alambic Brandy, Small Cask Brandy, Icewine Grappa, Varietal Grappas and Eaux de Vie

Stores: (7)

Toronto, Ajax, Richmond Hill, Waterloo, London, Winery Store Grimsby, Winery Inn

Public Tastings: All year round both wines and spirits

Additional facilities: Kittling Ridge Winery Inn (opens November 1, 1999)—79 rooms and suites, some with fireplaces and whirlpools. Restaurants: Vintages fine dining and Casablanca Bar & Grill; Kitchens of Kittling Ridge (gourmet take-away for picnic lunches and dinners); Distillations Roof Top Bar; Vineyard Gift Boutique; In-door swimming pool, sauna and hot tub, fitness exercise facility; Kittling Ridge wedding chapel, banquet facilities (up to 400 people), business convention facilities (8 stories); Shuttle service to Niagara Casino, Flamboro Downs Racetrack.

Public tastings: Yes

Winery tours: Yes

Recommended wines: Vidal Icewine, Icewine and Brandy, Vidal, Riesling, Riesling-Gewürztraminer

Konzelmann Winery

RR #3,
Lakeshore Road
Niagara-on-the-Lake, Ontario
L0N 1J0
Telephone: (905) 935-2866
Fax: (905) 935-2864
web site:
www.konzelmannwines.com

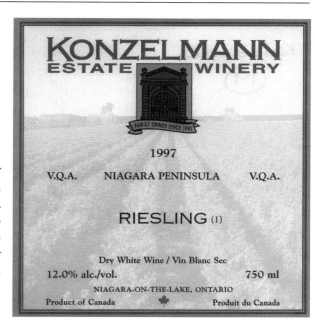

Herbert Konzelmann's family has been making wine in Württemberg since 1893, and a reproduction of the entrance to that winery can be seen on his Ontario labels. An oenology graduate from Weinsberg in Germany, Herbert ran the family facility for 25 years before visiting Canada on a hunting trip in 1980. He was so impressed by the potential of winemaking in Niagara that he took soil samples home with him in margarine containers and had them analyzed. Four years later he was back to purchase his 83-acre estate that backs onto Lake Ontario. He planted 32,000 vines and took his first crop off in the 1986 vintage, producing nine different varietals.

His Germanic winemaking style manages to coax subtle perfumes from his grapes, particularly Riesling, Chardonnay and Gewürztraminer. While he uses Allier, Nevers and Jugoslavian oak, especially for Chardonnay, his best results are from stainless steel, according to his own traditions. Herbert's Icewine is one of Canada's best.

In the German style, he believes in sweet reserve, back-blending fresh grape juice to the finished wines.

Winemaker: Herbert Konzelmann

Acreage: 83

Soil: Clay, sand. Ideal microclimate because of the proximity of the lake. Winds dry the vines, inhibiting fungus growth.

Grape varieties: Riesling, Chardonnay, Pinot Blanc, Gewürztraminer, Riesling-Traminer, Geisenheim 311, Vidal, Pinot Noir, Gamay, Zweigelt, Cabernet Sauvignon, Cabernet Franc, Merlot

Production: 40,000 cases

Average tonnage crushed: 460 tonnes

Annual tonnage purchased: 200 tonnes

Winemaking philosophy: "Konzelmann stands for quality."

Wines: LCBO: Golden Vintage, Johannisberg Riesling (Sugar Code 1 and Sugar Code 2), Chardonnay, Pinot Blanc, Pinot Noir, Merlot

Own store: *White*—Late Harvest Riesling Dry, Chardonnay Reserve, Late Harvest Vidal, Late Harvest Riesling Medium Dry, Gewürztraminer, Pinot Noir Rosé, Peach Wine, Riesling-Traminer Icewine, Vidal Icewine, Select Late Harvest Vidal, Chardonnay Grand Reserve, Riesling Icewine

Red—Pinot Noir (1), Gamay Noir, Baco Noir Late Harvest, Zweigelt Late Harvest, Cabernet/Merlot

Sparkling—Canadian Riesling

Store hours: *April to December:* Monday to Saturday, 10 am — 6 pm; Sunday, 12:30 pm — 5:30 pm; *January to March:* Wednesday to Saturday, 10 am — 6 pm

Winery tours: *May to September:* 2 pm daily

Public tastings: During store hours

Recommended wines: Chardonnay, Vidal Select Late Harvest, Riesling-Traminer Icewine, Vidal Icewine, Gerwüztraminer Late Harvest

Lakeview Cellars Estate Winery

RR #1, 4037 Cherry Avenue
Vineland, Ontario
L0R 2C0
Telephone: (905) 562-5685
Fax: (905) 562-0673
e-mail: Icew@waxxine.com
web site:www.lakeviewcellars.on.ca

Grower Eddy Gurinskas was a dedicated home winemaker who consistently won medals at national and international amateur competitions, especially for his Vidal Icewine. In 1991, he and his wife Lorraine followed in the footsteps of their friend John Marynissen in turning from grape grower to commercial winemaker when Lakeview Cellars got the second farm winery licence issued in Ontario.

From the start, Eddy's intention has been to bottle single vineyard wines with barrel ageing for his Chardonnay, Cabernet Sauvignon and Baco Noir.

Currently, he has 36 French and American oak *barriques*. The winery is a newly constructed barn with a gambrel roof.

In December 1996, neighbouring grower Larry Hipple joined the winery and in October 1997, Stu Morgan completed the partnership.

Winemaker: Eddy Gurinskas

Acreage: 13

Soil: The vineyard is located on the first plateau of the Niagara Escarpment, better known as "The Bench," approximately three km from Lake Ontario. The air drainage is very effective in the summer and provides considerable protection from extreme cold in winter. Soils are heavy clay loam.

Grape varieties: Cabernet Sauvignon, Chardonnay, Pinot Gris, Baco Noir, Vidal, Riesling

Production: 11,000 cases

Average tonnage crushed: 190 tonnes (15 per cent estate grown, 85 per cent from local farmers)

Winemaking philosophy: "Our aspirations are to make wine using only 100 per cent Ontario grapes that are locally grown. We intend to cap our production at 15,000 cases with sales of our wines through our winery store along with limited sales through the LCBO."

Wines: LCBO and Vintages: Chardonnay, Vidal, Pinot Gris, Baco Noir, Maréchal Foch, Gamay/Zweigelt, Riesling, Vidal Icewine, Cabernet Sauvignon

Own store: Merlot, de Chaunac, Zweigelt, Cabernet/Merlot, Baco Noir, Maréchal Foch, Gamay/Zweigelt, Chardonnay, Chardonnay Reserve, Riesling, Vidal, Kerner, Welschriesling, Gewürztraminer, Chardonnay Musqué, Late Harvest Vidal, Late Harvest Riesling, Select Late Harvest Vidal, Vidal Icewine, Apple Delight

Store hours: Daily, 10 am — 5:30 pm

Winery tours: Mid-May through October

Public tastings: During store hours (free)

───────────

Recommended wines: Cabernet Sauvignon, Cabernert/Merlot, Riesling, Chardonnay, Vidal Icewine, Pinot Gris

Le Blanc Estate Winery

4716-4th Concession, RR #2
Harrow, Ontario
N0R 1G0
Telephone: (519) 738-9228
Fax: (519) 738-2609
e-mail: leblanc@mnsi.net
web site: leblancestatewinery.com

In 1984, Alphonse and Monique LeBlanc planted their vineyard just north of Harrow. Their son Pierre and his wife Lyse got their winery licence in 1993, although Lyse (from Papineau, Que.) began fermenting in 1992, and even made an Icewine. They started with a single American oak barrel. In 1995 Lyse and Pierre bought the vineyard and now Lyse is running both vineyard and winery. The covered patio allows for cooking demonstrations by local chefs during the summer.

Winemaker: Lyse LeBlanc

Acreage: 50

Soil: Mostly clay, typical Lake Erie North Shore climate—higher heat units than Niagara, but colder winters.

Grape varieties: Pinot Blanc, Riesling, Seyval, Vidal (experimental plantings of Cabernet Sauvignon, Pinot Gris, Geisenheim, Merlot)

Production: 3,500 cases

Average tonnage crushed: 50 tonnes

Annual tonnage purchased: 20 tonnes

Winemaking philosophy: "To produce a wine that mirrors the quality of the grapes and the distinctive *gout de terroir*. We believe this to be achieved by merely guiding the grapes along to their natural conclusion."

Wines: Own store: *White*—Vidal, Riesling, Pinot Blanc, Gewürztraminer, Chardonnay, Vidal Icewine, Auxerrois, Pinot Gris, Vidal Select Late Harvest

Red—Pinot Noir, Cabernet Franc, Zweigelt, Cuvée Rouge

Rosé—Chant d'Eté

Store hours: *April to December*: Monday to Saturday, 11 am — 6 pm; Sunday, noon — 5 pm; *January to March:* closed Monday

Public tastings: During store hours

Winery tours: By appointment

––––––––––

Recommended wines: Cabernet Franc, Late Harvest Riesling, Pinot Gris

Magnotta Winery

271 Chrislea Rd.
Vaughan, Ontario
L4L 8N6
Telephone: (905) 738-9463
Toll free: 1-800-461-WINE
Fax: (905) 738-5551
web site:
www.magnotta.com

Unique among Ontario wineries, Magnotta built its business in eight years to become the fifth largest winery in Ontario — without sales through the LCBO (apart from the occasional Icewine). In 1990, Gabe and Rosanna Magnotta turned their successful juice operation (Festa) into a commercial winery having purchased the licence and stock of the defunct Charal winery in Blenheim. Taking advantage of the Ontario Wine Content Act (which then allowed 70 per cent offshore material to be blended with Ontario wines) their Argentinean winemaker produced a range of very inexpensive, very drinkable table wines.

In 1994, the Magnottas purchased the Montravin winery and renamed it Magnotta Cellars. They also acquired 72 acres of vineyard in the Niagara Peninsula to concentrate on VQA wines. Their art labels are some of the most attractive in Canada.

Magnotta has five locations across Ontario — Magnotta Vineyards in Mississauga, Magnotta Wines in Scarborough, Magnotta Vintners in Kitchener and the newly expanded Magnotta Cellars in Beamsville with its state-of-the-art crushing equipment.

The company flagship location, opened in 1997, is north of Toronto at Highway 7 and Highway 400 — a 60,000 square foot facility housing Festa Juice, the winery, a brewery and a distillery.

To supply its needs Magnotta has contracts with vineyards all over the world and owns 350 acres in Chile's Maipo Valley as well as 180 acres in the Niagara Peninsula producing VQA wines. An inveterate competition entrant, Magnotta has won over 800 medals, "more than any other Canadian winery."

Magnotta is a public company quoted on the Toronto Stock Exchange (MGN).

Winemakers: Peter Rotar and Simon LeChêne
Production: 250,000 cases

Average tonnage crushed: 1,054 tonnes

Annual tonnage purchased: 686 tonnes (Icewine juice purchased 13,000 litres)

Winemaking philosophy: "Affordable excellence. To make world-class wines available to the consumer as inexpensively as possible."

Wines: Own Stores: *Limited edition*—Riesling, Riesling Medium Dry, Gewürztraminer Dry, Gewürztraminer Medium Dry, Sauvignon Blanc, Chardonnay, Viognier, Cabernet Sauvignon, Cabernet Merlot, Merlot, Pinot Noir, Magnotta Millennium (Cabernet Sauvignon)

Gran Riserva—Gran Riserva White (Chardonnay), Gran Riserva Red (Cabernet Sauvignon)

Specialty product—"Sparkling Ice" (Sparkling Vidal Icewine — The World's First Sparkling Icewine)

Feature Wines: Dessert—Mirabella (Fortified Plum Dessert Wine), Iced Apple, Framboise (Raspberry Dessert Wine)

Icewine—1998 Vidal Icewine Limited Edition VQA (Niagara Peninsula), 1998 Riesling Icewine Limited Edition, 1998 Cabernet Franc Icewine Limited Edition

Special Reserve—1997 Pinot Gris, 1997 Fumé Blanc, 1997 Cabernet Sauvignon, 1997 Merlot, 1997 Gewürztraminer Dry, 19997 Gewürztraminer Medium Dry, 1997 Pinot Noir, 1996 Charonnay

Magnotta Winery also produces a fine selection of table wines, very affordable *varietal* Bag-in-Box wines, and an International Series of wines featuring Argentina, California, Chile, France, Italy, South Africa and Washington State.

Stores: (5) On winery premises *Store hours:* Monday to Friday, 9 am — 9 pm; Saturday, 8:30 am — 6 pm; Sunday, 11 am — 5 pm

Magnotta Wines: 1760 Midland Avenue, Scarborough, Tel: (416) 701-WINE (9463), Fax: (416) 701-1441. *Store hours:* Monday to Wednesday, 9 am — 6 pm; Thursday, 9 am — 8 pm; Friday, 9 am — 9 pm; Saturday, 9 am — 6 pm; Sunday, 11 am — 4 pm

Magnotta Vineyards: 2555 Dixie Rd., Mississauga, Tel: (905) 897-WINE (9463), Fax: (905) 897-5410. *Store hours*: Monday to Wednesday, 9 am — 6 pm; Thursday, 9 am — 8 pm; Friday, 9 am — 9 pm; Saturday, 9 am — 6 pm; Sunday, 11 am — 4 pm

Magnotta Vintners: 1585 Victoria Street N., Kitchener, Tel: (519) 571-0084, Fax: (519) 749-0037. *Store hours*: Monday to Wednesday, 9 am — 6 pm; Thursday, 9 am — 8 pm; Friday, 9 am — 9 pm; Saturday, 9 am — 6 pm; Sunday, 11 am — 4 pm

Magnotta Cellars: 4701 Ontario Street, Beamsville, Tel: (905) 563-5313, Fax (905) 563-8804. *Store hours*: Monday to Wednesday, 10 am — 6 pm, Thursday and Friday, 10 am — 7 pm; Saturday, 10 am — 5 pm; Sunday, 11 am — 4 pm

---

Recommended wines: Sparkling Vidal Icewine, Pinot Noir Special Reserve, Riesling Medium Dry, Vidal Icewine

Malivoire Wine Company

4260 King Street East
Beamsville, Ontario
L0R 1B0
Telephone: (905) 563-9253
Fax: (905) 563-9512
web site: www.malivoirewineco.com

MALIVOIRE

Moira Vineyard
1998
Chardonnay
VQA *Niagara Peninsula* VQA
DRY WINE · VIN SEC
750 mL   13% alc./vol.
PRODUCT OF CANADA · PRODUIT DU CANADA

Martin Malivoire and his wine-maker-contractor colleague, Wayne Philbrick, created a gravity-feed winery in 1998 by stretching a Quonset hut down an escarpment slope and painting it olive green. The ingenious design allows for gently processing of the juice on eight levels, from truck delivery of grapes to trucking of finished wines for ageing in a barrel cellar five minutes away. Martin and his partner, Moira Saganski, had to uproot a vineyard to plant grapes suitable for The Bench. Deborah Paskus, an early partner in Cave Spring, selects the grapes and the vineyard is now managed by Daryl Field. Ann Sperling is the general manager and consulting winemaker. All production is estate grown and produced. Martin has a penchant for rosé and plans to plant Grenache to augment the Gamay that it now produces.

Malivoire's first vintage was 1996, a Gewürztraminer Icewine.

Winemakers: Ann Sperling and Wayne Philbrick

Acreage: Two sites on the Beamsville Bench totalling 65 acres (plantings between 1990 and 1999)

Grape varieties: Gewürztraminer, Chardonnay, Pinot Noir, Pinot Gris, Gamay, Chardonnay Musqué, Maréchal Foch

Production: 2,000 cases (1998), potential 20,000 cases

Winemaking philosophy: "We are wine *growers* and will focus on low yields per vine by using 'green harvesting,' longer 'hang times' and botrytis where appropriate to increase the body and complexity of our wines. The winery is designed to use gravity and it will be possible to produce our reds entirely by gravity and our whites with a single pumping at the juice stage, i.e. prior to fermentation."

Wines: Gewürztraminer Icewine, Gewürztraminer Dry Late Harvest, Chardonnay, old vines Maréchal Foch, Rosé

Winery tours: By appointment

Public Tastings: Yes

———

Recommended wines: Gewürztraminer Dry Late Harvest, Chardonnay,
Maréchal Foch, Rosé

Maple Grove Estate Winery

4063 North Service Road
Beamsville, Ontario
L0R 1B0
Telephone: (905) 856-5700
Fax: (905) 856-8208

(See also Vinoteca, page 96)

Having established themselves at
Vinoteca in Woodbridge as the
first winery north of Toronto
since Prohibition, Giovanni
Follegot and his wife Rosanna
bought a property in 1992 at the
foot of the Niagara Escarpment
to make VQA wines. The winery,
according to Giovanni, is a
"miniature operation intended to grow slowly along with the production of grapes
from the estate, producing exclusively 100 per cent Ontario wines, particularly reds"
— a sentiment that reflects the predilection of his native Veneto.

Winemaker: Giovanni Follegot

Grape varieties: Chardonnay, Riesling, Pinot Noir, Cabernet Sauvignon

Winemaking philosophy: "My philosophy is quite simple, grow grapes the best way
I know how, transform each into a unique, characteristic Ontario wine experience and improve along the way."

Wines: Winery store: Chardonnay, Riesling, Trevin White, Pinot Noir, Cabernet
Sauvignon, Merlot, Trevin Red, Icewine

Store hours: Weekends, 10 am — 6 pm

Public tastings: Yes

Winery tours: Yes, telephone first

———

Recommended wines: Chardonnay, Cabernet Sauvignon, Merlot

Marynissen Estates

RR #6, 1208 Concession #1
Niagara-on-the-Lake,
Ontario
L0S 1J0
Telephone: (905) 468-7270
Fax: (905) 468-5784

MARYNISSEN
E S T A T E S

1997
GEWÜRZTRAMINER

MARYNISSEN VINEYARD

VQA • Niagara Peninsula • VQA

White Wine   ESTATE BOTTLED   Vin Blanc
750 ml   11.7% alc./vol.
Marynissen Estates Ltd., RR 6, Niagara-on-the-Lake, Ontario

As an amateur winemaker, grower John Marynissen has a cabinet full of trophies for his Chardonnays, Rieslings, Cabernet Sauvignons and Icewines won in national and international competitions. His family talked him into creating Ontario's first farm-gate winery, and with some backing from Tony Doyle (who used to own Willowbank — the stock was sold to Brights and the equipment went to Marynissen's barn), he started his own operation in 1990. A farmer for over 40 years, he sources his fruit from his two vineyards located between the Niagara Escarpment and the lake. Marynissen's Chardonnay, planted in the mid-1970s, and his Cabernet (1978) are some of the oldest in the Niagara region.

John is a believer in carbonic maceration for Ontario reds and favours the use of oak for fermenting and ageing. He currently uses Tronçais, Allier, Nevers and some American oak. In 1997 his daughter Sandra and her husband Glenn Muir assisted in the wine making.

Winemaker: John Marynissen, Sandra Marynissen and Glenn Muir

Acreage: 70 (55 in production)

Soil: Lot 31, sandy loam; Lot 66, more stoney, loam and gravel. The vineyards are protected from the more extreme air currents near the lake and from the escarpment.

Grape varieties: Chardonnay, Riesling, Gewürztraminer, Vidal, Cabernet Sauvignon, Cabernet Franc, Merlot, Gamay Noir, Syrah

Production: 10,000 cases

Average tonnage crushed: 140 tonnes

Winemaking philosophy: "We emphasize working with nature and producing wines as natural as possible. Growing all of our grapes for wine production here gives us an advantage in that we cut back our yields in order to produce a more concentrated premium grape and wine. We also use crop control depending on the weather, etc."

Wines: LCBO/Vintages: *White*—Chardonnay, Vidal Icewine

Red—Cabernet Sauvignon

Winery store: *White*—Riesling, Riesling Icewine, Chardonnay Barrel Fermented, Chardonnay (No Oak), Gewürztraminer, Cabernet Sauvignon Blanc de Noir, Vidal, Vidal Winter Wine (second pressing of Icewine), Sauvignon Blanc

Red—Merlot, Cabernet Sauvignon, Cabernet/Merlot, Riesling Icewine

Store hours: *November to April:* Monday to Saturday, 10 am — 5 pm; Sunday, 11 am — 5 pm; *May to October:* 10 am — 6 pm; Sunday, 11 am — 6 pm

Winery tours: Yes—group tours of 15 or more by appointment only ($2 per person)

Public tastings: Boutique hours, 50 cents per sample

––––––––––

Recommended wines: Cabernet Franc, Merlot Cabernet, Cabernet Sauvignon, Chardonnay, Vidal Icewine

Meadow Lane Winery

44892 Talbot Line
St. Thomas, Ontario
N5P 3S7
Telephone: (519) 633-1933
Fax: (519) 633-1355

Meadow Lane can be found on Highway #3 across from St. Thomas Airport. They produce the following fruit wines: Strawberry, Peach, Blueberry, Cherry, Cranberry, Raspberry, Nectarine, Elderberry, Gooseberry, Wild Blueberry, Plum, Rhubarb, Black Currant, Framboise, Strawberry-Rhubarb, Spiced Apple, Iced Apple, Apple, Wild Black Cap, Wild Raspberry.

RASPBERRY

Fruit Wine/Vin de Fruit
12.0% Alc./Vol.   750 ml
Meadow Lane Winery Ltd., R.R.# 3 St. Thomas, Ont.
Product of Canada/Produit du Canada

Milan Wineries

6811 Steeles Avenue West
Toronto, Ontario
M9V 4R9
Telephone: (416) 740-2005
Fax: (416) 740-8747

Cabernet Sauvignon
Dry Red Wine
Vin Rouge Sec

MILAN
W I N E R I E S
MISSISSAUGA, ONTARIO
PRODUCT OF CANADA / PRODUIT DU CANADA
750 ml 12% alc./vol.

Previously known as Lauro & Burden Fine Wines (founded in 1992, a 3,000 square foot facility in a commercial/industrial zone), the winery was bought in 1994 by Alberto Milan who ran a imported grape juice company named Vin Bon. Alberto was trained in oenology at the University of Conegliano in Italy and he intends to expand the production space and upgrade the product line "to include more wine types, grape varieties, sources and vintages — as well as oak-aged 'Riservas.'" The wines, a blend of imported material with Ontario grapes, are aged in French and American oak and sold at bargain prices.

Winemaker: Alberto Milan
Production: 16,000 cases
Average tonnage crushed: 50 tonnes
Annual tonnage purchased: 50 tonnes
Winemaking philosophy: "To provide wines of interest at reasonable prices."
Wines: Own store: *White*—Pinot Grigio, Chardonnay, Sauvignon Blanc, Vidal, Riesling, Riesling Icewine, Vidal Icewine
Red—Cabernet Franc, Cabernet Sauvignon, Merlot, Pinot Noir, Rosé
Sparkling—Dry, Semi-Dry, Prosecco Dry and Semi-Dry
Store hours: 9 am — 6 pm weekdays; Saturday 9 am — 5 pm
Tours: No
Public tastings: During store hours

 **FRUIT**

Norfolk Estate Winery

RR #1
St. Williams, Ontario
N0E 1P0
Telephone: (519) 586-2237
Fax: (519) 586-7995
e-mail: newine@simco.on.ca
web site: www.simcom.on.ca/~newine

The Benko family have been farming their 100-acre property southwest of Simcoe since 1946. Apples and tobacco were their crops but George Benko decided wisely there was no future in tobacco and concentrated on apples. In 1995, he and his wife Shirley opened the province's first apple winery. They produce a large portfolio of apple-based wines and have enjoyed much success with their Ice Apple Wine (an Icewine made from apples) and a curiosity — Ice Apple Ginseng — complete with root in bottle.

Winemaker: George Benko

Acreage: 100

Soil: Sandy loam

Apple varieties: Empire, Ida Red, Golden Delicious, Red Delicious, McIntosh, Spy

Production: 1,500 cases

Average tonnage crushed: 22 tonnes

Average tonnage purchased: 2 tonnes

Winemaking philosophy: "Nothing but the best — taste the difference for yourself. All production from fresh fruits — no colouring, flavouring or additives."

Fruit wines: *Dry*—Empire, Golden Delicious, Ida Red, Royal Empire, Royal Empress, Apple Raspberry

Medium—Amber Dry (Apple-Strawberry), Chariot Dry (Apple-Cherry), Apple-Elderberry, Jubilee (Apple-Sour Cherry)

Sweet—Sweet Amber (Apple-Strawberry), Sweet Chariot (Apple-Cherry), Blueboy (Apple-Blueberry), Late Harvest, Apple-Ginseng

Specialty— Apple Wine Liqueur, Chariot Wine Liqueur, Amber Wine Liqueur, Ice Apple Wine, Ice Apple Ginseng

Store hours: Monday to Saturday, 10 am — 5 pm; Sunday, noon — 5 pm (closed January)

Winery tours: Yes (by appointment)

Public tastings: Free

Ocala Orchards Farm Winery

971 High Point Road,
(RR #2)
Port Perry, Ontario
L9L 1B3
Telephone: (905) 985-9924
Fax: (905) 985-7794
e-mail: ocala@sympatico.ca

Irwin and Alissa Smith's farm winery (founded in 1995) is currently outside the VQA's designated wine-growing regions, located as it is five minutes south of Port Perry in the heart of Scugog Township. The winery is housed in a turn of the century dairy barn complete with timber beams, board floors and oak doors, surrounded by orchards and a young vineyard planted in 1992. From their first bottlings of Chardonnay and Riesling in 1992 they have expanded their portfolio into reds and Icewine.

Winemaker: Irwin Smith

Acreage: 12 (vineyard), 16 (orchard), 2 (berries)

Varieties: Chardonnay, Riesling, Vidal, Seyval, Pinot Gris, Auxerrois, Gewürztraminer, Muscat, Baco Noir, Maréchal Foch, Syrah

Production: 4,000 cases

Average tonnage crushed: (grapes and orchard fruit) 43 tonnes

Annual tonnage purchased: 11 tonnes

Winemaking philosophy: "To produce appealing wines from orchard fruit as well as grapes. As a young winery we will grow slowly while paying close attention to quality and customer approval of new wines."

Wines: Own store: *White*—Chardonnay, Riesling, Vidal, Vin de Glace (Vidal Icewine), Seyval, Cabernet Sauvignon, Baco Noir/Foch, Ocala Sparkling Wine

Fruit—several apple varieties, Cherry, Plum, Raspberry, Black Currant, Elderberry, Rhubarb, Gooseberry, Pear. (Not all wines are available year round)

Specialty—Iced dessert wines—Golden Apple, Golden Pear

Store hours: Monday to Saturday, 10 am — 5:30 pm; Sunday, noon — 5 pm

Winery tours: Yes

Public tastings: Yes

Recommended wines: Riesling, Golden Pear, Golden Apple

Pelee Island Winery

455 Seacliff Drive (County Road 20)
Kingsville, Ontario
N9Y 2K5
Telephone: (519) 733-6551
Fax: (519) 733-6553
e-mail: pelee@mnsi.net
web site:www.peleeisland.com

Pelee Island Wine Pavillion (on Pelee
Island)
Telephone: (519) 724-2469
Fax: (519) 724-2507

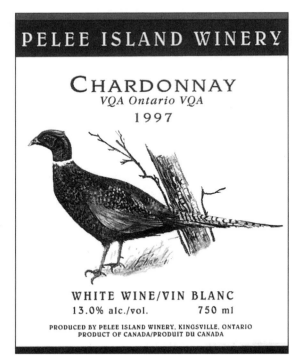

In 1980, Pelee Island Winery
planted Chardonnay, Riesling and
other German varietals on the
island, the first such planting since
the 1860s when Canada's first commercial winery, called VinVilla, was
founded on the island. Vineyards
here are the most southerly in
Canada enjoying the longest grow-
ing season and most heat units. The production facility and retail store (built in 1984)
are on the mainland. Tourists may tour the entire facility and see first hand how wine
is produced. The vineyards are on Pelee Island and tours are offered there as well.
One may taste wine in the vineyards or enjoy a BBQ'd lunch in the wine garden at
the island wine pavillion. The vineyards on the island are the most extensive *vinifera*
plantings of any estate winery.

Walter Schmoranz, the winemaster, is from Germany and has been making wine
for Pelee Island Winery since 1986. He produced Ontario's first red Icewine in 1989
(from Lemberger and Blaufrankisch).

Winemaker: Walter Schmoranz

Acreage: 500

Soil: Limestone bedrock close to surface, Toledo clay and sandy loam; moderating
  effect of Lake Erie

Grape varieties: Chardonnay, Riesling, Gewürztraminer, Zweigelt, Vidal, Gamay,
  Pinot Noir, Scheurebe, Merlot, Cabernet Franc, Cabernet Sauvignon, Pinot
  Gris, Sauvignon Blanc

Production: 150,000 cases

Average tonnage crushed: 1500 - 2000 tonnes

Annual tonnage purchased: 300 - 500 tonnes (Blenheim and Niagara)

Winemaking philosophy: "Our winemaking philosophy is to combine our extensive oenological and viticultural skills with our significant estate vineyards located in the most favoured climatic grape-growing region to produce quality wines as unique as the appellation of Pelee Island."

Wines: LCBO: *White*—Blanc de Blanc, Chardonnay, Hulda's Rock Chardonnay, Pelee Island Dry, Gewürztraminer, Pinot Gris, Riesling Dry, Late Harvest Riesling, Scheurebe

Red—Cabernet, Pinot Noir, Pelee Island Rouge, Merlot, Cabernet Merlot, Gamay Noir Zweigelt, Cabernet Franc

Winery Retail Store: Chardonnay Barrique, Vidal Icewine, Cabernet Sauvignon and Pelee Brut (sparkling)

Store: At the winery in Kingsville

Store hours: Monday to Saturday, 9 am — 6 pm; Sunday, 11 am — 5 pm

Winery tours: Daily — noon, 2 pm, 4 pm

Public tastings: Free during store hours

Pelee Island Wine Pavilion (on Pelee Island): Open daily May 1 to Canadian Thanksgiving. Tour times are co-ordinated with the arrival of the ferry.

Recommended wines: Cabernet Merlot, Gamay Zweigelt, Pinot Gris, Scheurebe, Vidal Icewine

Peller Estates

P.O. Box 10550
697 South Service Road
Winona, Ontario
L8E 5S4
Telephone: (905) 643-2151
1-800-668-9463
Fax: (905) 643-4515
website: www.peller.com

Andrew Peller was 58 when he founded Andrés Wines in Port Moody, B.C. in 1961. He would have opened up in Ontario, but provincial bureaucrats turned down his winery licence application because of his flagrant beer advertising on radio under the guise of selling his ice. (Under the Peller name, he owned a brewery and an ice factory.) After an early success, facilities in Calgary and Truro, N.S. were opened to get listings in those provinces, but business reversals forced Andrew's son, Dr. Joseph Peller, to take over the financial reins of the company. In 1969, Andrés bought their winery in Ontario, and five years later purchased a winery in St-Hyacinthe, Que. followed by the Rouge Valley Winery in Morris, Man.

The mid-1970s was Andrés era with the success of Baby Duck followed by the German-sounding Hochtaler. But the company got left behind in the *vinifera* revolution when the small wineries began to dictate public taste. It was not until 1991 that the company realized that the Andrés name — synonymous with Baby Duck — was not going to sell Chardonnay and Riesling, so it introduced the Peller Estates label to market its varietals which conform to VQA regulations. In 1991, Andrés made its first Icewine and limited amounts of Cabernet Sauvignon.

In July 1994, Andrés purchased Hillebrand Wines to remain competitive with Brights, who had merged a year earlier with Cartier-Inniskillin, to form Vincor.

Winemaker: Roger Summers

Production: 750,000 cases

Average tonnage crushed: 6,000 tonnes

Annual tonnage purchased: 3,000 tonnes

Winemaking philosophy: "Ensure the offering of a wide selection of quality wines to address the wants and needs of the wine consumer, from their 'good value' everyday wine selection to their premium varietal wines."

Wines: LCBO: *White*—Hochtaler, Hochtaler Gold Riesling, Cellar Reserve, Domaine D'Or, Domaine D'Or Superior, Peller Estates French Cross, Peller Estates Oakridge (Chardonnay, Sauvignon Blanc), Peller Estates Founder's Series VQA (Chardonnay, Riesling, Vidal, Late Harvest Vidal, Chardonnay Sur Lie)

Red—Domaine D'Or, Domaine D'Or Superieur, Peller Estates French Cross, Peller Estates Oakridge (Cabernet, Merlot), Peller Estates Founder's Series VQA (Cabernet-Merlot, Gamay Noir)

Vintages—Peller Estates Founder's Series Vidal Icewine

Own Stores: Oakridge Reserve

Wine Stores: 102 Wine Shoppes

Ajax:	Loblaws, 125 Harwood Avenue North
	IGA, 955 Westney Road South
Ancaster:	Sobey's, 977 Golf Links Road
Aurora:	Sobey's, 15500 Bayview Avenue
	IGA, 15278 Yonge Street
Barrie:	Zehrs, 11 Bryne Drive
	Zehrs, Glenronan, 201 Cundles Road, East
Bolton:	Zehrs, 487 Queen Street S.
Bramalea:	Miracle Ultra, Hwy #7 & Dixie Road
Brampton:	IGA, Westbram, 400 Queen Street West
	IGA, Congestoga Square, 29 - 380 Bovaird Drive

	IGA, MacKay Plaza, 930 North Park Drive
	Centennial Mall, 227 Vodden Street
Burlington:	Lakeside Shopping Village, 5353 Lakeshore Road
	Walkers Place, 3305 Upper Middle Road
	Sobey's, 1250 Brant St.
	Fortino's, 2025 Guelph Line
	Marilu's Market, 4025 New Street
Cambridge:	Zehrs, Hwy. #8 & Hwy. #97
	Zehrs, 180 Holiday Inn
Collingwood:	Blue Mountain Mall, 55 Mountain Road
	Loblaws, 12 Hurontario Street
Dundas:	Ultra Mart, 119 Osler Drive
East York:	Bruno's Fine Foods, 1605 Bayview Avenue
	IGA, Todmorden, 1015 Broadview Avenue
	Loblaws, Redway, 11 Redway Road
Etobicoke:	Bruno's Fine Foods, 4242 Dundas Street West
	Loblaws, Dixon, 245 Dixon Road
Gloucester:	Loblaws, Orleans, 1224 Place d'Orleans
Guelph:	Zehrs, 297 Eramosa Road
	Willow West Mall, 167 Silver Creek Parkway
	Zehrs, Hartsland Plaza, 160 Kortright Road, West
Hamilton:	Lloyd D. Jackson Square, 2 King Stret West
	Fortino's Eastgate, 75 Centennial Parkway, N.
	Fortino's, 50 Dundurn Street South
Keswick:	Zehrs, 24018 Woodbine Avenue
Kingston:	Loblaws, Cataraqui Town, 945 Gardiners Road
Kitchener:	Zehrs, 700 Strassburg Road
	Zehrs, Hi Way Market, 1375 Weber Street
	Highland Hills Mall, 46 - 875 Highland Road W.
London:	A&P, Byron Village, 1244 Commissioners Road
	Loblaws, 7 Baseline Road
	A&P, 395 Wellington South
	Oakridge Mall, 1201 Oxford Street W.
	A&P, Adelaide Centre, 1030 Adelaide Street, N.
Mississauga:	IGA, 6040 Glen Erin Drive
	Clarkson Village, 1865 Lakeshore Road W.
	Michael-Engelo's, 4099 Erin Mills Parkway
	Price Chopper, Deer Run, 4040 Creditview
	Dominion Plus, 1151 Dundas Street West

	Dominion Plus, 2550 Hurontario St.
	Loblaws, Credit Landing, 250 Lake Shore Road West
	South Common, 2150 Burnhamthorpe Road W.
	Loblaws, 620 Eglinton West
	Dominion Plus, 1240 Eglinton Avenue West
Nepean:	Loblaws, 59 Robertson Road
	Loblaws, Merivale, 1460 Mervale Road
Newmarket:	Loblaws, 20 Davis Drive
	Dominion Plus, 17725 Yonge St. N.
	Dominion Plus, 1111 Davis Drive
North York:	Loblaws, 3501 Yonge Street
	Steeles Heights Plaza, 1535 Steeles Avenue East
Oakville:	IGA, Abbey Plaza, 1500 Upper Middle Road W.
	IGA, Maple Grove, 511 Maple Grove Drive
	Loblaws, 2431 Trafalgar Road
Orangeville:	Zehrs, Heritage Mall, 54 - 4th Avenue
Oshawa:	A&P, 285 Taunton Road East
	Loblaws, 1300 King Street East
Ottawa:	Hunt Club Centre, 2 - 3320 McCarthy Road
	Southgate Shopping Centre, 2515 Bank Street
Owen Sound:	Zehrs, 1150 Sixteenth St. E.
Peterborough:	Loblaws, 661 Landsdowne Street
Richmond Hill:	Loblaws, 10909 Yonge Street
Scarborough:	Golden Miles S.C., 1880 Eglinton Avenue East
	IGA, Gerrard, 2490 Gerrard Street East
	Ultra Mart, 5085 Sheppard Avenue
	Maxi & Co., 1455 McCowan Road
	Dominion Plus, 3221 Eglinton Avenue East
Simcoe:	Sobey's, 470 Norfolk Street
St. Catharines:	Commisso's, 318 Ontario Street
	Super Fresh, 126 Welland Avenue
	Zellers, 366 Bunting Road
	Port Plaza, 600 Ontario Street
	Zehrs, Fairview Mall, 285 Geneva Street
	Zehrs, Pen Centre, 221 Glendale Avenue
	IGA, Ridley, 111 - 4th Avenue
St. Thomas:	Zehrs, 295 Wellington Street
Stoney Creek:	Fortino's, Fiesta Mall, 102 Hwy #8
Toronto:	Dominion, 656 Eglinton Avenue E.

The Beaches, 2144 Queen Street East
Bloor West Village, 2273 Bloor Street West
Bayview, 1689 Bayview Avenue
Forest Hill, 446 Spadina Road
Uxbridge: Zehrs, 321 Toronto St. S.
Vanier: Loblaws, 100 McArthur Road
Waterloo: Zehrs, Beechwood Plaza, 450 Erb Street West
Welland: Zehrs, 821 Niagara St.
Whitby: Loblaws, 3050 Garden Street
Willowdale: Loblaws, 3555 Don Mills Road
Save a Centre, 4775 Yonge Street
York: Loblaws, 3671 Dundas St. W.

Winery store hours: Monday to Friday, 10 am — 5 pm; Saturday and Sunday, 12 pm — 5 pm

Winery tours/tastings: During store hours: Daily—$1.95 per person. Introductory tasting with cheese and crackers— $3.95. Vintner's Choice — $7.95. Classic Selection — $10.95. Gold Medal Event — $13.95

————

Recommended wines: Founder's Series Chardonnay, Vidal, Late Harvest Vidal, Vidal Icewine

Pillitteri Estates Winery

1696 Highway 55
Niagara-on-the-Lake, Ontario
L0S 1J0
Telephone: (905) 468-3147
Fax: (905) 468-0398

It is, to say the least, unusual for a winery owner to be a federal Member of Parliament, but that's the case of Gary Pillitteri who launched his winery on June 5, 1993.

Gary emigrated to Canada from Sicily in 1948. A longtime grower and former Grape King, Gary was an amateur winemaker of distinction who won gold medals for his Icewine. The opera-

tion is very much a family affair involving his son Charles, daughter-in-law Lili, son-in-law Jamie Slingerland who manages the vineyard and his own grape farm, daughters Lucy and Connie and her husband Helmut Friesen. The winemaking is in the hands of Sue-Ann Staff who got her winemaking training at Australia's Roseworthy wine school.

The modern facility on the highway into Niagara-on-the-Lake features a wine garden, farm market, bakery, greenhouse and tasting room, as well as a hospitality room that can accommodate 100 people.

Winemaker: Sue-Ann Staff

Acreage: 37

Soil: Winery farm — sand; Line A farm — sand and clay

Grape varieties: Riesling, Chardonnay, Sauvignon Blanc, Vidal, Pinot Noir, Cabernet Sauvignon, Merlot

Production: 20,000 cases

Average tonnage crushed: 150 tonnes

Annual tonnage purchased: 130 tonnes

Winemaking philosophy: "Our approach is simple: to produce the finest wines possible from the highest quality Niagara Peninsula grapes. Our strategy, however, is much more complex. We treat each vineyard and wine individually for optimal quality and character. Our internal quality control measures maintain a very high standard throughout the year. From harvesting through to bottling, all processes are closely monitored. The result, award-winning VQA wines full of varietal character in a variety of styles to suit all palates."

Wines: LCBO/Vintages: Barrel Aged Chardonnay, Riesling Dry, Pinot Grigio, Rosé, Vidal Süssreserve, Gewürztraminer Icewine, Riesling Icewine, Select Late Harvest Vidal, Cabernet Sauvignon, Baco Noir

Winery store: Barrel-fermented Chardonnay, Barrel-aged Chardonnay, Chardonnay (No Oak), Riesling Extra Dry, Riesling Dry, Sauvignon Blanc, Pinot Grigio, Auxerrois, Riesling Dry, Gewürztraminer/Riesling, Seyval Blanc, Riesling Sweet Reserve, Vidal Sweet Reserve, Riesling Dolce, Rosé, Blanc de Noir, Merlot, Cabernet Sauvignon, Cabernet Franc, Pinot Noir, Baco Noir, Carretto Rosso Secco, Canadian Port Ghiacco, Late Harvest Riesling, Select Late Harvest Vidal, Select Late Harvest Riesling, Riesling Icewine, Vidal Icewine

Winery tours: Yes

Public tastings: Yes

Recommended wines: Vidal Icewine, Riesling Icewine, Cabernet Franc Family Reserve, Barrel-Ferminated Chardonnay, Pinot Grigio

Quai Du Vin Estate Winery

RR #5
St. Thomas, Ontario
N5P 3S9
Telephone: (519) 775-2216
Fax: (519) 775-0168
e-mail: quai@execulink.com
web site: www.execulink.com/nquai/

Roberto Quai, like Jim Warren of Stoney Ridge and John Marynissen, was an accomplished prize-winning amateur winemaker who went professional. He created his small winery in 1988 with the determination to keep his operation small so that he could control all of its aspects. His father, Redi, had planted the vineyard 25 years ago. The winery itself is spartan and its unique philosophy of offering a 25-cent return deposit on bottles may be the future of an industry that is becoming more environment-conscious. (It's also a good marketing ploy to keep customers coming back.)

Winemaker: Roberto Quai

Acreage: 20

Soil: Clay-loam, gravel base; highest point in Elgin County, 5 km from Lake Erie.

Grape varieties: Vidal, Chardonnay, Aurore, Seyve-Villard 23-512, Riesling, Pinot Noir, De Chaunac

Production: 5,000 cases

Average tonnage crushed: 36.6 tonnes

Annual tonnage purchased: 16 tonnes

Winemaking philosophy: "To produce good quality wine at reasonable prices. Simple winemaking techniques, no sophisticated equipment. Low overheads, no employees."

Wines: Winery store only: Aurore (Semi-Dry), Riesling Semi-Dry, Late Harvest Riesling, Chardonnay, SV 23-512; De Chaunac, Oak Aged Chardonnay

Store hours: Monday to Saturday, 10 am — 5 pm; Sunday, Noon — 5 pm

Winery tours: Yes (no set hours)

Public tastings: Yes (no set hours)

Recommended Wines: not tasted

Reif Estate Winery

RR #1
Niagara Parkway
Niagara-on-the-Lake, Ontario
L0S 1J0
Telephone: (905) 468-7738
Fax: (905) 468-5878
e-mail: wine@reifwinery.com
web site: www.reifwinery.com

The Reif family has been making wines for 13 generations in Germany. This tradition and winemaking knowledge was moved to Canada in 1977 when Ewald Reif purchased vineyards on the scenic Niagara Parkway. After years of uprooting *labrusca* and hybrids and replacing them with Rieslings, Chardonnays, Boredeaux reds and other *viniferas,* Reif officially opened its doors in 1983.

The winemaking was all done in the historic stagecoach house on the property which is still used today as the retail and tour centre. Even today you can see some of the original large German casks brought in from the family estate.

The winemaking took on a new look when in 1987, Klaus Reif (Ewald Reif's nephew, a Geisenheim-trained winemaker) came to Canada to take control of the winemaking operations. One of his first wines, a 1987 Vidal Icewine, was judged by Robert Parker, Jr. to be one of the 10 best wines of the year.

The Reif winemaking style is described as Germanic in tradition with New World flair. Klaus and his co-winemaker Roberto Di Domenico use a combination of stainless steel tanks, large German oak casks and an underground barrel cellar which houses over 200 French and American barriques.

Winemaker: Klaus Reif and Roberto DiDomenico

Acreage: 135

Soil: Sand and loam. The moderating effects of Lake Ontario and the Niagara River provide the vineyards with optimum growing conditions.

Grape varieties: Riesling, Chardonnay, Gewürztraminer, Vidal, Seyval Blanc, Trollinger-Riesling, Cabernet Sauvignon, Merlot, Cabernet Franc, Pinot Noir, Gamay, Baco Noir, Pinot Gris, Sauvignon Blanc; Zinfandel

Production: 35,000 cases

Average tonnage crushed: 500 tonnes

Winemaking philosophy: "Using a combination of Tradition, Technology and Art to create outstanding wines by growing and vinifying premium grape varieties from our own vineyards, thereby maintaining complete control over quality from the vineyard to the glass."

Wines: LCBO/Vintages: *General List*—Chardonnay, Riesling Off-Dry, Vidal, Seyval Blanc, Vintners Cuvée White, Vintners Cuvée Red

Vintages—Vidal Icewine, Cabernet Franc, Pinot Noir

Winery store: *White*—Chardonnay, Chardonnay Reserve, Riesling Dry, Riesling Reserve, Riesling Kabinett, Riesling Clones, Riesling Off-Dry, Riesling Late Harvest, Trollinger-Riesling, Gewürztraminer Dry, Gewürztraminer Medium Dry, Pinot Gris, Sauvignon Blanc, Vidal, Vidal Late Harvest, Seyval Blanc, Vintners Cuvée White, Sparking Wine

Red—Cabernet Franc, Cabernet Sauvignon, Pinot Noir, Pinot Noir Reserve, Merlot, Baco Noir, Cabernet/Gamay Late Harvest, Tesoro (Bordeaux blend)

Rosé—Gamay Rosé

Dessert whites—Riesling BA, Vidal Select Late Harvest, Riesling Icewine, Vidal Icewine

Store hours: *May to October:* 10 am — 6 pm; *November to April:* 10 am — 5 pm

Winery tours: May — September: Daily — 1:30 pm. Groups by appointment.

Public tastings: Yes, year round during business hours

———

Recommended wines: Tesoro, Vidal Icewine, Riesling Icewine,
Cabernet Sauvignon, Select Late Harvest Vidal

Royal DeMaria Wines

4551 Cherry Avenue	Telephone: (905) 563-9692
Vineland, Ontario	Fax: (905) 563-9001
L0R 2C0	e-mail: royald@idirect.com

In 1997, Joseph DeMaria, a Toronto-based hair stylist, bought 25 acres of vineyard planted with Riesling, Cabernet Franc and Vidal. He recently added another 20-acre parcel in which he is planting Pinot Noir, Gewürztraminer, Cabernet Franc and Cabernet Sauvignon. By 2000 he will have a retail outlet but in the meantime he is concentrating on exporting to the United States.

Winemaker: Joseph DeMaria and Brian Alexander (consultant)

Acreage: 45

Soil: Clay loam

Grape varieties: Gewürztraminer, Cabernet Sauvignon, Cabernet Franc, Merlot, Riesling, Vidal

Production: (1998) 5,000 cases (five year plan — 40,000 cases)

Average tonnage crushed: 110 tonnes

Wines: *White*—Vidal, Riesling, Icewines (Riesling, Gewürztraminer, Vidal and
   Cabernet Franc)

Red—Cabernet Sauvignon, Merlot, Cabernet Franc

Blush—Gewürztraminer

Store hours: Monday to Saturday, 10 am — 5 pm; Sunday, 11 am — 5 pm

Winery tours: Conducted and self-guided

Public tastings: Charge for specialty wines

Rush Creek Wines

RR #2
Aylmer, Ontario
N5H 2R2
Telephone: (519) 773-5432
Fax: (519) 773-5431
e-mail: rushcreek@Kanserv/ca
web site: www.elgin.net/RUSH
CREEK WINES/

Rush Creek is a small family-owned fruit winery, the first in Elgin County. Kim and Wendy Flintoff's orchards are close to the north shore of Lake Erie. From 1997 they have enjoyed much success in local competitions with their raspberry, gooseberry and dessert elderberry wines.

Winemaker: Kim Flintoff

Acreage: (orchards) 7 acres, (berries) 3 acres

Soil: Sandy loam

Fruit varieties: Peaches, nectarines, plums, raspberries, gooseberries, black currants, elderberries, strawberries, blueberries. Apples and rhubarb purchased

Production: 3,000 cases

Winemaking philosophy: "One hundred per cent pure fruit wines made without blending apple or grape. To make fruit wines that taste like fruit wines traditionally did in the past, not a mimic of the grape wines (which never result in a satisfactory product). We have no plans to make any grape wines in the foreseeable future. There are too many fruit wines we haven't made yet."

Wines: *Fruit: White*—Peach Classic, Harvest Peach, Light Peach, Sweet Peach, Nectarine, Apple, Spiced Apple, Strawberry-Rhubarb, Plum (rosé), Mead
Red—Elderberry Select, Blueberry, Raspberry, Strawberry
Fortified—Maple Rush
Specialty—Black Currant, Dessert Elderberry, Gooseberry, Framboise
Store hours: Tuesday to Saturday, 10 am — 6 pm; Sunday, noon — 5 pm
Winery tours: Yes (by appointment)
Public tastings: Free

Southbrook Farms Winery

1061 Major McKenzie Drive
Maple, Ontario
L0J 1E0
Telephone: (905) 832-2548
Fax: (905) 832-9811
e-mail:
office@southbrook.com
web site:
www.southbrook.com

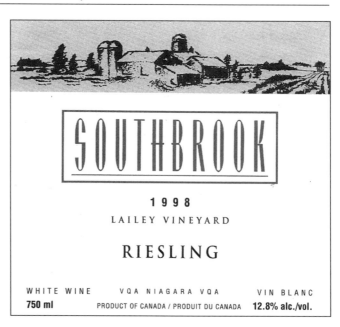

Southbrook, located north of Toronto, is a farm winery with a difference. There are no vineyards but Bill Redelmeier and his wine-maker Derek Barnett truck in grapes from the Niagara Peninsula to vinify them in a century-old barn. Their first crush was in 1991 and they augmented the Ontario grapes with fruit from California. Now they are strictly a VQA winery with all their grapes coming from Niagara vineyards. In fact their new series of wines under the Triomphe label are selected from two specific Niagara-on-the-Lake vineyards. Their Lailey Vineyard bottlings have enjoyed great success for several years as have their fruit wines, Framboise and Cassis. Southbrook has been making Icewine since 1995.

Winemaker: Derek Barnett
Production: 6,000 cases (wine), 1,100 cases (Icewine), 6,000 cases (fruit wine)
Average tonnage crushed : 100 tonnes
Winemaking philosophy: "Fruit focused wines with superior texture and complexity. Interfere as little as possible or necessary and let time and nature work their

magic as much and as often as possible. Extended aging both in barrel and bottle allow wine the chance to develop complex flavours. Yeast fermentation and malo-lactic fermentation are controlled carefully to ensure bold clean flavours."

Wines: *White*—Chardonnay Barrel Fermented, Riesling, Lailey Vineyard, Sauvignon Blanc, Pinot Gris, Vidal, Auxerrois, Chardonnay Lailey Vineyard, Triomphe Chardonnay, Vidal Icewine, Riesling Icewine, Gewürztraminer Icewine

Red—Cabernet Sauvignon Lailey Vineyard: Triomphe Cabernet Merlot, Triomphe Pinot Noir, Cabernet Franc Lailey Vineyard, Zweigelt, Merlot Lailey Vineyard, Maréchal Foch

Fruit—Fortified Dessert Wines—Canadian Framboise, Canadian Cassis, Framboise Noir, Framboise D'or, Blueberry

Store hours: *May 1 to December 24:* 9 am — 6 pm; *January 1 to April 30:* Friday, Saturday, Sunday, 10 am — 5 pm

Winery tours: *May 1 to December 24:* Daily; *January 1 to April 30:* by appointment

Public tastings: Yes, during store hours. Donations for local charities in lieu of tasting charge.

―――――――

Recommended wines: Sauvignon Blanc, Pinot Gris, Chardonnay Lailey Vineyard, Triomphe Chardonnay, Lailey Vineyard Cabernet Sauvignon, Cabernet Franc, Merlot, Vidal Icewine

―――――――――――――――――――――――――――――

Stonechurch Vineyards

1270 Irvine Road, RR #5
Niagara-on-the-Lake, Ontario
L0S 1J0
Telephone: (905) 935-3535
Fax: (905) 646-8892
e-mail:wine@stonechurch.com
web site:stonechurch.com

Stonechurch, founded in 1989, was the first of a new wave of small farm-gate winery enterprises, but the Hunse family had been in the business of growing grapes since 1972. Their holdings make them the

largest family-owned and operated winery in Ontario and their vineyards have been described as looking "as neat and tidy as a hospital bed." Rick Hunse took over the running of the family business in 1995 when his parents, Lambert and Grace Hunse, officially retired but Lambert still retains an active part in maintaining the vineyards.

Winemaker Jens Gemmrich, who gained his winemaking experience in Germany and Austria, joined the company in 1995.

Stonechurch is the most westerly of the Niagara-on-the Lake wineries, situated just off Lakeshore Road.

Winemaker: Jens Gemmrich

Acreage: 150

Soil: Ranging from clay-loam to gravel

Grape varieties: Chardonnay, Morio Muscat, Riesling, Gewürztraminer, Seyval Blanc, Vidal, Cabernet Sauvignon, Cabernet Franc, Pinot Noir, Baco Noir

Production: 30,000 cases

Average tonnage crushed: 6000 tonnes

Winemaking philosophy: "We grow quality grapes and use modern technology to make superb wines which reflect their varietal character."

Wines: LCBO/Vintages: *White*—Chardonnay, Riesling, Morio Muscat, Vidal, Vidal Icewine, Semper White

Red—Cabernet Sauvignon, Cabernet Franc, Baco Noir, Semper Red

Winery store: All of the above plus Barrel-fermented Chardonnay, Gewürztraminer, Vidal Late Harvest, Pinot Noir, Reserve Cabernet Sauvignon, Reserve Chardonnay and selected older vintages

Store hours: *May to September:* Monday to Saturday, 10 am — 6 pm; Sunday, 11 am — 6 pm; *October to April:* Monday to Saturday, 10 am — 5 pm; Sunday, 11 am — 5 pm

Winery tours: Self-guided vineyard tour

Public tastings: During store hours

Private tastings: By appointment

Recommended wines: Morio Muscat, Riesling, Cabernet Franc, Cabernet Sauvignon, Vidal Icewine

Stoney Ridge Cellars

3201 King Street
Vineland, Ontario
Telephone: (905) 562-1324
Fax: (905) 562-7777
L0R 2C0
e-mail: info@stoneyridge.com
web site: www.stoneyridge.com

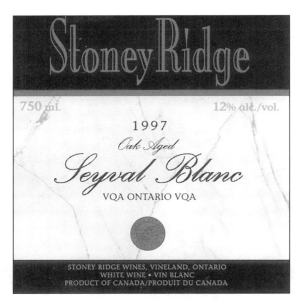

Jim Warren was a gifted and high-ly successful amateur winemaker in the 1970s and early '80s. In 1985, he took the commercial plunge, establishing a tiny winery at Vinemount in a tin shed the size of a small bungalow. In 1990, he went into partnership with grapegrower Murray Puddicombe and they built a winery in Winona. Jim is known for the number of wines he produces (35 — he likes to work with small lots) and his full-flavoured wines with their exotic flavours caught on with the consuming public. In 1997, he was voted "Winemaker of the Year" at the annual Air Ontario Wine Competition. When a group of Ottawa investors bought Stoney Ridge in 1998, Jim found himself presiding over three labels — Stoney Ridge Cellars, Cuesta Estates (premium wines) and Woods End (bargain-priced). Ray Cornell, formerly Hernder Estate's winemaker, shares the winemaking duties. The new winery in a spectacular rural setting is designed to attract visitors. Jim produced the first Ontario port and sherry under VQA regulations and in spite of a huge portfolio of wines he still manages to produce specialty products and a line of fruit wines. Currently most of the grapes are brought in until the Cuesta vineyard comes on stream.

Winemakers: Jim Warren and Ray Cornell

Acreage: 40 (newly planted)

Grape varieties: Pinot Noir, Gewürztraminer, Chardonnay

Production: 50,000 cases

Winemaking philosophy: "We like to produce wines with abundant flavour and bou-
quet — wines that are top quality yet very appealing, well-balanced and honest to
the grape variety. In a word — well-balanced, varietal character, good fruit."

Wines: LCBO: *White*—Bench Chardonnay, Bench Riesling, Bench
Gewürztraminer, Seyval Blanc Fume, Woods End Chardonnay

Red—Pinot Noir, Bench Cabernet Franc, Cabernet/Merlot, Woods End Cabernet
Sauvignon, Woods End Zweigelt, Woods End Rosé

Vintages: *White*—Reserve Chardonnay (Butlers Grant), Charlotte's Chardonnay (Sur Lie), Viognier

Vintages *Red*—Reserve Merlot (Butler's Grant), Reserve Cabernet (Byl Vineyards)

Winery store: *White*—Single Vineyard Chardonnay, Pinot Gris, Sauvignon Blanc, Bench Colombard

Red—Reserve Pinot Noir, Reserve Single Vineyard Cabernet Francs

Specialty— Gewürztraminer Icewine, Vidal Icewine, Select Late Harvest Riesling-Traminer, Forte (VQA Port-Style Wine), Topaz (VQA Sherry-Style Wine)

Fruit— Cranberry, Plum, Ice Apple, Ice Pear, Wild Blueberry

Store hours: Daily, 10 am — 5 pm (6 pm in summer)

Tours and tastings: Daily complimentary tours at 11 am, 2 pm; large selection of wines for tasting; a variety of group and specialty tour packages available

---

Recommended wines: Chardonnay Old Vine, Chardonnay Reserve, Gewürztraminer, Pinot Noir Butler's Grant, Bench Reserve Riesling, Cabernet Merlot, Select Late Harvest Vidal, Riesling-Traminer Icewine

Strewn Estate Winery

1339 Lakeshore Road
Niagara-on-the-Lake, Ontario
L0S 1J0
Telephone: (905) 468-1229
Fax: (905) 468-8305
e-mail:strewnwines@sympatico.ca
web site:strewnwinery.com

Joe Will trained as a winemaker at Roseworthy in Australia. He spent several years as Pillitteri's winemaker before purchasing a disused fruit cannery on Lakeshore Road. With his wife Jane Langdon he transformed the vast empty space (35,000 square feet) into a winery, a cooking school (the first such winery enterprise in Canada), their own home and ultimately an on-premise restaurant devoted to regional cuisine.

Their first crush was the 1994 vintage at Pillitteri.

Winemaker: Joe Will
Acreage: 26

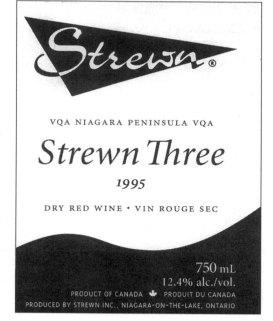

VQA NIAGARA PENINSULA VQA
Strewn Three
1995
DRY RED WINE · VIN ROUGE SEC
750 mL
12.4% alc./vol.
PRODUCT OF CANADA ♦ PRODUIT DU CANADA
PRODUCED BY STREWN INC., NIAGARA-ON-THE-LAKE, ONTARIO

Soil: Varies — sand, sandy loam, clay

Grape varieties: Cabernet Sauvignon, Cabernet Franc, Chardonnay, Riesling, Sauvignon Blanc, Pinot Blanc, Gewürztraminer, Vidal

Production: 17,000 cases

Average tonnage crushed: 282 tonnes

Annual tonnage purchased: 210 tonnes

Winemaking philosophy: "Strewn is committed to producing premium wines from grapes grown in the Niagara Peninsula."

Wines: *White*—Chardonnay Barrel-aged, Chardonnay Unwooded, Riesling (dry), Riesling Süssreserve (semi-dry), Gewürztraminer-Riesling, Pinot Blanc Barrel-aged, Riesling Late Harvest, Vidal, Riesling Icewine

Red—Strewn 3 (Merlot 50%, Cabernet Sauvignon 25%, Cabernet Franc 25%), Cabernets (Cabernet Sauvignon 50%/Cabernet Franc 50%), Merlot, Cabernet Sauvignon, Cabernet Franc, Cabernet Rosé

Sparkling—"In the future, traditional method."

Store hours: Daily, Summer 10 am — 6 pm; other months: 11 am — 5 pm

Winery tours: Weekends at 1 pm, daily in summer. Groups by appointment

Public tastings: Free

———————

Recommended wines: Cabernets, Chardonnay Barrel-aged, Riesling Select Late Harvest, Riesling Late Harvest, Riesling Süssreserve, Vidal Icewine

Sunnybrook Farm Estate Winery

1425 Lakeshore Road
RR #3
Niagara-on-the-Lake, Ontario
L0S 1J0
Telephone: (905) 468-1122
Fax: (905) 468-1068

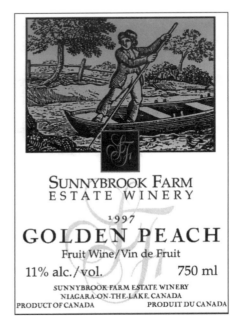

Gerald and Vivien Goertz have been long-time fruit growers in Niagara (and yes, they do have a daughter named Rebecca). While they dabbled in turning their fruit into wine, it wasn't until a vicious hailstorm in 1992 left them with 80 tonnes of bruised and unsalable peaches that they turned winemaking into a proper business. The next fall they got their winery licence in time to open for Christmas. They grow peaches, cherries, pears, plums, apricots, and berries. They also make their fruit version of Icewine — an artificially frozen fermented fruit salad of most of the above. All fruit wines range in alcohol from 10 per cent to 11.5 per cent by volume.

Winemakers: Gerald Goertz and Rebecca Goertz

Production: 8,000 cases

Winemaking philosophy: "Our goal is to make quality wines from fruit other than grapes. All wines are made from 100 per cent Ontario fruit, most of which is grown on our own farm in Niagara-on-the-Lake. The fruit is tree ripened so that the full fruit flavour is captured in the wines. No artificial flavours or colours are used. The wines are not fortified, they are not grape based."

Wines: Winery store: They sell approximately 18 varieties of wine made from peaches, pears, cherries, apples, plums, and berries, from off-dry to dessert styles.

Store hours: *May through October:* Monday to Saturday, 10 am — 6 pm, Sunday, 10 am — 5 pm; *November through December:* Daily, 10 am — 5 pm; *January through April:* Wednesday to Sunday, 10 am — 5 pm

Winery tours: Group tours only, by appointment. (We have a very small facility, so large groups will be crowded.)

Public tastings: During store hours, nominal charge

The Thirteenth Street Wine Company

RR #1 (13th Street South)
Jordan Station, Ontario
L0R 1S0

Telephone/Fax: (905) 562-5900
e-mail: funkwine@vaxxine.com

Thirteenth Street is an association of grape-growing and amateur winemaking talent that could prove to be the most exciting new winery in the province. Grapes are drawn from three very distinct Niagara Peninsula sites and terroir. The three sites (see below) are all Beamsville Bench vineyards: Sandstone Vineyard will specialize in Gamay Noir; Funk will concentrate on grapes for sparkling wines; and Paskus will select grapes for her signature barrel-aged Chardonnays. In appropriate years Pinot Noir, Merlot and Late Harvest Riesling will be produced. The goal is to make ultra-premium, single-vineyard wines that are hand-crafted. The first wines will be released in the fall of 1999.

Winemakers: Deborah Paskus, Herb Jacobson and Erwin Willms (with assistance from Guenther Funk and Ken Douglas)

Acreage: Funk Vineyard — 8.8 acres (sandy clay soil); Willms Sandstone Vineyard (stoney loam soil), plus assorted Bench sites under contract to Deborah Paskus

Grape varieties: Pinot Noir, Chardonnay, Gamay, Cabernet Sauvignon, Cabernet Franc

Production: 1,200 – 2,500 cases

Winemaking philosophy: "Reduced yields in the vineyard for optimum quality. Handpicked followed by processing within a few hours. Soft pressing — whole berry where applicable. Every viticultural effort to grow the best grapes possible."

Thirty Bench Vineyard & Winery

4281 Mountainview Road
Beamsville, Ontario
L0R 1B0
Telephone: (905) 563-1698
Fax: (905) 563-3921
e-mail: wine@thirtybench.com
web site: www.thirtybench.com

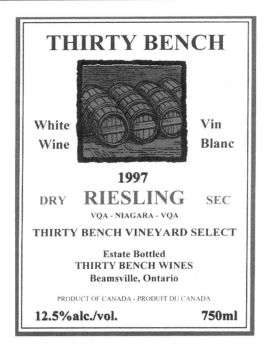

The first crush of Thirty Bench was in 1994, but its origin goes back to 1980 when some gifted amateur winemakers bought 35 acres on the Beamsville Bench and planted it with Riesling. Today Thirty Bench is led by Dr. Tom Muckle (who is also the CEO), Yorgos Papageorgiou and Frank Zeritsch, all three members of the original team. An additional 41 acres of adjacent prime land was purchased at the end of 1998, and its development will begin in the spring of 1999.

The emphasis is on Riesling in a range of styles, but Vidal, Chardonnay and red *viniferas* have become increasingly important. In order to achieve best results, every effort is made to control the winemaking process both at the vineyard and in the winery. This is why grape quality is crucial to Thirty Bench. The vineyard manager, Marek Maniecki, relies heavily on rigorous bunch thinning and late harvesting. Both French and air-cured American barrels are used in the production of the preomium red and white wines. In addition to bunch thinning at the vineyard, barrel ageing for these wines lasts considerably longer than average.

Winemakers: Tom Muckle, Yorgos Papageorgiou and Frank Zeritsch

Acreage: 30 (further 10 in development)

Soil: Beamsville Bench, plus limestone clay-loam. "The driest vineyard on the Bench."

Grape varieties: Riesling, Cabernet Franc, Cabernet Sauvignon, Pinot Noir, Merlot, Pinot Meunier

Production: 7,000 cases

Winemaking philosophy: "Geography, small scale and meticulous attention to detail are necessary for wine quality and character."

Wines: Winery store: *White*—Riesling: Limited Yield, Dry, Semi-Dry, Select Early Harvest, Botrytis Affected Late Harvest, Icewine; Vidal Riesling, Vidal Icewine, Chardonnay "Tradition", Chardonnay Kocsis Vineyard, Chardonnay Reserve

Red—Meunier Red, Cabernet Franc "Tradition", Merlot Reserve, Cabernet Franc Reserve, Cabernet Sauvignon Reserve

Store hours: Daily, 10 am — 6 pm

Winery tours: Yes, on weekends during store hours; at other times by appointment

Public tastings: During store hours

Recommended wines: Chardonnay Reserve, Cabernet Franc, Merlot, Riesling Limited Yield, Riesling Botrytis Affected, Riesling Icewine

---

Thomas & Vaughan Vintners

4245 King Street
Beamsville, Ontario
L0R 1B1
Telephone: (905) 563-7737

Barbara Vaughan and Thomas Kocsis established their winery in 1998 just below the ridge of the Niagara Escarpment between Beamsville and Vineland. Thomas has over 20 years experience of grape growing in the area and has done much to upgrade the Kocsis vineyard in terms of fruit quality. The winery will focus mainly on red varieties. Their first crush was in 1997.

Winemaker: Thomas Kocsis

Acreage: 52 (21 acres planted with *vinifera*, 31 with hybrids)

Soil: Predominantly red clay

Grape varieties: Chardonnay, Riesling, Pinot Gris, Vidal, Cabernet Franc, Cabernet Sauvignon, Merlot, Baco Noir, Maréchal Foch

Production: 1,300 cases (3,500 cases in 1999; 5,000 cases in 2000)

Winemaking philosophy: "The belief that great wines are made in the vineyard.

A technique of minimal interference in the winery and the use of premium quality grapes allows for optimum integrity in the finished product."

Wines: *White*—Chardonnay, Riesling, Vidal, Vidal Icewine, Late Harvest Vidal

Red—A blend of Cabernet Franc, Cabernet Sauvignon and Merlot, Maréchal Foch

Store hours: Thursday to Sunday, 11 am — 6 pm

Winery tours: Yes, special tours by appointment

Public tastings: Free

Recommended Wines: Chardonnay, Riesling, Cabernet blend

Vincor International Inc.

441 Courtney Park Drive, East	Telephone:	(905) 564-6900
Mississauga, Ontario		1-800-265-9463
L5T 2V3	Fax:	(905) 564-6909
	web site:	www.winerack.com
		www.inniskillin.com
		www.atlaswines.com

In 1993, T. G. Bright and Co. merged with Cartier and Inniskillin, thus effectively ending the corporate history of two of the most influential wineries in the history of Canadian wine — Brights and Cartier (formerly Château-Gai). In the following spring all the wine stores operated by these entities (apart from Inniskillin's winery boutique) were consolidated as Wine Rack stores, a number that would eventually reach 161 outlets. In 1996, the company went on a buying spree after raising $38 million on the Toronto Stock Exchange. They acquired Dumont Vins et Spiriteux in Quebec, Okanagan Vineyards (to give Inniskillin its own vineyards in British Columbia) and London Winery to enhace their position as Canada's largest winery.

In 1997, Vincor bought R.J. Grape Products in Kitchener to get into the home winemaking market and the next year, Spagnols, a home winekit producer in Vancouver. To secure supplies of off-shore wines Vincor went into a joint venture with the Boisset group in France and most recently purchased the Paul Masson facility in Montreal.

Vincor will be planting 2000 acres over five years in the Okanagan.

The company has wineries in British Columbia, Ontario, Quebec and New Brunswick and imports wines, spirits and beers under its importing agency, Atlas Wine Merchants. While Inniskillin, the flagship of the group, operates independently, Vincor has a vast portfolio of wines, led by the Jackson-Triggs label (Allan Jackson, the former winemaker at Cartier and Donald Triggs, Vincor's CEO).

Wines: *Jackson-Triggs label* (Winemaker: Mira Ananicz) — Proprietor's Reserve Chardonnay, Riesling, Gewürztraminer, Meritage, Blanc de Noir, Proprietor's Selection, Chardonnay, Sauvignon Blanc, Cabernet Sauvignon, Merlot, Blanc de Noir

Okanagan Vineyards label (BC)—Chardonnay, Sauvignon Blanc, White Zinfandel, Cabernet Sauvignon, Merlot, Vidal Icewine

Braeburn Cellars label—Merlot, Gamay, Cabernet, Sauvignon Blanc, Seyval, Chardonnay

Sawmill Creek label—Chardonnay, Fume Blanc, Riesling, Dry White, Cabernet, Merlot, Dry Red, Autumn Blush, Reserve Series: Chardonnay Bin 55, Cabernet Sauvignon Bin 67, Humidor Cigar Dessert Wine (port style)

London Vineyard Selection label—Baco Noir, Icewine, Late Harvest Vidal, Reserve: Chardonnay, Merlot

Cedar Springs Reserve label—Riesling, Maréchal Foch

Capistro label—White, Dry

House Wine label—White, Dry White, L'Oiseau Bleu, London Chablis, Vintner's Choice, Manor St. David's, Heritage Estates Chablis, L'Escapade

Ambiance label—White, Red

Entre-Lacs label—White, Red, Maria Christina White and Red

Alpenweiss label—White

Fortified wines: *Sherry*—President Sherry, Pale Dry Sherry, Dry Sherry, Cream Sherry, 74 Sherry, Imperial Sherry, Private Stock, London Supreme, London Westminster, London XXX

Port—Private Stock, President Port, 74 Port

Vermouth—London Sweet (Red), London Dry (White)

Sparkling wines: President Canadian Champagne — Canadian Dry White, Special Moments, Canadian Pink, Canadian Brut, Imperial Dry Champagne Spumante Bambino, Rosato Bambino, Spumante Bianco

Stores: Wine Rack Stores

Ajax: Discovery Bay Pl., 570 Westney Road S.

Barrie: 37 Molson Park Drive W.

    409 Bayfield Avenue

Beamsville: 4961 King Street E., Unit 2A

Belleville: Dewe's, 420 Dundas Street E.

    Ultra Food & Drug, 180 N. Front Street

    540 Dundas Street

    Quinte Mall, 390 N. Front

Bowmanville: Bowmanville Mall, 243 King Street E.

Bramalea: Bramalea CC, 25 Peel Centre Drive

Brampton: SW Brampton, Hwy. 10 & Steeles Avenue

    City South Centre, 7700 Hurontario Street

Brantford: Lynden Park Mall, 84 Lynden Road

    290 King George Road

Brockville: 1000 Island Mall, 2199 Parkdale Avenue

Burlington: Longo's, 2900 Walkers Line
 2075 Fairview Street
 Ultra-Mart, 3365 Fairview Street
Cambridge: 35 Pine Bush Road
Chatham: Chatham Centre, 100 King Street W.
North Maple Village, 801 St. Clair Street
Cobourg: Northumberland Mall, 111 Elgin Street W.
Cornwall: Eastcourt Mall, 1390 - 2nd Street E.
 31 - 9th Street E.
Don Mills: Don Mills SC, 919 Lawrence Avenue E.
 Parkwoods Village, 1277 York Mills Road
East York: East York TC, 45 Overlea Blvd.
Etobicoke: 201 Lloyd Manor Road
 Thorncrest Plaza, 1500 Islington Avenue
 Cloverdale Mall, 250 The East Mall
Fort Erie: 200 Garrison Road, Unit 3A
Georgetown: Northview Centre, 211 Guelph Street
Gloucester: 1619 Orleans Avenue
Goderich: Suncoast Mall, 397 Bayfield Road
Grimsby: 44 Livingston Avenue
Guelph: 500 Edinburgh S.
 Stone Road Mall, 435 Stone Road
Hamilton: Mountain Plaza, 665 Upper James Street
 Centre Mall, 1147 Barton Street E.
 505 Rymal Road E.
Huntsville: 70 King William Street
Kingston: Kingston SC, 1080-1096 Princess Street
 675 Dath Road
 2435 Princess Street
Kitchener: 95 King Street W.
 Zehrs, 123 Pioneer Drive
Lindsay: Lindsay Square, 401 Kent Street W.
London: First London Centre, 1080 Adelaide Street N.
 155 Clarke Side Road
 540 Wharncliffe Road S.
 Argyle Mall, 1925 Dundas Street E.
 1255 Wonderland Road N.
 615 Southdale Road
 Northland Mall, 1274 Highbury Avenue

White Oaks Mall, 1105 Wellington Road

Masonville Place, 1680 Richmond Street N., Unit 33

Markham: Markville SC, 5000 Hwy. #7 East

Midland: Mountainview Mall, Hwy #93 and Hugel Avenue

Milton: A&P, 500 Laurier Avenue

75 Nipissing Road

Mississauga: Town Centre, 6677 Meadowvale Blvd.

Sheridan Mall, 2225 Erin Mills Parkway

1250 S. Service Road

3100 Dixie Road

Square One SC, 100 City Centre Drive

Iona Plaza, 1585 Mississauga Valley Blvd.

Central Parkway Mall, 377 Central Parkway

Nepean: Barrhaven Mall, 900 Greenbank Road

Newmarket: Upper Canada Mall, 17600 Yonge Street

17730 Leslie Street

Niagara Falls: 6770 McLeod Road S.

6940 Morrison Street

Portage Plaza, 3714 Portage Road

4887 Dorchester Road

6777 Morrison Street

Nobleton: Nobleton Plaza, Hwy #27 North

North Bay: Northgate Square, 1500 Fisher Street

North Bay Mall, 100 Lakeshore Drive

North York: Lawrence Square, 700 Lawrence Avenue W.

5383 Yonge Street

1694 Avenue Road

NOTL: Line 3 and Niagara Parkway

Oakville: Bronte Village, 2441 Lakeshore Road W.

338 Dundas Street E.

Sherwood Heights, 2828 Kingsway

1011 Upper Middle Road

Orangeville: 150 - 1st Street

Orillia: Orillia Square Hwy #11 and West Street

Oshawa: 481 Gibb Street

500 Howard Avenue

Midtown Mall, 200 John Street

Ottawa: Bayshore S.C., 100 Bayshore Drive

Herongate Mall, 1670 Heron Road

Gloucester Centre, 1980 Ogilvie Road, Unit 131

    Merrivale Mall, 1642 Merrivale Road
    Westgate SC, 1309 Carling Avenue
    708 George Street
    Billings Bridge, 2269 Riverside Drive
    Lincoln Heights, 2525 Carling Avenue
    Carlingwood SC, 2121 Carling Avenue
    Place D'Orleans SC, 110 Place D'Orleans
    296 Bank Street
    11 Metcalfe Street
    2210C Bank Street
Parry Sound: Parry Sound Mall, 70 Joseph Street
Pembroke: Pembroke Mall, 1100 Pembroke Street E.
Peterborough: 370 George Street N.
    Portage Pl. SC, 1154 Chemong Road
    900 Lansdowne Street
Pickering: Supercentre, 1792 Liverpool Road
    1822 Whites Road
Port Colborne: Port Colborne Mall, 287 West Side Road
Sarnia: 600 Murphy Road
Scarborough: Bridlewood Mall, 2900 Warden Avenue
    Morningside Mall, 255 Morningside Avenue
    Cedarbrae Mall, 3401 Lawrence Avenue E.
    Malvern TC, 31 Tapscott Road
    Warden Power Centre, 725 Warden Avenue
    Woodside Square, 1571 Sandhurst Circle
    2650 Lawrence Avenue E.
St. Kitts: Glenridge Plaza, 216 Glenridge Avenue
St. Thomas: Elgin Mall, 417 Wellington Street
Stoney Creek: Eastgate Square, 75 Centennial Parkway
Stratford: Queensland Plaza
Strathroy: 626 Victoria Street
Sudbury: 1485 Lasalle Blvd.
    1836 Regent Street
Thornhill: Thornhill Square, 100 John Street
    Shops on Steeles, 2900 Steeles Avenue E.
    800 Steeles Avenue W.
    The Promenade SC, 1 Promenade Circle
Thunder Bay: 600 Harbor Expressway
Timmins: 654 Algonquin Blvd. E.

Toronto: 1354 Queen Street W.
    731 Queen Street E.
    403 Parliament Street
    560 Queen Street W.
    77 Wellesley Street E.
    SW Danforth, 1003 Danforth Avenue
    2447 Yonge Street at Erskine Avenue
    17 Leslie Street at Lakeshore Blvd.
    103 Cosburn Avenue at Pape Avenue
    746 King Street West
    Honest Eds, 581 Bloor Street W.
    710 Mt. Pleasant Road
    St. Clair Centre, 12 St. Clair Avenue
    Dufferin Mall, 900 Dufferin Street
    Woodbine SC, 500 Rexdale Blvd.
Trenton: Trenton TC, 226 Dundas Street E.
Waterloo: Waterloo Town Square, 75 King Street S.
    550 King Street W.
    70 Bridgeport Road E.
Welland: Rose City Plaza, 815 Ontario Street
    Seaway Mall, 800 Niagara Street
Weston: 2549 Weston Road
Whitby: 70 Thickson Road
Windsor: 880 Goyeau Street
    Malden Village Centre, 5890 Malden Road
    Central Mall, 3669 Tecumseh Road
    Parkway Mall, 7201 Tecumseh Road East
    Dougall Square, 2430 Dougall Avenue
Woodstock: 379 Springbank Avenue N.
    969 Dundas Street
    645 Dundas Street

————

Recommended Wines: Jackson Triggs: Okanagan Vidal Icewine, Ontario Gewürztraminer, Meritage, Riesling

Vine Court Estate Winery

4279 Cherry Avenue
Beamsville, Ontario
L0R 1B0
Telephone: (905) 562-8463

Geisenheim-trained Joseph Zimmermann has been around the Canadian wine industry longer than his looks would suggest. In 1976, he was the winemaker for Jordan-Ste. Michelle in Victoria, BC, before moving to that company's operations in Ontario. When Jordan was bought out by Brights, Joseph took a job with Ontario's Grape Adjustment Program. In 1993, he had accumulated 90 acres of vineyard and sold his juice mainly to out-of-province wineries. To create his own winery he took over Ron Speranzini's Willow Heights facility (visible from the QEW at Beamsville) where he plans to make his own wines and continue to sell juice and wine to producers outside Ontario.

Winemaker: Joseph Zimmermann

Acreage: 35

Soil: Sandy loam to sandy clay

Grape varieties: Auxerrois, Riesling, Chardonnay, Vidal, Baco Noir, Gamay Noir, Pinot Noir, Zweigelt

Production: 3,500 cases

Winemaking philosophy: "Vine Court Estate is dedicated to vinify only the best varietal grapes."

Wines: *White*—Auxerrois, Chardonnay, Riesling, Icewines (Vidal, Cabernet Franc, Riesling)

Red—Baco Noir, Gamay Noir, Zweigelt, Cabernet Franc, Pinot Noir Rosé

Sparkling: Chardonnay

Fortified: Sovereign Coronation

Store hours: *July 1 to Labour Day:* Daily, 10 am — 5 pm; *Labour Day to December 24:* Saturday and Sunday, 11 am — 5 pm; *February to June:* Saturday and Sunday, 10 am — 5 pm

Tours: Yes

Public tasting: Free

Recommended Wines: not tasted yet

Vineland Estates Wines

RR #1, 3620 Moyer Road
Vineland, Ontario
L0R 2C0
Telephone: (905) 562-7088
Fax: (905) 562-3071
e-mail: wine@vineland.com
web site: vineland.com

Vineland Estates has been producing premium VQA wines since 1988. Eighty per cent of the winery's grapes are estate grown, and the location of their vineyards on the much heralded growing area of the Bench of the Niagra Escaprment provides a terroir and soil particularly suited to Riesling. Today, Vineland Estates' winemaker Brian Schmidt continues the tradition begun at the property by his brother and General Manager, Allan Schmidt. Riesling, in the trademark style exacted by Allan, continues to be the hallmark of Vineland Estates' wines. In the future, Brian plans to expand the winery's red wine production and is branching out to new varietals and styles such as Sauvignon Blanc and a Riesling sparkling wine.

Since the purchase of the winery by John Howard in 1992, the winery has undertaken significant expansion projects, and the change which has characterised the winery over the last five years is set to continue. In 1999, the century barn was renovated to house an expanded retail store, and plans are in place to open a 10,000 square foot underground barrel cellar. Improvements are also planned for the on-site restaurant, in keeping with the new look of the winery as it enters the millennium.

Set on the bench of the Niagara Escarpment, Vineland Estates is the most picturesquely situated winery in Ontario with its 1845 farmhouse (now the tasting room and boutique wine shop), small bed-and-breakfast cottage on the edge of the vineyard, and Ontario's first winedeck serving light bistro-style lunches. A newly restored 1857 stone carriage house is the venue for winemaker dinners and catered events.

Winemaker: Brian Schmidt
Acreage: 50 acres on site, 250 acres off site
Soil: Gently sloping vineyards, clay loam soil, well-drained, rolling hills
Grape varieties: Riesling, Chardonnay, Pinot Noir, Cabernet, Seyval Blanc, Gewürztraminer, Vidal (Icewine), Chardonnay Musqué, Merlot
Production: 30,000 cases (projected 70,000 by 2002)
Average tonnage crushed: 450 tonnes
Annual tonnage purchased: 50 tonnes

Winemaking philosophy: "Riesling not overripe. Cool fermentations giving slightly higher acidity than normal."

Wines: LCBO: *White*—Dry Riesling, Riesling Semi-Dry, Vidal Icewine

Own store: *White*—Riesling Reserve, Select Late Harvest Riesling, Chardonnay, Chardonnay Estate, Chardonnay Reserve, Chardonnay Musqué, Gewürztraminer, Seyval Blanc

Red—Pinot Noir, Cabernet Sauvignon, Carriage House Red, Merlot, Meritage

Sparkling — Riesling Cuve Close

Store hours: Weekdays, 10 am — 5:30 pm; Saturday and Sunday, 11 am — 9 pm; *January to April:* Weekdays, 10 am — 5 pm; weekends, 11 am — 5 pm

Public tastings: During store hours

Winery tours: Daily, 11 am, 1 pm, 3 pm (May 24th weekend through October 31)

Recommended wines: Riesling Dry and Semi-Dry, Riesling Reserve, Vidal Icewine, Chardonnay Reserve, Meritage, Gewürztraminer, Select Late Harvest Riesling, Riesling Cuve Close

Vinoteca Inc.

527 Jevlan Drive
Woodbridge, Ontario
L4L 8W1
Telephone: (905) 856-5700
Fax: (905) 856-8208

VQA NIAGARA PENINSULA VQA

Chardonnay
96 RESERVE
WHITE WINE / VIN BLANC
750 ml - 11.5% alc./vol.
PRODUCT OF CANADA / PRODUIT DU CANADA
VINOTECA INC., WOODBRIDGE, ONTARIO

Giovanni Follegot and his wife Rosanna, natives of Veneto in northern Italy, began by importing grape juice for the Italian community to make their own wine.

In 1989, the Follegots set up a fermenting operation in a Woodbridge industrial park, using Ontario grapes trucked in from the Niagara Peninsula and imported juice. The winery produces VQA wines and off-shore blends.

French and American oak barrels are used and the winery began making small batches of Icewine in 1990. In 1992 they purchased vineyards in Vineland.

Vinoteca wines are only available at the winery. See also Maple Grove Estate Winery page 62.

Winemaker: Giovanni Follegot

Winemaking philosophy: "Our total dedication and hard work has enabled us to produce valid wines that are well accepted by consumers, whose use is mainly to complement their meals. With confidence we are able to progress and improve our wines to reach the highest standards."

Wines: Winery store only: *White*—Pinot Grigio, Sauvignon Blanc, Chardonnay, Riesling, Vidal Icewine

Red—Pinot Noir, Cabernet Sauvignon, Merlot

Store hours: 9 am — 6 pm; Sunday, 11 am — 4 pm (except July and August)

Winery tours: By appointment

Public tastings: During store hours

Recommended wines: Chardonnay, Cabernet Sauvignon, Cabernet Franc

---

Willow Heights Winery

Box 551
3751 Regional Road
#81, R.R. #1
Vineland, Ontario
L0R 2C0
Telephone: (905) 562-4945
Fax: (905) 562-5761
e-mail: willowheights@sympatico.ca
web site: www.willowheightswinery

Ron and Avis Speranzini opened Willow Heights in Beamsville in 1994. Ron was a basement winemaker for 12 years who won many awards for his wines in amateur competitions. He studied oenology through university home-learning programs for five years and paid his dues by working the crush at local wineries in the peninsula. Like Jim Warren of Stoney Ridge and John Marynissen of Marynissen Estates before him, Ron made the leap from amateur to professional and he set his sights high. In 1998 he purchased a Vineland property and has subsequently expanded the patio area to serve higher fare.

Winemaker: Ron Speranzini
Acreage: 12 acres on new property to be planted

Grape varieties: Chardonnay, Riesling, Seyval Blanc, Vidal, Gewürztraminer, Auxerrois, Gamay Noir, Merlot, Cabernet Franc, Pinot Noir

Production: 6,000 cases

Average tonnage crushed: 83 tonnes

Winemaking philosophy: "To produce the highest quality wines possible bearing the VQA trademark. This can only be achieved through the dedicated co-operation between the grower and vintner throughout the harvest year. We intend to produce wines which are distinctive to the *terroir* of the Niagara Peninsula."

Wines: LCBO/Vintages: Chardonnay Reserve, Seyval Blanc, Late Harvest Vidal Villard Noir, Cabernet Franc

Store hours: Monday to Saturday, 10 am — 5 pm; Sunday, 11 am — 5 pm

Winery tours: By appointment

Public tastings: During store hours

———————

Recommended wines: Chardonnay Pinot Noir, Seyval Blanc, Gamay Noir, especially Reserve Wines

BRITISH COLUMBIA

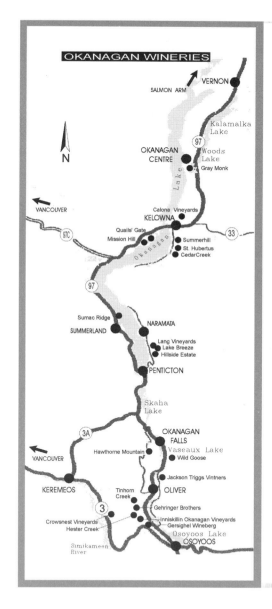

OKANAGAN WINERIES

SALMON ARM
VERNON

Kalamalka Lake

OKANAGAN CENTRE
97
Woods Lake
Gray Monk

VANCOUVER

N

97C

Calona Vineyards
KELOWNA
Quails' Gate
Mission Hill
Summerhill
St. Hubertus
CedarCreek
33

Okanagan Lake

97

Sumac Ridge
NARAMATA
SUMMERLAND
Lang Vineyards
Lake Breeze
Hillside Estate

PENTICTON

Skaha Lake

3A

OKANAGAN FALLS
Vaseaux Lake
Hawthorne Mountain
Wild Goose

VANCOUVER

Jackson Triggs Vintners

KEREMEOS
3
Tinhorn Creek
OLIVER
Gehringer Brothers
Crowsnest Vineyards
Hester Creek
Inniskillin Okanagan Vineyards
Gersighel Wineberg
Osoyoos Lake
OSOYOOS
Similkameen River

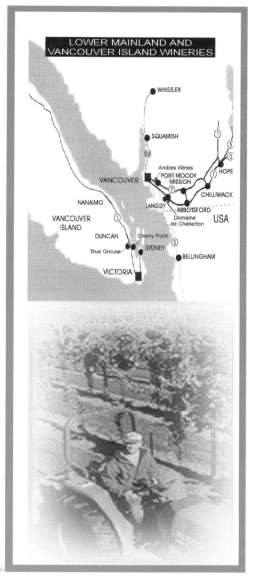

LOWER MAINLAND AND VANCOUVER ISLAND WINERIES

WHISTLER

SQUAMISH
1
6
5
89
3
Andres Wines
VANCOUVER
PORT MOODY
MISSION
HOPE
1
NANAIMO
7
CHILLIWACK
LANGLEY
ABBOTSFORD
VANCOUVER ISLAND
1
Domaine de Chaberton
USA
DUNCAN
Cherry Point
5
Blue Grouse
SYDNEY
BELLINGHAM
VICTORIA

Wine Regions of British Columbia

There have been few transformations as swift and profound as the one experienced in the last decade by the British Columbia wine industry. From a crisis in 1988-89 when two thirds of its predominantly hybrid grape acreage was literally pulled out of the ground, the industry has been able to reinvent itself as an internationally recognized premium *vinifera* wine producer.

The crisis initiating the change was the signing of the Canada-U.S. Free Trade Agreement which basically told the industry that to survive as a wine producing region it would have to convert from growing mainly hybrid varieties to premium *viniferas*. The response was the massive pull out program.

The early 1990s was a transition period for grape growers who took advantage of government incentives to replant to *vinifera* varieties. The road was a long one. Even by 1994 total grape acreage had only recovered 1,712 acres of the 3,400 that had existed before the pull out program. By that time however, growth was becoming swift. The 3,400 acre level was recovered by 1997 and major planting programs were aiming toward 5,000 acres around the turn of the millennium.

Compared to this hectic pace, most of the history of the British Columbia grape and wine industry was leisurely.

Early History

The wine industry in B.C. did not really start until the 1930s. While the combined insanity of Prohibition and the Depression almost destroyed the Ontario wineries, ironically it provided the impetus for the birth of B.C. commercial winemaking in the Okanagan and Similkameen River valleys when *labrusca* varieties such as Campbell, Concord, Diamond, Patricia, Sheridan, Bath and Delaware were first planted.

The story goes back to the 1860s when Father Charles Pandosy planted a few vines at the Oblate Fathers' Mission, built seven miles south of Kelowna. But the farmers who followed were more interested in fruit crops such as apples, peaches and apricots than in grapes. The first commercial vineyard in the province was planted by W.J. Wilcox some 55 miles north of Kelowna, at Salmon Arm. This three-quarter-acre plot yielded such Ontario varieties such as Concord, Niagara, Delaware and Agawam for the table trade. Six years later, Jim Creighton planted a small vineyard in Penticton, an area which would ultimately prove to be one of the best sites for grape growing along the shore of Okanagan.

The narrow serpentine lake, carved out by prehistoric glaciers, stretches north for over 100 kilometres and the land rises steeply from the water on either side. Technically, the area is a desert since there is little rainfall (the southern end of the lake around Oliver gets no more than six inches of precipitation a year). In terms of latitude, the Okanagan Valley is in the same belt as the Champagne region of France and the Rheingau of Germany (a fact which seduced many pioneers into believing that they could produce wines to rival the great Rieslings and sparkling Chardonnays) but the climate is very different from Europe. During the summer days, the Okanagan vines experience tremendous heat and at night the temperature dips dramatically. Intense sunlight builds up the grape sugars and the freezing nights do not allow the acids to metabolise, so the berries have very high acid readings. Because of the lack of rainfall, the vineyards have to be irrigated during the growing season.

The Okanagan experiences long, mild autumns, as does northern Germany, but by mid-October the temperature has fallen to a point where the grapes will no longer mature and they will have to be harvested. On the plus side, British Columbian summers, like those in California, are consistent and predictable, which ensures an even quality of grape from year to year. In spite of fluctuating temperatures, there are pockets along the valley's southern slopes that protect the vines from the killing frost that rolls down the lake from October on, and the body of water ameliorates the air temperature on the coldest nights. Many of these microclimates have been identified by infrared aerial photography, through a program conducted by the Summerland Research Station in conjunction with the provincial government. Without the advantage of such technology, the early grape growers could only plant their vines, sit back and pray.

The first wines in British Columbia were not made from grapes at all, but from loganberries which flourished in southern Victoria Island on the Saanich Peninsula. They rejoiced in such names as Slinger's Logan and Logana. But a few inspired souls turned their attentions to wine grapes. Charles Casorso of Kelowna was a grape-growing pioneer who planted a vineyard on a 35-acre property at Rutland near Kelowna in 1925 and in 1926 a farmer by the name of Jesse Willard Hughes, encouraged by the Hungarian oenologist Dr. Eugene Rittich, bought a 45-acre vineyard in Kelowna near the Oblate Fathers' Mission and planted vines that had been locally propagated. He also purchased a 20-acre site on Black Mountain. The larger vineyard near Kelowna prospered to such an extent that four years later wines made from these grapes were vinified at the Growers' Wine Company in Victoria.

Encouraged by his success, Hughes was to expand his vineyard to 300 acres, but the experiment at Black Mountain proved a disaster since the vines were wiped out by winter kill.

Rittich and his viticulturist brother Virgil, however, were convinced that grapes could be grown on Black Mountain. It was just a question of finding the right variety and employing the correct viticultural practices to prevent winter kill. As the first champions of *vinifera* grapes in the province, they experimented with 44 varieties on this site and one in the barren Oliver region. They summed up their work together with grape variety recommendations in cooler districts where winter protection is necessary in 1934 in a book called *European Grape Growing*.

In the same year Eugene Rittich was hired as the winemaker for the Growers' Wine Company, which had previously specialized in loganberry wine. A freak of nature was to give the fledgling industry the boost it needed. Successive abundant harvests of apples caused a glut on the market and many farmers were forced to tear out their orchards and plant grapes instead. Growers' Wine Company was paying $100 a tonne for grapes (compared to $65 a tonne in Ontario) while apples were left rotting under the trees. "A cent a pound or on the ground," was the farmers' anguished cry. "A dollar a box or on the rocks."

At the height of the Depression in 1932, an immigrant Italian winemaker named Guiseppe Ghezzi came to Kelowna with the idea of creating a winery to use the worthless apple crop.

The idea had also occurred to a local hardware store owner, William Andrew Cecil Bennett, who had discussed just such a possibility with his neighbour on Kelowna's main street, an Italian grocer named Pasquale "Cap" Capozzi. Both men were teetotallers, but they joined with Ghezzi to form a company called Domestic Wines and By-Products. The company would manufacture not only wines but a whole gamut of products including "apple cider ... brandy, alcohol, spirits of all kinds, fruit juices, soft drinks, fruit concentrates, jelly jams, pickles, vinegar, tomato paste, tomato catsup, tomato juice and by-products of every kind." The debonair Guiseppe Ghezzi stayed long enough to set up the winery before emigrating to California where he established a "champagne" plant.

Bennett and Capozzi set about raising money to finance their new operation. At a time when soup kitchens meant more to the public than wineries, they began selling shares in the company for one dollar. They raised $4,500, and although they were under-capitalized, they bought fermenting tanks and other equipment to begin this multifaceted business. In September 1932, they took up residence in an old rented building on Kelowna's Smith Avenue. The following year they hired Guiseppe Ghezzi's son Carlo as winemaker to complete their staff of eight employees. Their initial production included four apple-based wines — Okay Red, Okay Clear, Okay Port and Okay Champagne. But the products were far from "okay." Even the company's official history records that the wines "were a bitter disappointment. Many bottles refermented on liquor store shelves and had to be thrown out. Liquor stores were reluctant to stock the ill famed domestic wines and people were reluctant to buy them." Sales in the company's first full year of operation were a disaster, amounting to a mere few thousand dollars.

After three years of ineffectual competition against the genuine wines of the Growers' Company, Bennett and Capozzi realized that B.C. consumers just did not want apple wines. They switched to grapes which they bought in California, and soon Growers' and the Victoria Wineries on Vancouver Island did likewise, perpetuating the fiction of making domestic wines by using whatever local grapes were available.

With the change of style, the former apple winery needed a change of name, and in 1936 the directors chose a phonetic spelling of the Indian place name where the company was born: Calona Wines Limited. Okay Clear apple wine became Calona Clear grape "wine," a white semi-sweet product whose label read ominously "When Fully Mature: About 28% Proof Spirit."

In 1940, W.A.C. Bennett left Calona to pursue a career in politics. One year later he was elected to the B.C. parliament and he sold his shares to Capozzi. When he became premier of the province in 1952, he took a serious look at the wine industry he had helped to create. If the wineries were to sell their products through the government-controlled liquor stores, then they should do their part in promoting the grape-growing sector, he argued. In 1960, the B.C. government passed a law stating that wines vinified in the province had to contain a minimum percentage of locally grown grapes. Since there were only 585 acres under vines in the Okanagan Valley, that figure was set at 25 per cent. To encourage the planting of new vineyards, the Liquor Board stated that the quota would rise to 50 per cent in 1962 and 65 per cent by 1965.

Farmers in the Okanagan Valley began planting French and American hybrids (Okanagan Riesling, De Chaunac, Maréchal Foch, Verdelet, Rougeon, Chelois and Baco Noir) with a vengeance and within four years the total acreage had risen by 400 per cent. In 1961, Andrew Peller built Andrés' spanking new winery at Port Moody; six years later a company called Southern Okanagan Wines of Penticton opened for business, but it soon changed its name to Casabello. At the same time, the beautifully situated Mission Hill Winery was built on a ridge overlooking Okanagan Lake at Westbank. This facility was acquired in 1969 by the ebullient construction king and brewer, Ben Ginter, who promptly renamed it with characteristic flamboyance (if little understanding of consumer sophistication) Uncle Ben's Gourmet Winery. He also put a portrait of himself on his labels. Among the products Ginter was to market were such items as Fuddle Duck and Hot Goose.

In 1973, the Growers' Wine Cooperative, which had merged with Victoria Wineries and changed its name to Castle Wines, was acquired from Imperial Tobacco by Carling O'Keefe. Another corporate name change was in store. Castle Wines became Ste-Michelle Wines (a subsidiary of Jordan and Ste-Michelle Cellars Ltd.) in 1974. The company had long outgrown its facility in Victoria and looked to the mainland to build a modern winery to service the growing demand in the province for table wines. Four years later, it began building at Surrey, just south of Vancouver, and opened its operation in April 1978.

From 1974 to 1979, growers turned their attention to grape varieties imported from California and Washington. Experimental plantings of Cabernet Sauvignon, Merlot, Chenin Blanc, Gewürztraminer, White and Grey Riesling, Semillon and Chardonnay were evaluated at 18 sites throughout the Okanagan. In 1975, George Heiss brought in Auxerrois, Pinot Gris and Gewürztraminer from France to plant in his Okanagan Centre vineyard.

In March 1977, the B.C. Ministry of Consumer and Corporate Affairs, responding to a strong lobby from the wineries and grape growers, announced a new liquor policy "to recognize the health and social costs caused by the abuse of alcohol on the one hand and consumer demand for better products, better prices and better premises in which to have a drink, on the other hand." The thrust of the new legislation was to encourage the consumption of wine, both imported and domestic, at the expense of hard liquor and beer.

To help the provincially based wineries compete with low-cost imports, the government lowered the markup on table wines from 66 per cent to 46 per cent (at the same time reducing imports from 117 per cent to 100 per cent markup). To give their products a sales boost, B.C. wineries were allowed to open a retail store on their premises, and under the aegis of the federal and provincial Ministries of Agriculture a five-year grape-growing program was introduced, at a cost of $133,000, to upgrade the quality of the grapes they had to use. The program was directed by world-famous viticulturist, the late Dr. Helmut Becker, then head of the Research Institute of Grape Breeding and Grape Propagation at Geisenheim in Germany. At the invitation of Andrés Wines, Dr. Becker selected 27 European varieties for testing in B.C. soil.

Two three-acre plots were chosen for the experiment "a southern site on light, sandy soil near Oliver, and a northern site in the heavier soil at Okanagan Mission." The first wines made from these grapes were vinified by the Summerland Research Station in 1980. The most promising varietals turned out to be Auxerrois, Ehrenfelser, Pinot Blanc, Bacchus, Gewürztraminer, Müller-Thurgau, Schönburger and Scheurebe.

Looking south to the Napa and Sonoma valleys of California, the B.C. government realized that there was great tourist potential for a thriving wine industry in the beautiful Okanagan Valley setting. After years of bureaucratic foot-shuffling, the politicians finally agreed to the creation of cottage or estate wineries; the first in the field was Claremont. In 1979, the late Bob Claremont took over a facility built by Marion John who had planted vineyards on a steep slope just north of Peachland 19 years earlier. John's first wines were made and bottled at Mission Hill Winery, but Claremont, who had worked as a winemaker at Calona as well as at Jordan's Ontario plant, set up a crusher, fermentation tanks and a bottling line, and began to vinify B.C.'s first estate-bottled wines in 1979.

The B.C. Liquor Control and Licensing Branch, not knowing how to deal with the novel enterprise, hastily introduced regulations which both encouraged and inhibited the new winery. To be an estate winery, the company had to cultivate 20 acres of vines and could only make a maximum of 30,000 gallons (later increased to 40,000 gallons). All the grapes used in the wine had to be grown in the province and 50 per cent of these had to come from Claremont's own vineyards. The winery was allowed to open a retail store on its premises and could sell directly to licensees without having to pay the government's markup.

Claremont could sell two products through the specialty liquor stores only, but these would only carry the then markup of 15 per cent.

Within the next three years, Bob Claremont was joined by four other small producers in the Okanagan — Sumac Ridge, Vinitera (which went into receivership in 1982), Uniacke Cellars (now CedarCreek), Gray Monk, and in the spring of 1983, Divino Wines in Oliver. In those early days, there was a feeling of camaraderie among the operators of these small wineries and they helped each other out when they could by sharing facilities and equipment, such as hand-labelling machines or storing one or the other's wines. They were the pioneers of a new phase of B.C.'s growing wine industry.

Meanwhile, Uncle Ben's Gourmet Wines, suffering the consequences of marketing dubious wines, fell foul of the banks and reemerged briefly under the name of Golden Valley Wines. However, its reincarnation did not help its balance sheet; thanks to union animosity following troubles at Ginter's Red Deer Brewery, Ginter was forced to sell and the company was bought in 1981 by Anthony Von Mandl's Mark Anthony Group, a successful Vancouver-based firm of wine importers, who immediately restored its original name of Mission Hill and began a massive reorganization.

The last commercial winery to open in B.C. was Bright's, who built a spectacular modern winery in 1981 on Inkameep Indian Band land to ferment grapes grown on the Band's adjacent Inkameep Vineyards. The building alone cost $2 million and was funded by development money from the provincial and federal governments. Bright's invested $3.5 million in equipment for the new facility. In 1994, Bright's merged with Cartier-Inniskillin to form Vincor International, and for economies of scale the company enlarged this facility for its combined winemaking operations.

The Rebuilding

After the extensive *vinifera* replanting that followed the 1988-89 pull out program there was a lull while the new vines came into production. For the wine consumer, the impact of the fundamental changes began to become apparent in 1993 when many of the vines from the new plantings started to come into production to augment the established white Germanic *viniferas*.

Additional volumes of familiar Riesling, Gewürztraminer, and Ehrenfelser were joined by Pinot Blanc, Pinot Gris and Chardonnay. On the red *vinifera* side, existing Pinot Noir and a bit of Merlot and Cabernet suddenly blossomed into appreciable releases of these premium varietals at an increasing number of wineries.

Essentially, 1993 marked the turning point for the British Columbia wine industry and from that time forward there was no looking back. Consumers responded with increasing purchases of B.C. produced VQA wines, in turn spurring additional plantings.

On the quality side, lessons were being learned rapidly as well. In the early 1990s a white *vinifera* wine priced at over $9 per bottle was virtually unheard of. By combining quality fruit with advanced winemaking techniques, premium releases of Pinot Blanc and Chardonnay were soon fetching around $13 per bottle. This provided a better return to growers, prompting improved vineyard practices and additional plantings.

In the wine cellar, new techniques included judicious barrel ageing combined with lees contact and malolactic fermentation to produce wines with more complexity. By continuing to cold ferment a portion of the wine in stainless steel to retain fruitiness and acid, the resulting blends soon earned British Columbia a solid reputation as a premium producer of Pinot Blanc, Pinot Gris and Chardonnay. This accomplishment was marked when Mission Hill's 1992 Grand Reserve Chardonnay won the Avery Trophy for Best Chardonnay in the World at the 1993 International Wine and Spirits Competition in London.

White *vinifera* plantings in the later 1990s built on this foundation and expanded into successful releases of Sauvignon Blanc and Semillon.

Following the initial success of the white *viniferas*, recognition for premium red *viniferas* soon followed. Sumac Ridge Estate Winery's 1995 Merlot was named Canada's Best Red Wine as well as Canada's Wine of Year at the All Canada Wine Championships in 1997 while their 1995 Cabernet Sauvignon won a Gold medal at Sélections Mondiales in Montreal, marking the first time that a Canadian red wine ever won a Gold medal in this international competition.

Red wine momentum continued to grow as increasing volumes of quality Pinot Noir, Merlot, Cabernet Franc and Cabernet Sauvignon came on stream in the late 1990s. The dramatic rebirth of the British Columbia wine industry is reflected in the growth of VQA wine sales which increased from $6.8 million in 1991-92 to $39.7 million in 1997-98, an increase of almost 500 per cent.

What we have been discussing here are the true British Columbia wines which are grown and produced in the province, not wines that are imported from other wine growing regions and only bottled in the province as proprietary releases by major wineries and labeled as "Product of Canada."

Up until 1998, British Columbia liquor control regulations divided the wine industry into three categories: major, estate and farm wineries.

- Farm wineries had to have a minimum of four acres of vines and were limited to producing 10,000 gallons of wine from B.C. grapes. Their wines had be sold from their own store on the property or directly to restaurants.
- Estate wineries were required to have at least 20 acres of vines and were limited to 40,000 gallons of wine made from B.C. grapes for domestic sale through their own wine shop, licensed outlets and BCLDB stores.
- Major wineries were not required to own their own vineyards and could produce B.C. VQA wines as well as blended imported wines. Major wineries had access to the full range of liquor outlets.

In 1998, in consultation with all of the players, the B.C. provincial government established a new licensing policy which in effect created only one winery license for all wineries, similar to arrangement in Ontario.

As far as consumers were concerned, the change in winery licensing made very little difference. In the first two years after the change only one estate winery, Domaine de Chaberton in Langley in the Fraser Valley, added a line of imported proprietary releases to its otherwise VQA wine list. Except for the former major wineries, all other wineries continued to focus on B.C. grown and vinted wines, either designated VQA or "B.C. Grown."

With the expansion of the British Columbia industry, VQA wine sales rose to 2.4 million litres in 1998 which represented about 20 per cent of the volume of imported "bottled in B.C." wines sold in the province. While the former major wineries, Vincor International (Jackson-Triggs, Sawmill Creek, etc.), Mission Hill, Calona and Andrés continued to build their VQA programs, they still relied on imported products for most of their sales volume up until the late 1990s. A significant change at this time was when these same large wineries became directly involved in grape growing.

This new phase was launched in 1997 when Anthony von Mandl announced that Mission Hill Wines was planting a new 225-acre vineyard across the lake from Osoyoos at the southern end of the Okanagan Valley, virtually on the U.S. border. This vineyard, in addition to other extensive cooperative vineyard projects in the south of the valley, laid the framework for Mission Hill increasingly to replace imported wines with B.C. grown VQA wines for its varietal releases.

This move was soon followed by Calona Wines in close cooperation with the extensive Burrowing Owl Vineyards, also in the southern Okanagan. Andrés Wines announced a 65-acre joint vineyard venture in the neighbouring Similkameen Valley to the west, but the most dramatic step was taken in 1998 by Vincor International. That year Vincor planted 130 acres of new vineyards at the northeast corner of

Osoyoos Lake on land leased from the Osoyoos Indian Band. A further 370 acres was planted in 1999, however the site has the potential to be Canada's most extensive premium vineyard with up to 2,000 acres possible over the following eight years.

Again, one of the main objectives of the project was to replace formerly imported products with premium B.C. grown VQA wines.

B.C.'s Grape Growing Regions

The British Columbia viticultural spotlight in the late 1990s was definitely on the near-desert portion of the Okanagan Valley stretching from Oliver in the south to the U.S. border at Osoyoos. Long hours of sunshine, the highest daytime heat units in Canada, ample irrigation water and winter conditions buffered by Osoyoos Lake have produced consistently high quality Chardonnay, Sauvignon Blanc, Merlot, Cabernet Franc and Cabernet Sauvignon as well as the less demanding *viniferas*.

Full fruit ripeness lends body and intensity to the wines which have a lively flavour profile. This is partly due to the contrast between high daytime and cool nighttime temperatures which produces a higher tartaric to malic acid balance than is found, for example, in Niagara Region wines.

The west side of the southern valley is designated as the "Golden Mile" of contiguous vineyards and wineries. From the south are Gersighel Wineberg, Golden Mile Cellars, Domaine Combret, Inniskillin Okanagan, Hester Creek, Gehringer Bros., Tinhorn Creek and Fairview Vineyards. Across the valley on Black Sage Road there is Carriage House Wines, Manola's Vineyard and the new Burrowing Owl Vineyards winery to the south and the extensive Inkameep Vineyards and Vincor International to the north.

As well as new vineyard plantings, the Similkameen Valley over the mountain to the west has two wineries, St. Laszlo at Keremeos and an expanded Crowsnest Vineyards near Cawston. The Simikameen is also a near-desert area with high summer heat units and cooler night temperatures tempered only by the meandering Similkmeen River.

Back over Highway 3 to the Okanagan Valley, the lake and mountain area around Okanagan Falls has impressive heat units and is home to Hawthorne Mountain Vineyards on the west and Wild Goose Vineyards, Stag's Hollow, Blue Mountain and Prpich Vineyards on the east side.

This brings us to Skaha and Okanagan Lakes at Penticton. On the east bench overlooking Okanagan Lake are the clustered Naramata area vineyards including Hillside Estate, Poplar Grove, Lake Breeze, Lang Vineyards, Red Rooster, Kettle Valley and Nichol Vineyard which together produce a wide range of wines from Syrah to Ehrenfelser.

Across the lake there is Sumac Ridge and Scherzinger Vineyards in Summerland and Hainle Vineyards and First Estate Cellars in Peachland.

Immediately north in Westbank, Mission Hill, Quails' Gate and Slamka Cellars overlook Okanagan Lake from west side bench land. Radiating southeast from Kelowna, Pinot Reach Cellars and Summerhill, St. Hubertus and CedarCreek Estate Wineries command views of the valley and lake from the southeast.

Calona Wines in Kelowna and the nearby House of Rose are complemented by the dramatically situated Gray Monk on the east bench Okanagan Lake which lends a taste of the slightly cooler central part of the Okanagan.

In the northern end of the valley, Bella Vista Vineyards in Vernon hands over to two new Shuswap area wineries, Larch Hills in Salmon Arm and Recline Ridge west of Salmon Arm near Tappen. From Kelowna north, crisp, flavourful Germanic white wines rule, though Pinot Noir, Chardonnay and other varieties are also successfully grown.

Overshadowed by the growth of the Okanagan wine region are two other designated British Columbia wine regions, the Fraser Valley and Vancouver Island.

The Fraser Valley has two wineries including Domaine de Chaberton in Langley which produces award winning Bacchus, Madeleine Sylvaner and Madeline Angevine reflecting the softer profile of this temperate growing area. The other winery is Columbia Valley Classics near Chilliwack which is adding grape wines to its list of lively, intense fruit wines.

Vancouver Island is a rapidly emerging wine district with six wineries in the Duncan area; Cherry Point, Vigneti Zanatta, Blue Grouse, Venturi-Schulze, Alderlea and the transplanted Divino Winery, as well as Chateau Wolff in Nanaimo. Saturna Island winery and Vineyard at Bowen Island share a similar terroir, sometimes cosseted, at other times buffeted by the proximity to the ocean.

In heat units the Cowichan Valley does very well over the summer in average years, with the added feature of mild overnight temperatures that create a shallow temperature gradient, the exact opposite of the Okanagan. As in the Niagara region which is tempered by the great reservoir of Lake Ontario, the more level temperatures favour a softer acid balance, nudging the more forward tartaric acid into balance with the mellower malic acid in the grapes. The resulting wines reflect this with a softer flavour profile that frames subtle but rich fruit character with clean, discrete acid.

At the millennium British Columbia has 55 operating wineries with more planning to open within a year or two.

BRITISH COLUMBIA WINERIES

Alderlea Vineyards

1751 Stamps Road
RR1
Duncan, B.C.
V9L 5W2
Telephone: (250) 746-7122
Fax: (250) 746-7122

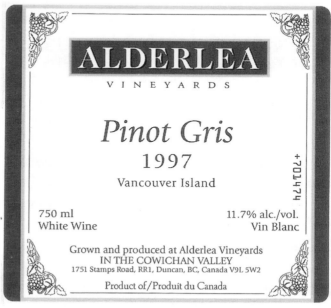

Alderlea Vineyards was created in 1992 when Roger and Nancy Dosman moved from Vancouver to the rural setting of the Cowichan Valley. Their south-facing vineyard overlooks Quamichan Lake five kilometers north-east of Duncan. The new winery, which opened in July 1998, is situated in a converted barn on the property. Their first crush was in 1996 producing two wines, Auxerrois and Bacchus, from their own grapes. White wines are fermented and aged in stainless steel, reds in American and French oak.

Winemaker: Roger Dosman

Acreage: 10

Soil: Rocky

Grape varieties: Bacchus, Pinot Gris, Pinot Noir, Maréchal Foch

Winemaking philosophy: "100 per cent of our wines are crafted from grapes grown in our own vineyard. Our careful vineyard management and dedication to winemaking produces distinctive Cowichan Valley wines."

Wines: *White*—Bacchus, Pinot Gris, Angélique (blend)

Red—Clarinet (Maréchal Foch), Hearth (port style)

Store hours: Saturday and Sunday, 1 pm — 5 pm or by appointment

Public tastings: Store hours

Recommended wines: Pinot Gris, Pinot Noir, Clariet (Maréchal Foch)

Andrés Wines (B.C.) Ltd.

2120 Vintner Street
Port Moody, B.C.
V3H 1W8
Telephone: (604) 937-3411
Fax: (604) 937-5487
e-mail: into.bc@andreswines.com
web site: www.wineroute.com/peller/

Andrés Wines began operating in Vancouver's western suburb of Port Moody in 1961 and opened wineries within a year in Nova Scotia and Alberta, followed quickly by Quebec, Manitoba and Ontario. Although the commercial heart has now shifted to the Winona plant in Ontario, the Port Moody facility is the historic soul of the company. This winery on Vintner Street was built when Andrew Peller could not acquire a going concern at the price he wanted. The original winemaker, Wallace Pohl, like the equipment, came from California. Early bottlings used California grapes which increased their price in the marketplace against wines of other B.C. houses. The public equated the expense with higher quality and bought Andrés' products to such a degree that Andrew Peller expanded quickly into other provinces. The growth took its toll on the founder's health so his son, Dr. Joe Peller, gave up his medical practice to run the company. Now his grandson John is at the helm.

In the 1970s, on advice from Dr. Helmut Becker of the Geisenheim Institute, Andrés developed 300 acres of French hybrid and *vinifera* vines on Indian land near Oliver, called Inkameep Vineyards. Andrés has made a commitment to VQA wines in B.C. with 95 per cent of its contracted vineyards acreage being *vinifera*. A recent investment of $1 million in new equipment is beginning to show in the quality of the wines.

The company markets a variety of wines under different labels corresponding to the grape source: Franciscan California, Gold Coast (Australia), Santa Anna (Chile), Di Conti (Italy) and Bighorn Vineyards and Peller Estates for its VQA varietal wines.

The Domaine D'Or Chardonnay is a blend of several wine regions — Australia, California and Chile.

The company has invested in the 75-acre Rocky Ride Vineyard with Roger Hol in Cawston, B.C. They planted Pinot Blanc, Chardonnay, Gewürztraminer, Merlot, Pinot Noir and Gamay.

Winemaker: Tony Vlcek
Acreage: 200 contracted
Production: 500,000 cases

Average tonnage crushed: 950 tonnes

Winemaking philosophy: "Andrés Wines produces good quality for good value, without compromise. Our philosophy in making wine is to associate art and technology."

Wines: LDB: *Peller Estates label white VQA:* Pinot Blanc, Ehrenfelser, Dry Riesling, Chardonnay, Gewürztraminer Trinity Icewine, Pinot Gris

Peller Estates label Non-VQA white: Proprietors Reserve, Oakridge Chardonnay and Sauvignon Blanc, Cellar Reserve House, Domaine D'Or, Domaine D'Or Chardonnay, Domaine D'Or Dry, Hochtaler, Hochtaler Dry, Similkameen Superior, Similkameen Chablis

Franciscan California label white: California Chablis

Gold Coast label white: Chardonnay, Semillon/Chardonnay, Vintage Reserve

Other whites: Santa Anna Semillon/Chardonnay, Chardonnay, Sauvignon Blanc, Di Conti Bianco

Sparkling: Baby Duck, Baby Champagne

Red—Peller Oakridge Estates Cabernet and Merlot, Peller Estates Proprietors' Reserve, Similkameen Superior, Domaine D'Or, Domaine D'Or Dry, Gold Coast Cabernet/Shiraz, Franciscan Californian Burgundy, Santa Anna Cabernet Sauvignon, Merlot, Di Conti Rosso

Sherry: Almond Cream, Golden Cream, Medium Dry

Red—VQA Showcase Peller Estates Merlot, Pinot Noir, Gamay Noir

Fortified: Dune Port

Recommended wines: Peller Estates Pinot Blanc, Peller Estates Chardonnay, Peller Estates Riesling, Bighorn Chardonnay, Bighorn Pinot Blanc, Peller Estates Limited Edition Merlot

---

Bella Vista Vineyards

3111 Agnew Road
Vernon, B.C.
V1T 5J8

Telephone: (250) 558-0770
Fax: (250) 542-1221
e-mail: BVV@workshop.com.ca
web site: www.webtec.com.au/bvv

Larry Passmore's large colonial-style winery on three floors, finished in 1994, used to be the most northerly in the Okanagan until Hans Nevrkla took that distinction two years later with Larch Hills. An amateur winemaker, Larry started up a U-brew store in his native Vernon. He purchased the Bella Vista farm with its 15-acre vineyard in 1991 and invited a group of local friends to buy minority shares in the enterprise. The first crush was in 1993. A restaurant licence has been applied for.

Winemaker: Larry Passmore (consultant Gary Strachan)
Acreage: 15
Grape varieties: Maréchal Foch, Pinot Noir, Gewürztraminer, Pinot Auxerrois

Production: 5,000 cases
Wines: *White*—Gewürztraminer, Auxerrois, Seyval Blanc
Red—Pinot Noir, Maréchal Foch
Stores hours: *May 24 to September 30:* noon — 4 pm
Winery tours: Call ahead
Public tastings: Call ahead

Blue Grouse Vineyards

4365 Blue Grouse Road
Duncan, B.C.
V9L 6M3
Telephone: (250) 743-3834
Fax: (250) 743-9305

Hans Kiltz, a former veterinarian from Germany, established Vancouver Island's second winery in 1989 with his wife Evangeline and their children, Sandrina and Richard. After experimenting with over 100 grape varieties, the Kiltzes have settled upon a dozen vines best suited to their cool climate acreage in the Cowichan Valley. The enterprise is a true family business in which Hans, with his training in microbiology and biochemistry, makes the wine, his wife manages the vineyard, Richard assists them both and even helps out his sister Sandrina who runs the wine shop.

The winery, on the ground floor of the house, sits on a hill overlooking the bowl-shaped vineyard, recognised as one of the best microclimates on the island.

The style of the wines is decidedly Germanic. Notable are the Ortega Special Selection 1996, the first botrytis affected Late Harvest wine produced on Vancouver Island and the interesting Black Muscat.

In summer you can picnic under the arbour to enjoy the picturesque view.

Winemaker: Dr. Hans Kiltz
Acreage: 8
Soil: Sandy loam, the warmest spot in the Cowichan Valley, protected by evergreen hills
Grape varieties: Pinot Gris, Ortega, Müller-Thurgau, Bacchus, Pinot Gris,
Siegerrebe, Gamay Noir, Pinot Noir, July Muscat

Production: 1,500 cases

Winemaking philosophy: "Vancouver Island is the most recent viticultural region. It is important to us that we produce distinctive wines which clearly reflect the unique growing conditions on the island and our continuous search for quality."

Wines: Own store: *White*—Ortega, Müller-Thurgau, Bacchus, Pinot Gris, Dry Muscat *Red*—Gamay Noir, Pinot Noir

Winery tours: Yes (up to 12 people)

Public tastings: Wednesday, Friday, Saturday, Sunday, 11 am — 5 pm

---

Recommended wines: Bacchus, Müller-Thurgau, Pinot Gris, Pinot Noir

---

Blue Mountain Vineyard & Cellars

RR #1, S3, C4
Okanagan Falls, B.C.
VOH 1R0
Telephone:
(604) 497-8244
Fax: (604) 497-6160

Ian Mavety spent 21 years growing grapes on his Okanagan property before deciding to produce wine. He and his wife Jane made their first wines in 1991 — a barrel-fermented Pinot Blanc and a blended barrel-and-tank fermented Pinot Gris. With their first effort they also produced one of the best Pinot Noirs that B.C. consumers had ever enjoyed. And as if this wasn't enough, they went on to make a series of *methode champenoise* sparklers of distinction with help from oenologist Raphael Brisbois, who worked at Iron Horse in Sonoma. Then the Mavetys turned their attention to barrel-fermented Chardonnay. Taking their cue from Burgundy, whose climate resembles their own, they decided to concentrate on Chardonnay and Pinot Noir rather than the Valley's ubiquitous Riesling.

Ian's son, Mark, graduated from UBC in agricultural economics and spent an exchange year in New Zealand studying viticulture and oenology. He now shares the winemaking duties with his father.

Situated in the hills south of Okanagan Falls, Blue Mountain is one of the region's most picturesque sites and well as being one of its best producers.

Winemaker: Ian and Mark Mavety
Acreage: 60

Soil: Light, sandy

Grape varieties: Pinot Blanc, Pinot Gris, Chardonnay, Pinot Noir (reserve wines have Stripe Label), Gamay

Production: 7,000 cases (ultimately 12,000 planned)

Winemaking philosophy: "The quality of the wines reflect the quality of the grapes, and winemaking at Blue Mountain begins in the vineyard where restricted yields concentrate the grape flavours. In the cellars, our winemaking is traditional. French oak barrels are used extensively to soften and add complexity to the wines."

Wines: Own store only: *White*—Pinot Gris, Pinot Blanc, Chardonnay

Red—Pinot Noir, Gamay Noir

Sparkling—Vintage Brut, Brut Rosé

Winery tours: By appointment

Public tastings: By appointment

Recommended wines: Pinot Blanc, Pinot Gris, Chardonnay, Pinot Noir, Blue Mountain Brut

Burrowing Owl Vineyards

620 West 8th Avenue
Suite 200
Vancouver, B.C.
V5Z 1CS
Telephone: (250) 498-0620
Fax: (250) 498-0621
e-mail:
bovwinery@bc.sympatico.ca
web site: bovwine.com

In late 1993 and early 1994, Vancouver businessman Jim Wyse acquired approximately 220 acres in the southern Okanagan to the south of the Inkameep Vineyard. He bought the property from Albert LeComte to whom he now supplies grapes. The acquisition and replanting costs will reach $3.3 million, and in full production the L-shaped vineyard will produce 1,100 tonnes of *vinifera* grapes. In addition to the original 20-acre block of Pinot Blanc planted in 1985, there will be Chardonnay, Pinot Noir, Merlot and Cabernet Franc. The winery, built in 1998, is set into the hillside in the centre of the vineyard, with a fabulous view of the valley, the mountains to the west and Osoyoos Lake to the south.

In 1997, former Sterling winemaker Bill Dyer from Napa took over the wine making and produced some California-style Merlot, as well as Pinot Gris and Chardonnay.

Winemaker: Bill Dyer

Acreage: 290

Soil: Sandy loam

Grape varieties: Currently 19 but the winery only processes Merlot, Cabernet Sauvignon, Cabernet Franc (for blending), Chardonnay and Pinot Gris

Production: 9,000 cases in 1998; maximum capacity, 12,000 cases

Average tonnaged crushed: 150 tonnes

Winemaking philosophy: "To focus on a relatively small number of varieties that we can produce at world class level."

Wines: *White*—Chardonnay, Pinot Gris

Red—Merlot, Cabernet Sauvignon (blended with Cabernet Franc)

Winery tours: No

Public tastings: A tasting room is under construction and will be ready for the summer of 2000

Recommended wines: Pinot Gris, Chardonnay, Merlot, Cabernet Sauvignon

Calona Wines

1125 Richter Street
Kelowna, B.C.
V1Y 2K6
Telephone: (250) 762-3332
Toll Free: 1-800-663-5086
Fax: (250) 762-2999
e-mail:
wineboutique@cascadia.ca
web site:
www.discoverywines.com/calona

In 1932, when the original company was formed, apples were the raw material for their products. Later, other fruits were introduced under the Jack line (Cherry Jack is still in Calona's portfolio). Since its founding during the Depression, the winery has been associated with the Capozzi family who make no bones about the fact that they modelled their products and sales strategies on those of Ernest & Julio Gallo, the world's largest winery. In fact, in 1969 there was talk about an amalgamation of the two wineries. Calona's continuing prosperity has historically been based on its blended products, including such popular labels as Schloss Laderheim, Sommet Blanc and Sommet Rouge. The winery also bottles imported wines from California, Washington, Chile and Australia under The Heritage Collection label.

Since 1988 Calona has made a commitment to VQA wines. Their red and white varietal wines have been winning medals in competitions. Their prestige VQA wines are bottled under the Private Reserve and Artist Series labels. The winery uses 70 per cent French and 30 per cent American oak.

Winemaker: Howard Soon

Acreage: 360

Soil: Sandy loam

Production: 30,000 cases

Tonnage crushed: 600 tonnes

Annual tonnage purchased: 500 tonnes

Grape varieties: Johannisberg Riesling, Chardonnay, Rougeon, Chelois, Souvereign Opal

Winemaking philosophy: "My challenge as a winemaker is to balance the artistic elements in order to create winning wines of distinction."

Wines: Trilogy Series: *White*—Gewürztraminer, Riesling, Bacchus

Red—Cabernet Franc, Pinot Noir, Merlot

Artist Series: *White*—Chardonnay, Semillon Chardonnay, Pinot Blanc, Gewürztraminer, Sovereign Opal, Riesling, Semillon

Red—Rougeon, Cabernet Franc, Merlot, Chancellor

Private Reserve Series (in good years only): *White*—Late Harvest wines, Barrel-fermented Chardonnay

Red—Cabernet Sauvignon

Heritage Collection (imported wines with B.C. blend): *White*—Chardonnay, Fumé Blanc, White Cabernet

Red—Cabernet Sauvignon, Merlot, Shiraz, Cabernet Merlot

Store hours: *Summer:* 9 am — 7 pm; *Winter:* 10 am — 5 pm

Winery tours: Daily, *Summer:* 1:00, 3:00, 5:00 pm; *Winter:* 2 pm

Public tastings: During store hours

————

Recommended wines: Artist Series Chardonnay, Artist Series Pinot Gris, Private Reserve Semillon, Sauvignon Blanc, Sangiovese

Carriage House Wines

RR #1, S46, C19
Oliver, B.C.
V0H 1T0
Telephone/Fax: (250)
498-8818

Dave and Karen Wagner made their first crush in 1994. They used the Kerner they grew on their 8.5-acre vineyard located at the north end of Black Sage Road, on the east side bench between Oliver and Osoyoos. This has become their signature wine. In 1995, they added Pinot Noir, Merlot and Cabernet Sauvignon to their red varieties. They use French oak only. Low yields are the aim here. The winery also has a picnic site with a breathtaking view of the Southern Okanagan Valley.

Winemaker: Dave Wagner

Acreage: 8.5

Soil: Rich sandy clay, southwest exposure

Grape varieties: Kerner, Chardonnay, Pinot Noir, Merlot, Cabernet Sauvignon

Production: 2,500 cases

Average tonnage crushed: 30 tonnes

Annual tonnage purchased: 3 - 5 tonnes

Winemaking philosophy: "Small quantities, high quality with the customer's satisfaction in mind."

Wines: Own store: Kerner (Dry and Semi-Sweet); 1996—Chardonnay, Kerner, Ebonage (Pinot Blanc/Kerner/Chardonnay) Merlot, Pinot Noir

Store hours: 10 am — 6 pm (November through April by appointment only)

Winery tours: Yes

Public tastings: Yes

Recommended wines: Kerner, Pinot Blanc

CedarCreek Estate Winery

5445 Lakeshore Road
Kelowna, B.C.
V1W 4S5
Telephone: (250) 764-8866
Fax: (250) 764-2603

In 1986, David Ross Fitzpatrick of Kelowna bought Uniacke winery and vineyards (founded by grower David Mitchell in 1980). The contemporary Mediterranean-style winery built above the cellar was designed by a Uniacke partner, David Newman-Bennett. The winemaker then was the youthful Weinsberg-trained oenologist Tilman Hainle who went on to create his own winery with his grape grower father, Walter, in 1985.

CedarCreek is situated 12 km south of Kelowna near Okanagan Mission at an elevation of 300 metres. Fitzpatrick originally hired winemaker Vienna-born Helmut Dotti, who had worked at Ste. Michelle facilities across the country and for Mission Hill. Ann Sperling took over the winemaking duties but she now consults. There is extensive use of French oak in barrel fermenting and ageing. Chardonnay is a combination of barrel fermentation, barrel ageing and stainless steel. CedarCreek's first Icewine was produced from Riesling grapes in 1991.

Winemaker: Kevin Willenborg

Acreage: 40 (CedarCreek), 40 (Greata Ranch)

Soil: Well-drained sandy loam that ranges from light to heavy from top to bottom of the steep southwest facing slope. Moderately saline and calcareous.

Grape varieties: Specializing in Pinot Blanc, Chardonnay, Pinot Noir and Merlot. Also producing Riesling, Ehrenfelser, Gewürztraminer, Auxerrois, Cabernet Franc and Cabernet Sauvignon for Cabernet Merlot blend

Production: 30,000 cases

Average tonnage crushed: 470 tonnes

Annual tonnage purchased: 270 tonnes

Winemaking philosophy: "Each wine has its own life. That life begins with the planting and development of the vine. It is then transferred as the grapes are harvested, crushed, fermented into wine, aged and bottled. The role of the winemaker is to steward this life with care and attention to detail so as to preserve its flavours throughout the process into each glass."

Wines: Own Store: *White*—Proprietor's White (blend), Chardonnay, Pinot Blanc, Dry Riesling, Ehrenfelser, Gewürztraminer

Red—Proprietor's Red (blend), Pinot Noir, Merlot, Cabernet Merlot

Store hours: *April to October:* Daily, 9:30 am — 5:30 pm; *November to March:* Monday to Saturday, 9:30 am — 5 pm

Winery tours: 11 am, and 2:00 pm through 4:00 pm

Public tastings: During Wineshop hours

———

Recommended wines: Chardonnay, Ehrenfelser, Merlot, Cabernet Merlot

Chateau Wolff

2534 Maxey Road	Telephone: (604) 753-4613
RR #3	Fax: (604) 753-0614
Nanaimo, B.C.	
V9S 5V6	

Harry von Wolff, a native of Riga in Latvia, discovered his love of wine while at hotel school in Lucerne, Switzerland. After a stint in the hotel business in B.C., he became a shoemaker whose business in Nanaimo on Vancouver Island flourished and grew into the Island Boot and Saddle Shop. An amateur vineyardist who grew vines around his house, he indulged his hobby by buying an eight-acre farm with its two-storey farmhouse in 1987. He cut down the trees to subsidize the creation of a commercial vineyard and planted it with Pinot Noir and Chardonnay in the upper portion and Müller-Thurgau, Bacchus and Siegerrebe in the lower belt. He also has some Viognier in the 4.5-acre vineyard.

His goal is to create cellars tunnelled into the hillside and remain small, producing around 1,000 cases a year.

Picnic tables are in the garden in front of the tasting room.

Winemaker: Mike Farkas

Grape varieties: Pinot Noir, Dornfelder, Chardonnay, Pinot Blanc, Riesling-Sylvaner, Viognier, Bacchus, Siegerrebe

Winemaking philosophy: "We endeavour to make big wines in the style of the '20s, Pinot Noir to be aged a minimum of six years prior to consumption … we crop Pinot Noir and Chardonnay at three-quarters to one tonne per acre."

Wines: Pinot Noir, Viva (Chardonnay Riesling-Sylvaner blend), Pinot Blanc and Viognier

Store hours: Saturday, 10 am — 5 pm and by appointment

Cherry Point Vineyard

840 Cherry Point Road
RR #3
Cobble Hill, B.C.
V0R 1L0
Telephone: (250) 743-1272
Fax: (250) 743 -1059
web site:
cherrypointvineyards.com

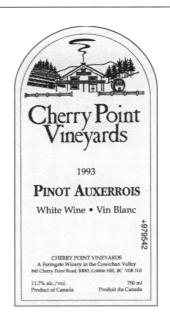

Wayne Ulrich's farming background, interrupted by a stint with Agriculture Canada, gave him the necessary background to open his own winery in 1993 with his wife Helena. The introduction of B.C.'s farmgate winery legislation in 1989 was the only spur they needed to start looking for a farm in the Cowichan Valley. They settled on a former mink ranch and moved there in January 1990, raising sheep while they waited for their vines to mature. The Ulrichs have planted an experimental plot with 32 varieties to augment in future the six already in the ground.

Winemaker: Todd Moore
Acreage: 26
Soil: Upper bench—gravel moraine; lower level— silty clay
Grape varieties: Pinot Blanc, Pinot Noir, Gewürztraminer, Ortega, Auxerrois, Agria
Production: 4,000 cases
Average tonnage crushed: 50 tonnes
Annual tonnage purchases: 10 tonnes
Winemaking philosophy: "To make wine in a way that reflects the natural advantages of our site and climate."
Wines: Own store: *White*—Pinot Blanc, Pinot Gris, Ortega, Pinot Noir Reserve, Agria Valley Sunset, Gewürztraminer, Auxerrois
Red—Pinot Noir
Store hours: Daily, 11:30 am — 6 pm
Winery tours: Guided tours by appointment
Public tastings: During store hours; wine bar and restaurant open 11:30 am — 6 pm. Extensive picnic area and conference facilities available.

Recommended wines: Siegerrebe, Auxerrois, Müller-Thurgau, Ehrenselser, Ortega, Pinot Noir

Columbia Valley Classics

1385 Frost Road
Lindell Bench, B.C.
V2R 4X8
Telephone/Fax: (604) 858-5233
e-mail: cvcwines@dowco.com
web site: www.cvcwines.com

John Stuyt and Dominic Rivard own a 40-acre berry farm in the Columbia Valley, east of Vancouver, surrounded by views of the mountains. In addition to fruit and wine grapes, they also grow hazelnuts. Peacocks and golden pheasants collected by John add interest to a winery visit. Picnic facilities are available.

Winemaker: Dominic Rivard
Acreage: 40
Grape varieties: Madeleine Angevine, Ortega
Fruit: Blackberry, Raspberry, Blueberry, white, red and black Currant, Gooseberry, Kiwi
Production: 6,000 cases
Winemaking philosophy: "Our wines are a true expression of the blessing that Mother Nature has given this land."
Wines: *White*—Madeleine Angevine
Red—Chancellor
Fruit—White Currant, Blackberry, Blueberry, Red and Black Currant, Raspberry
Fortified— Black Currant and Raspberry liqueur
Store hours: Monday to Saturday, 10 am — 5 pm; Sunday, 11 am — 4 pm
Winery tours: Yes, during store hours

Crowsnest Vineyards

Box 501
Keremeos, B.C.
V0X 1N0
Telephone/Fax: (250) 499-5129

A course in food processing at B.C.'s
Institute of Technology set Andrea
McDonald in pursuit of the grape. As
a lab technician at Okanagan
Vineyards (and subsequently at
Brights), she married fruit farmer
Hugh McDonald and together they
planted their first two acres of Pinot
Auxerrois in 1990 on the family prop-
erty overlooking the Similkameen

River on an eastern slope. Their first crush was in 1994. The MacDonalds have
planted sunflowers at the start of the vineyard rows.

Winemaker: Andrea McDonald

Acreage: 12

Soil: Well-drained sandy loam soils, high heat units

Production: 500 cases

Average tonnage crushed: 7 tonnes (will increase yearly)

Winemaking philosophy: "K.I.S.S. We want the flavours that have developed in
   the vineyard to come through."

Wines: Own store: *White*—Auxerrois, Riesling, Chardonnay, Kerner,
   Gewürztraminer, Harvest Moon (Riesling and Icewine)

Red—Merlot, Pinot Noir

Winery tours: Yes

Public tastings: Yes

Recommended wines: Auxerrois, Kerner

Divino Estate Winery

1500 Freeman Road
Cobble Hill, B.C.
V0R 1L0
Telephone: (250) 743-2311
Fax: (250) 743-1087

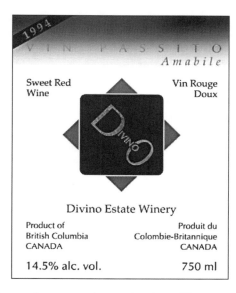

Joseph Busnardo is something of a maverick in the B.C. wine industry, choosing not to be part of the B.C. Wine Institute. He has been growing grapes for 27 years, experimenting with over 100 varieties, most of which came from his native Veneto. Currently he is planting and experimenting at his new location on Vancouver Island. He is also diversifying and growing kiwis, blackberries, figs and apples, plus some table grapes. His winemaking technique is defiantly Italian and Veneto in particular. He favours whole berry fermentation *à la maceration carbonique*. He uses only stainless steel for his grapes.

Winemaker: Joseph Busnardo

Acres: 39.5

Soil: Clay

Grape varieties: Merlot, Cabernet Franc, Cabernet Sauvignon, Gamay Noir, Chardonnay, Trebbiano, Tocai, Pinot Noir, Pinot Bianco, Pinot Grigio, Malvasia, Pinot Nero

Production: new vineyard; 1999 vintage — should be 60 per cent in production

Winemaking philosophy: "My style of winemaking could be classed as *primitivo* and 'earthy.' In order to have a good wine, you must have good grapes. My philosophy is that 'if the wine is good enough for me, then it is good enough for the general public!'"

Wines: Own stores: All varieties produced

Red—Bacaro, Cabernet, Merlot, Rosso di Giuseppe, Pinot Nero

Sparkling—Il Segreto Brut (Charmat process)

Dessert —Tocai Late Harvest, Passito Amabile Rosso, Passito Amabile Bianco

Stores: Vancouver: Corks 'n Candles, 1610 Robson St.
New Westminster: Divino's Quayside Cellar, 910 Quayside

Recommended Wines: not tasted yet

Domaine Combret

P.O. Box 1170, Road 13
Oliver, B.C.
V0H 1T0
Telephone: (250) 498-8878
Fax: (250) 498-8879
e-mail: domainecombret@bc.sym-
patico.ca

Robert Combret, his wife Maité
and Montpellier-trained winemaker son Olivier had a triumph
before they even had an on-site
store to sell their first wines
(Chardonnay and Riesling 1993)
to visitors. Their '93 Alsace-style
Riesling won a silver medal at
the Challenge International du Vin at Blaye-Bourg in Bordeaux in 1994. In March
1995, they had an even bigger success: Domaine Combret Chardonnay 1993 was
judged among the best "Chardonnay of the World" at the annual international
Chardonnay challenge in Burgundy.

Robert, who emigrated from Provence to Canada with his family in 1992, comes
from a long line of winemakers stretching back ten generations to 1638, and was
himself president of the AOC Coteaux d'Aix-en-Provence and owner of Château
Petit Sonnailler (cattle bell). The spanking new 7,700-sq.-ft. gravity-feed winery
with wooden catwalks and arched wooden doors is a model of efficiency and state-
of-the-art technology with its computer-controlled double-jacketed tanks, below-
ground barrel-aging cellar and selection of barrels from puncheons (Seguin Moreau)
and *foudres* to a 7,500-litre oak tank. The facility enjoys a panoramic view of Osoyoos
Lake and the town of Oliver.

The Chardonnay is barrel-fermented and aged in oak. Wines are exported to
Europe and Asia.

Winemaker: Olivier Combret

Acreage: 30

Soil: Volcanic origin — granite and schist, elevation 400 metres with a south eastern exposure and low percentage of relative humidity

Grape varieties: Chardonnay, Riesling, Cabernet Franc, Gamay, Pinot Noir

Production: 10,000 cases

Average tonnage crushed: 60 tonnes

Winemaking philosophy: "Traditional French winemaking, grapes 100 per cent
grown, matured and processed on site: origin guaranteed."

Wines: Own store: Chardonnay, Riesling, Cabernet Franc, Gamay, Pinot Noir
Winery tours: By appointment
Public tastings: By appointment

Recommended wines: Riesling, Chardonnay, Gamay Noir, Cabernet Franc

---

Domaine de Chaberton

1064 - 216th Street
Langley, B.C.
V2Z 1R3
Telephone: (604) 530-1736
Toll free: 1-888-332-9463
Fax: (604) 533-9687
e-mail: cviolet@direct.ca
web site:www.domainedechaberton.com

In July 1991, Claude Violet opened his winery named after the farm he owned in southern France. A Parisian by birth, Claude comes from a French Catalan family that can trace itself back through nine generations of winemakers over a period of 350 years to Manaut Violet, cooper and grape grower. When Claude came to Canada in 1981, he brought his winegrowing experience that encompassed dealings in France, Switzerland and Spain. Instead of choosing the Okanagan, he bought a 55-acre farm in South Langley and converted it into vineyards, becoming the first commercial grape grower in the Fraser Valley. His winery is the most southerly on the B.C. mainland.

Winemakers: Claude Violet
Acreage: 55
Soil: Top quality soil; 60 per cent less rain than Vancouver.
Grape varieties: Bacchus, Madeleine Angevine, Madeleine Sylvaner, Ortega, Chardonnay, Chasselas Doré
Average tonnage crushed: 130-150 tonnes
Winemaking philosophy: "In winemaking there must be love. I grew up in the atmosphere of wine so it is so natural, so normal. For me, it's quality before quantity."
Wines: Own store: Madeleine Angevine, Madeleine Sylvaner, Bacchus, Ortega,

Chardonnay, Optima, Pinot Noir (and imported wines under Cellar Selection label)

Store hours: Monday to Saturday, 10 am — 6 pm; Sunday, noon — 5 pm

Winery tours: Public: *mid-April to end of August:* Saturday and Sunday, 2 pm — 4 pm; Private: By appointment only (groups of 15 - 20, please)

Public tastings: During store hours

Recommended wines: Madeleine Angevine, Madeleine Sylvaner, Bacchus

---

Fairview Cellars

RR #1 S66/C15
Oliver, B.C.
V0H 1T0
Telephone: (250) 498-2211
e-mail: beggert@IMG.net

Located at the northern end of the "Golden Mile" region, Bill Eggert has created a small red wine-only boutique winery with a concrete "cave" and an old log cabin which he has converted into his wine shop. His first crush was in 1997, two beefy reds based on Cabernets and Merlot.

Winemaker: Bill Eggert

Acreage: 65

Soil: Heavy, rocky, variable with some sandy areas

Grape varieties: Cabernet Sauvignon, Cabernet Franc, Merlot, Syrah, Gamay Noir

Production: 1,500 cases

Average tonnage crushed: expanding to 25 tonnes

Winemaking philosophy: "Benevolent neglect, quality from vineyard, neutral oak, two years before release, gravity flow processing, extended maceration."

Wines: *Red*—Cabernet Merlot blend, Merlot Cabernet blend

Store hours: By appointment — starting summer 2000

Winery tours: By appointment

Public tastings: Charges

Recommended Wines: Merlot Cabernet

Gehringer Brothers Estate Winery

RR #1, S23, C4
Oliver, B.C.
VOH 1T0
Telephone: (250) 498-3537
Fax: (250) 498-3510

Walter and Gordon Gehringer made their first wine 1985, but not before both had acquired sound experience in oenology and viticulture at Germany's famed schools Geisenheim and Weinsberg, respectively. During their summer vacations, the brothers brought back winemaking equipment as well as techniques they had learned to apply to the grapes grown by their father Helmut and his brother Karl. Slowly, they evolved the style which has become the benchmark for the company's white wines: fermentation to dryness and then backblending with 10 per cent fresh juice just before bottling.

In 1981, the Gehringers selected their vineyard site eight km north of Osoyoos, which lies north of Mount Kobau, and one year later Gordon returned to manage it. All white varieties were planted. In 1984, Walter, who spent five years as winemaker for Andrés both in Ontario and B.C., joined the enterprise. The following year they began construction of the winery. In 1995, the brothers bought their neighbour's land, augmenting their property to 60 acres.

No oak is used in the winemaking process. In 1991, the brothers produced their first Icewine. A consistent gold medal winner.

Winemakers: Walter and Gordon Gehringer

Acreage: 60

Soil: Located on a narrow upper bench of the valley above the frost zone at the southern end of the Okanagan. South-facing slope offers good exposure and air drainage.

Grape varieties: Riesling, Pinot Gris, Auxerrois, Pinot Blanc, Ehrenfelser, Schönburger, Pinot Noir, Merlot, Cabernet Franc

Production: 15,000 cases

Average tonnage crushed: 220 tonnes

Annual tonnage purchased: 30 per cent

Winemaking philosophy: "In the fall, the grapes are pressed and a portion of the juice is stored fresh and unfermented. Before bottling in the spring, we blend the unfermented juice, which has retained its rich flavour, back into the dry wine. This results in the varietal fruit flavour components being combined with the developed wine, yielding a complex, full-bodied wine. All our wines have a pleasant, harmonious taste, bringing out the subtle, yet distinctive flavours of each grape variety."

Wines: LDB: *White*—Ehrenfelser, Ehrenfelser Dry, Riesling, Riesling Dry, Auxerrois, Pinot Gris, Pinot Blanc and Riesling Icewine

Red—Pinot Noir, Cuvée Noire (Chancellor & Pinot Noir)

Boutique: Schönburger, Pinot Gris, Desert Sun, Auxerrois, Riesling, Pinot Noir, Cuvée Noire, Cabernet, Merlot Icewine

Store hours: *June to Mid-October:* Daily, 10 am — 5 pm; *Mid-October to May:* Monday to Friday, 10 am — 5 pm

Winery tours: By appointment

Public tastings: During store hours

Recommended wines: Riesling, Ehrenfelser, Auxerrois, Gewürztraminer, Pinot Noir, Riesling Icewine

Gersighel Wineberg

RR #1, S40, C20
Oliver, B.C.
V0H 1T0
Telephone: (250) 495-3319

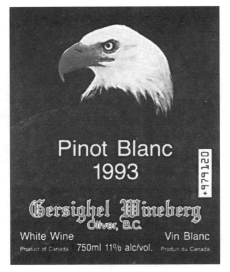

Dirk De Gussem and his wife, Gerda Torck founded their winery in 1995. They are located the furthest south on Highway #97, across the valley from some of the large vineyard plantings on the east bench between Oliver and Osoyoos. Their tasting room is "at home," and at the time of writing they offer wines of several vintages reflecting all the varieties they have in the ground. The winery's unusual name is drawn from the names of their three children — Gerd, Sigrid and Helgi — and Wineberg because it "sounds better than Wine Mountain," derived from the ski hill Mount Baldy, visible on the eastern horizon. This concept inspired the label featuring the head of a bald eagle.

Winemaker: Gerda and Helgi De Gussem

Acreage: 7.5

Soil: Loam and sand, fertile top soil; southeastern slope backed by a heat-retaining mountain

Grape varieties: Pinot Blanc, Chardonnay, Tokay, Perle of Csaba, Viognier, Pinot Noir, Merlot, Riesling, Gewürztraminer

Production: 2,500 cases

Winemaking philosophy: "It will take more than one generation to determine which variety a vintner will plant in his vineyard and where. Only time can tell but being farmers for generations and travelling all over Europe, living in France for three years, and visiting the wine regions of South Africa, I am convinced that the Okanagan will produce Grand Cru wines — but as everywhere else in the world, not too many. I looked for the microclimate of an open hill and the structure of the soil; that's the first step in making great wines."

Public tastings: Daily, 9:30 am — 8 pm

————————

Recommended wines: Pinot Blanc, Sauvignon Blanc

Golden Mile Cellars

13140 - 316A Avenue
Road 13
Oliver, B.C.
V0H 1T0
Telephone: (250) 498-8330
Fax: (250) 498-8331

Peter and Helga Serwo planted their vineyard in the 1970s and eventually saw their dream come true when they opened their farm winery in the summer of 1998. The building is a cross between a chateau and a castle. Made of concrete blocks, it comes complete with a drawbridge, ramparts and a cone-shaped roof above the wine shop.

Winemaker: Ross Mitco

Acreage: 25

Soil: Gravel, sand, humus, clay — many different spots

Grape varieties: Merlot, Pinot Noir, Chardonnay, Riesling, Ehrenfelser, Optima, Kerner, Bacchus

Production: 1500 cases

Average tonnage crushed: 15 - 20 tonnes

Winemaking philosophy: "To be soft and simple from start to finish."

Wines: *White*—Riesling, Riesling Botrytis Affected, Bacchus, Kerner, Chardonnay, Blanc de Noir, "All Vinifera" blends

Red—Pinot Noir, Merlot

Store hours: Daily, 10 am — 5 pm during the season; *Winter:* By appointment only

Winery tours: Conducted 11 am and 2 pm daily during season

Public tastings: Free

————

Recommended wines: Bacchus, Riesling, Kerner, Chardonnay, Pinot Noir

Gray Monk Cellars

P.O. Box 63
1055 Camp Road
Okanagan Centre, B.C.
V4V 2H4
Telephone: (250) 766-3168
Toll free: 1-800-663-4205
    (B.C. Only)
Fax: (250) 766-3390
e-mail:
mailbox@graymonk.com
web site: www.graymonk.com

The vineyards sweep down the eastern slope from the winery which commands a spectacular view of Okanagan Lake. It used to be the most northerly estate winery on the continent until Bella Vista opened its doors. George Heiss, born and raised in Vienna, started building his classically simple farmhouse-style winery in January 1982, ten years after he had torn out acres of aged orchard and planted his first European vines. The winery name is a translation of what the Austrians call the Pinot Gris grape — Gray Monk.

George, his wife Trudy and German-trained son, George Jr., make some of the best white wines in B.C. as evidenced by the number of medals the winery has won in provincial, national and international competitions. The style, as you would expect, is Germanic but remarkably delicate. All of the wines are made in stainless steel. Some are exported to Japan.

Winemaker: George Heiss, Jr./Christine Leroux
Acreage: 49

Grape varieties: Auxerrois, Pinot Gris, Ehrenfelser, Bacchus, Kerner, Rotberger, Seigerrebe, Gewürztraminer, Gamay Noir, Pinot Noir, Cabernet Franc

Production: 42,000 cases

Average tonnage crushed: 500 tonnes

Annual tonnage purchased: 150 tonnes

Winemaking philosophy: "We take pride in producing 100 per cent varietals and showing the marketplace what can be done in the Okanagan."

Wines: LDB: *White*—Bacchus, Ehrenfelser (Auslese, Spätlese), Gewürztraminer, Unwooded Chardonnay, Chardonnay Riesling, Kerner Late Harvest, Müller-Thurgau, Pinot Auxerrois, Pinot Blanc, Pinot Chardonnay, Pinot Gris, Siegerrebe

Red—Pinot Noir, Rotberger Rosé, Merlot, Gamay Noir, Cabernet Franc

Sparkling: Odyssey (Riesling and some Chardonnay)

Speciality— Ehrenfelser Icewine (weather dependent), Late Harvest Ehrenfelser

Own store: Latitude Fifty

Store hours: *May 1 to October 31:* Daily, 10 am — 5 pm; *November 1 to April 30:* Monday to Saturday, 11 am — 5 pm; Sunday (until New Years), noon — 4 pm

Winery tours: *Summer:* 11 am — 4 pm on the hour; *Winter*: 2 pm

Public tastings: During store hours

Recommended wines: Pinot Auxerrois, Latitude Fifty, Chardonnay, Rotberger Rosé, Merlot, Pinot Noir, Gamay Noir

---

Hainle Vineyards

5355 Trepanier Bench Road
Box 650
Peachland, B.C.
V0H 1X0
Telephone: (250) 767-2525
Fax: (250) 767-2543
e-mail: tilman@hainle.com
sandra@hainle.com
web site: www.hainle.com

The Hainle family has been making wine in the Okanagan for over 22 years, and before that for ten generations in Germany. Father Walter made Canada's first Icewine from Okanagan Riesling in

1977 for the benefit of family and friends. First commercial production was in 1978. Sadly, Walter died in a hiking accident on the property on January 1, 1995.

His son Tilman had become winemaker at Uniacke Cellars at age of 24. He left when the winery was sold (to become CedarCreek) and joined his father across the lake near Peachland to create Hainle Vineyards in 1985.

Father and son built up an inventory of wines until they had sufficient to receive an estate winery licence in 1988. The winery is a 3,000-sq.ft. block-construction building.

In 1991, Tilman began making champagne-method sparkling wine (60 per cent Pinot Blanc, 20 per cent Chardonnay, 10 per cent Pinot Noir and 10 per cent Pinot Meunier). He adds sulphur dioxide only after fermentation to preserve the wine, believing that some oxidation of the fresh juice helps to clarify the wine so that little or no fining and filtering — which can rob the wine of varietal character — is necessary.

A second floor addition to the winery was completed in May, 1993, affording an additional 3,000 sq. ft., including a tasting room, Bistro Amphora, a lab and office space.

Hainle, the first Canadian winery to produce Icewine, holds a library of products going back to 1978. Tilman has made an experimental batch of port from Baco Noir and has two sparklers, one a traditional Cuvée, the other from Riesling. Starting with the 1995 vintage, all Estate Bottled wines were made from organically grown grapes. Starting in 1997, Elisabeth's Vineyard were made this way as well.

Winemaker: Tilman Hainle

Acreage: 18.5 (Fully certified as organic. Yields are kept low to make plants more resistant to disease and pests.)

Soil: Very light sandy soils, pH 6.5 — 6.8. High gravel content; glacio-fluvial slopes with south to southeast exposure. Very good air circulation.

Grape varieties: Riesling, Traminer, Chardonnay, Chasselas, Pinot Noir and small plantings of Merlot, Pinot Meunier, Perle of Csaba

Production: 5,500 cases

Average tonnage crushed: 60 tonnes

Annual tonnage purchased: 20 - 25 tonnes Fischer Vineyard, Elisabeth Harbeck, Knollvine Vineyard

Winemaking philosophy: "We specialize in fully fermented, completely dry wines which are ideal for matching with food. We strive for as natural a product as possible, starting with organic grape-growing, and continuing with minimal intervention in the cellar. Sulphite levels are kept as low as possible. The wines age well in the bottle for an average of five to seven years."

Wines: LDB: *White*—Kerner Fischer Vineyard, Riesling Estate Bottled, Pinot Blanc Elisabeth's Vineyard

Own store: *White*—Chardonnay Estate Bottled, Pinot Gris Okanagan Valley, Traminer Estate Bottled, Riesling Icewine

Red—Merlot, Pinot Noir (Estate Bottled and Elisabeth's Vineyard), Lemberger

Store hours: *November to April:* noon — 5 pm. *May to October:* Tuesday to Sunday, 10 am — 5 pm

Winery tours: None

Public tastings: During shop hours

Bistro hours: Noon — 3 pm on days when wineshop is open. Phone to confirm winter hours.

————

Recommended wines: Kerner, Pinot Noir, Traminer, Riesling-Traminer

Hawthorne Mountain Vineyards

Green Lake Road
PO Box 480
Okanagan Falls, B.C.
V0H 1R0
Telephone: (250) 497-8267
Fax: (250) 497-8073
e-mail: hawthorn@vip.net
web site: www.hmvineyard.com

The Hawthorne Mountain Vineyards site was settled in the early 1900s by the homesteading Hawthorne Brothers. Formerly the LeComte winery, it was purchased by Sumac Ridge's Harry McWatters in 1995. (The LeComte name survives on an eponymous line of labels.) The winery, located five kilometers southwest of Okanagan Falls, is set high above the Okanagan affording it a panoramic view of the valley and surrounding lakes, best experienced from the large garden deck where visitors can picnic. The original vineyard, one of the region's first plantings, was established in the early 1960s and some of the original vines are still there. Harry McWatters has undertaken an extensive expansion program, upgrading the hardware and planting new vineyards, now numbering 170 acres.

The delightful tasting room and shop are in the original settler's home, a stone heritage building.

Winemaker: Bruce Ewart

Acreage: 170

Grape varieties: Chardonnay, Riesling, Gewürztraminer, Pinot Gris, Pinot Noir, Gamay Noir, Merlot, Cabernet Franc, Lemberger

Production: 20,000 cases

Average tonnage crushed: 300 tonnes

Winemaking philosophy: "We strive to make wines with distinctive character, and we concentrate on maximizing the flavours in our wines."

Wines: LDB: *White*—Chardonnay, Gewürztraminer, Riesling, Ehrenfelser Icewine

Red—Gamay Noir, Merlot, Pinot Noir

Sparkling—HMV Brut

Own store: All above plus: *White*—Chardonnay/Semillon, Pinot Meunier, Select Late Harvest Optima

Red—Cabernet Franc, Meritage, Lemberger

Store hours: *Winter:* Monday to Friday, 9 am — 5 pm; Saturday and Sunday, 11 am — 5 pm; *Summer:* Daily, 9 am — 5 pm

Winery tours: *Summer:* Daily, hourly between 10 am and 4 pm; *Winter:* On request

Public tastings: During store hours

Recommended wines: Riesling, Pinot Noir, Lemberger, Ehrenfelser Icewine, Gewürztraminer Icewine

Hester Creek Estate Winery

Box 1605
13163-326 Street
Oliver, B.C.
V0H 1T0
Telephone: (250) 498-4435
Fax: (250) 498-0651
e-mail: info@hestercreek.com
web site: hestercreek.com

Originally the property of Joe Busnardo of Divino Estate, this 70-acre vineyard with mature *vinifera* vines (the oldest cultivars along South Okanagan's "Golden Mile") was sold to Hans Lochbichler, Henry Rathje and former Vincor winemaker Frank Supernak in 1996. (Busnardo took the Divino name to Vancouver Island.) The trio invested in a beautifully decorated reception and tasting room and wine boutique with high beamed ceilings and wrought iron fittings. You can take a light lunch on the patio overlooking the vineyards.

Winemaker: Frank Supernak

Acreage: 70

Soil: Gravel, clay

Grape varieties: Pinot Blanc, Chardonnay, Trebbiano, Merlot, Cabernet Franc, Cabernet Sauvignon, Gamay

Production: 25,000 cases

Average tonnage crushed: 350 tonnes

Annual tonnage purchased: 90 tonnes

Winemaking philosophy: "To produce premium wine to strict VQA standards."

Wines: *White*—Pinot Blanc Estate, Pinot Blanc Signature, Pinot Gris, Kerner, Chardonnay Estate, Chardonnay Signature Release, Blanc de Noir (Pinot Noir and Merlot)

Red—Merlot, Cabernet Franc, Cabernet, Merlot, Cabernet Sauvignon, Pinot Noir

Specialty —Late Harvest Trebbiano, Pinot Blanc Ice Wine

Store hours: *May 1 to October 31:* Daily, 10 am — 5 pm

Winery tours: By appointment only

Public tastings: Free ($2 charge for dessert wines)

Recommended wines: Pinot Blanc (three styles), Chardonnay, Merlot, Cabernet Franc, Late Harvest Trebbiano

---

Hillside Estate Winery

1350 Naramata Road
Penticton, B.C.
V2A 8T6
Telephone:
(250) 493-6274
Fax: (250) 493-6294
web site: www.hill-sideestate.com

Started in 1990 by Vera and Bohumir Klokocka, Hillside Cellars was one of the first farm-gate wineries in the Okanagan. A Czechoslovakian by birth, Vera taught herself winemaking in Canada. In 1900, she released her first 25 cases. In the next six years she and Bohumir enlarged their vintage to 1200 cases annually.

In the summer of 1996 Vera sold the winery to a consortium of Alberta and British Columbia investors who financed a huge expansion from Vera's garage winery to a 15,000 square foot building.

On May 1, 1998, Hillside Estate Winery opened their new premises to the public. This stylish building is a 15,000 square foot timber-framed structure that enhances the incredible views of the lake. The winery produces a large portfolio of wines some of which are aged in a combination of French and American oak barrels.

Winemaker: Eric von Krosigk

Acreage: 5.6

Soil: Mostly stony, sloping vineyard overlooking Naramata Road and Lake Okanagan

Grape varieties: Johannisberg Riesling, Auxerrois, Muscat d'Ottonel, Gamay, some Cabernet Sauvignon, Pinot Noir

Production: 15,000 cases

Average tonnage crushed: 10 - 15 tonnes

Annual tonnage purchased: 270 tonnes

Winemaking philosophy: "We have made a commitment to producing quality wines with only the best Okanagan Valley grapes."

Wines: *White*—Auxerrois, Chardonnay, Ehrenfelser, Gewürztraminer, Kerner, Pinot Blanc, Pinot Gris, Semillon

Red—Cabernet Franc, Gamay, Merlot, Pinot Noir, Syrah, Cabernet Sauvignon

Rosé—Gamay Blush

Specialty—Hillside Brut, Riesling Icewine, Late Harvest Vidal, Vidal Icewine

Store hours: *April 1 to October 31:* Daily 10 am — 6 pm; *November 1 to March 31:* Tuesday to Sunday, 11 am – 5 pm

Winery tours: *Summer:* Daily; *November to March*: Friday to Sunday

Public tastings: During store hours

––––––––––

Recommended wines: Semillon, Gamay Noir

House of Rose Vineyards

2270 Garner Road
Kelowna, B.C.
V1P 1E2
Telephone/Fax: (604) 765-0802

The White Rose

Verdelet

1992

WHITE WINE / VIN BLANC

OKANAGAN VALLEY

750 mL

Product of / Produit du
British Columbia,
Canada

11.4% Alc./Vol.

HOUSE OF ROSE VINEYARDS LTD., KELOWNA, BRITISH COLUMBIA, CANADA

Vern Rose, a former Alberta school teacher, bought his farm that sits high above the lake on the old Belgo Bench in 1982. He began making wine for himself from the established vineyard. He took two courses in winemaking at UC Davis and at Okanagan College and attended a symposium on cool climate viticulture in New Zealand in 1988 and Germany in 1992 before establishing his winery in 1992. His vineyard favours hybrids and his northerly location and distance from the lake make it possible for him to grow Icewine.

Winemaker: Vern Rose

Acreage: 16

Soil: Alluvial bench soil, good gravel sub-soil; semi-arid valley conditions require irrigation

Grape varieties: Chardonnay, Verdelet, Perle of Zala, Semillon, Okanagan Riesling, Maréchal Foch, Pinot Noir

Production: 5,000 cases

Average tonnage crushed: 75+ tonnes

Annual tonnage purchased: 6 tonnes

Winemaking philosophy: "Grow top-quality grapes to produce the best possible wine. Keeping as close as possible in harmony with nature, avoiding the use of additives to wine wherever possible.

Wines: Own store: *White*—Chardonnay, Verdelet Dry, Verdelet (2), Johannisberg Riesling, Perle of Zala, Semillon, Vintner's Choice Dry (Verdelet, Chardonnay, Okanagan Riesling, Perle of Zala), Vintner's Choice (2), Okanagan Trocken, Late Harvest Chardonnay

Red—Proprietors' Reserve (Pinot Noir, Maréchal Foch, Merlot, De Chaunac), Maréchal Foch

Rosé—Rosé

Store hours: 10 am — 6 pm

Winery tours: 10 am — 5 pm

Public tastings: During store hours

Inniskillin Okanagan Vineyards

Road 11, RR 1 S24 C5
Oliver, B.C.
Telephone: (250) 498-6663
Fax: (250) 498-4566
web site: www.inniskillin.com

When Inniskillin became part of Vincor, following their merger with Cartier in 1992, it opened the opportunity for Donald Ziraldo and Karl Kaiser to make wines in British Columbia at the former Bright's facility in Oliver, using fruit from the Inkameep Vineyard. The initial vintage of 1994 was auspicious and production doubled the following year to 6,000 cases. Encouraged by their success, the partners, with Vincor's backing, purchased Okanagan Vineyards, an existing winery, and its 22-acre Dark Horse Vineyard to source grapes for their Inniskillin Okanagan Vineyards label.

In 1998 they hired Australian winemaker Philip Dowell, formerly with Coldstream Hills in the Yarra Valley, as general manager of the new project; and by 2001 they hope to begin construction of a dramatic four-storey winery whose top level will be linked by a bridge to the vineyard. The new facility will have a capacity to produce 100,000 cases.

Winemaker: Sandor Mayer

Acreage: 22

Soil: Granite based, gravelly-rocky loam

Grape varieties: Merlot, Cabernet Sauvignon, Cabernet Franc, Pinot Noir, Chardonnay, Pinot Blanc, Riesling, Gewürztraminer

Production: 18,000 cases

Average tonnage crushed: 150 tonnes

Annual tonnage purchased: 70 tonnes

Winemaking philosophy: "Making world class wine, distinct wine styles for Inniskillin. Quality wine comes only from vineyard and winemaking — an unbreakable marriage."

Wines: *White*—Chardonnay, Pinot Blanc, Gewürztraminer, Riesling Icewine, Vidal Icewine

Red—Merlot, Cabernet Sauvignon, Meritage, Pinot Noir

Store hours: Monday to Friday, 10 am — 5 pm; Saturday and Sunday: in summer months

Winery tours: Yes

Public tastings: Free

Recommended wines: Gewürztraminer, Pinot Blanc, Cabernet Sauvignon, Red Meritage, Vidal Icewine

---

Jackson-Triggs

(See Vincor International)

Kettle Valley Winery

2988 Hayman Road
Naramata, B.C.
V0H 1N0
Telephone: (250) 496-5898
Fax: (250) 496-5298
e-mail:
KettleValleyWinery@BC.sympatico.ca

Drawing its name from the Kettle Valley Railway, which travelled through the Naramata area on the east side of Okanagan Lake, the winery opened to the public in 1996. Brothers-in-law, Tim Watts, a geologist, and Bob Ferguson, a chartered accountant, planted their first vineyard with Pinot Noir and Chardonnay in the mid-1980s, followed up with additional plantings of the same varieties in 1989 and in 1991-1992 with Cabernet and Merlot plantings. Recent plantings include more Cabernet and Merlot with a Shiraz planting planned for 1999.

The first commercial release was the 1992 Pinot Noir, followed with the 1994 Chardonnay. A new winery facility is in the planning stages with anticipated construction to commence in the summer of 2000.

Winemakers: Bob Ferguson and Tim Watts

Acreage: 11

Soil: A mix of clay, sand and gravel, south and west facing slopes

Grape varieties: Chardonnay, Pinot Noir, Cabernet Sauvignon, Cabernet Franc, Merlot, Shiraz

Production: 1,650 cases (1998)

Average tonnage crushed: 26 tonnes (1998)

Winemaking philosophy: "We operate a small farm-based winery. Our goal is to produce quality barrel-aged wines. We produce three wines only: a Chardonnay, a Pinot Noir and a blend of Cabernet and Merlot. Our focus is quality and by staying a small farm-based winery we hope our passion will show through in our wines."

Wines: Own store: Chardonnay, Pinot Noir, Cabernet, Merlot

Store hours: *Summer months:* Thursday to Monday, noon — 5 pm; otherwise by appointment

---

Recommended wines: Chardonnay, Pinot Noir, Cabernet, Merlot

Lake Breeze Vineyards

Sammet Road off Naramata
Road
Box 9
Naramata, B.C.
V0H 1N0
Telephone: (250) 496-5659
Fax: (250) 496-5894
e-mail: lakebreezevine-
yards@sympatico.bc.ca

Wayne and Joanne Finn took over Lake Breeze from the Mosers in the fall of 1998. They have a licensed patio (brunch on weekends, light snacks and lunches during the week) offering a panoramic view of Okanagan Lake from Penticton and Peachland. This is the first Canadian winery to produce a varietal wine from the South African grape, Pinotage (a cross betwen Pinot Noir and Cinsaut).

Winemaker: Garron Elmes

Acreage: 14 (12.59 planted with grapes)

Soil: Sandy soils with a westerly slope (Pinot Blanc, sandy/clay; Chardonnay and Ehrenfelser, slightly heavier soils, east/west exposure)

Grape varieties: Pinot Blanc, Gewürztraminer, Ehrenfelser, Chardonnay, Semillon, Morio Muscat, Pinot Noir, Cabernet Franc, Merlot, Pinotage

Production: 4,500 cases

Average tonnage crushed: 75 tonnes

Winemaking philosophy: "At Lake Breeze we believe in taking the natural fruit flavours of the grape and transferring them to the bottle with the minimum amount of manipulation. Through careful and meticulous vineyard management we receive fruit of the highest quality, from which our wines make themselves."

Wines: *White*—Pinot Blanc, Gewürztraminer, Ehrenfelser, Chardonnay, Semillon, Ehrenfelser Icewine, Pinot Blanc Icewine

Red—Pinot Noir, Pinot Noir Reserve, Cabernet Franc, Merlot, Pinotage

Sparkling— Zephyr Brut

Specialty— Delice (Morio Muscat dessert wine)

Store hours: *May 15 to October 15:* Monday to Saturday, 10 am — 5 pm; Sunday, 11 am — 5 pm; *Off season:* By appointment or by chance

Winery tours: Yes, through the summer months

Public tastings: Free (Icewine - $2)

Recommended wines: Pinot Blanc, Semillon

Lang Vineyards Ltd.

RR #1, S11, C55
2493 Gammon Road
Naramata, B.C.
V0H 1N0
Telephone: (250) 496-5987
Fax: (250) 496-5706
e-mail: langwines@img.net

Lang Vineyards has the distinction of being the first farm winery in Canada. In 1980, Guenther and Kristina Lang moved from Nuertingen, Germany, and settled in the Okanagan Valley. They bought the existing old vineyard in Naramata on the sunny east side of the Okanagan Lake. First they built their house and then they started to replant the vineyard with new grape varieties.

What started as a hobby for the Langs turned into a business. In 1985, Guenther approached the B.C. government and asked if he could sell the wines he made. After some years of lobbying, a proffered bottle to then-premier Bill Van der Zalm seemed to oil the wheels of government because in 1990 the legislation was passed to set up farm wineries. In 1993, the Langs built a 4,000-sq. ft. winery with an on-site wine store.

Winemakers: Guenther and Kristina Lang

Acres: 15

Soil: West-facing slope, sandy-stone/clay soil

Grape varieties: Riesling, Gewürztraminer, Pinot Noir, Pinot Meunier, Maréchal Foch, Merlot, Auxerrois, Viognier

Production: 5,000 cases plus

Average tonnage crushed: 50 plus tonnes

Winemaking philosophy: "We strive for the highest quality grapes possible by controlling every step of viticulture, especially thinning to have a lighter crop. We harvest as late as possible to have a high degree of ripeness. We only make wine from healthy, truly ripe grapes using only *Vitis vinifera* varietals (apart from Maréchal Foch)."

Wines: Own store only: *White*—Riesling Dry, Riesling Farm Winery Reserve, Riesling Late Harvest Dry, Medium Dry and Select, Riesling Icewine, Gewürztraminer, Pinot-Auxerrois, Viognier

Sparkling Wines—(Methode Classique) Pinot Auxerrois, Pinot Meunier

Red—Maréchal Foch Medium, Pinot Noir Dry, Pinot Meunier Dry, Merlot Dry

Store hours: *May 1 to October 15:* Daily, 10 am — 5 pm; *October 16 to April 30:* by appointment

Winery tours: By arrangement

Public tastings: During store hours

Recommended wines: Riesling all styles, Maréchal Foch

Larch Hills Winery

110 Timms Road
Salmon Arm, B.C.
V1E 2P8
Telephone: (250) 832-0155
Fax: (250) 832-9419
e-mail:
Lhwinery@shuswap.net
web site:
www.Larchhillswinery.bc.ca

Hans and Hazel Nevrkla's winery, established in 1996, is the most northerly in the Okanagan situated on bench land south of Salmon Arm. Five years before this they had planted a four-acre

vineyard on the steeply raked south-facing slopes. Hans was an award-winning amateur winemaker who turned pro with his first vintage in 1995. The winery has an attractive wine shop and boutique with an outdoor patio for picnicers. Hans' style is Germanic though his drier wines are more Austrian in style.

Winemaker: Hans Nevrkla

Acreage: 4.5

Soil: Loam, clay, rocks

Grape varieties: Ortega, Siegerrebe, Madeleine Angevine, Madeleine Sylvaner, Agria

Production: 1,500 cases

Average tonnage crushed: 22 tonnes

Winemaking philosophy: "German style, cool climate, lots of fruit."

Wines: *White*—Oretga, Gewürztraminer, Riesling, Northern Lights (blend of Siegerrebe, Madeleine Angevine, Madeleine Sylvaner, Ortega)

Red—Gamay, Pinot Noir

Store Hours: *May 1 to October 31:* Daily, 12 noon — 5 pm; *Winter:* by appointment only

Winery tours: Yes, on request (conducted tour and tasting $3)

Recommended wines: Ortega, Gewürztraminer, Gamay

Mission Hill Winery

1730 Mission Hill Road
Westbank, B.C.
V4T 2E4
Telephone: (250) 768-7611
Fax: (250) 768-2267
e-mail:
kmoul@markanthony.com

Mission Hill, one of B.C.'s most beautifully sited wineries atop Boucherie Mountain, is a major vineyard owner in the Okanagan with holdings in Oliver (Black Sage Road Vineyard), Osoyoos (Osoyoos Estate) and Westbank (Mission Hill Estate). This is a large enterprise that thinks and acts like a sophisticated California estate winery and consistently produces award-winning wines. Kiwi winemaker John Simes won the prestigious Avery Trophy for the best Chardonnay worldwide in 1994 for his 1992 vintage.

Mission Hill's flamboyant owner Anthony von Mandl is the president of the Mark Anthony Group, a wine, beer, spirit and cider conglomerate which also owns beverage alcohol stores. His winery boasts state of the art technology and much emphasis is put on clonal selection from the vineyards. Currently under construction is a $30 million visitors' centre featuring two underground barrel-ageing cellars with a capacity to hold 6,000 barrels, a wine and food centre with test kitchen, reception hall, private dining and tasting rooms, amphitheatre, audio-visual theatre, all surmounted by a 75-foot bell tower which will afford a magnificent view of the region.

Currently, Mission Hill has 4,000 French and American Oak barrels. In 1992, it released its first champagne method sparkling wines — Cuvée Chardonnay and Cuvée Chenin Blanc.

Mission Hill bottles under four labels — Grand Reserve (VQA wines and non-VQA wines), Private Reserve and Vintner's Selection.

Winemaker: John Simes

Production: Over 205,000 cases

Average tonnage crushed: 1,100 - 1,200 tonnes

Annual tonnage imported: 300 - 400 tonnes (mainly Washington fruit)

Winemaking philosophy: "At Mission Hill, we have been inspired by the vision Robert Mondavi brought to the Napa Valley. In this spirit, our focus has been on quality and innovation. As the Okanagan Valley is a relatively young wine-producing district, we felt it was important to experiment with a wide variety of *vinifera* varietals, allowing us over time to focus on those wines we believe have the greatest potential. Our focus is principally on dry wines, both white and red, and where we see exceptional potential to produce strictly limited quantities of specialty wines. Our primary objective is to produce wines that show true varietal character and have excellent ageing potential."

Wines: LDB: *VQA wines white*—Mission Hill Grand Reserve Bacchus Icewine, Grand Reserve Optima Late Harvest, Grand Reserve Pinot Blanc, Grand Reserve White; Private Reserve Chenin Blanc Bin 66, Private Reserve Late Harvest Riesling, Private Reserve Pinot Blanc, Private Reserve Riesling, Private Reserve Sauvignon Blanc, Private Reserve Semillon Bin 1, Private Reserve Chardonnay, Private Reserve Verdelet/Riesling (organic), Private Reserve Gewürztraminer; Mission Hill 49 North

VQA wines red—Mission Hill Grand Reserve Red, Mission Hill Vin Nouveau; Private Reserve Maréchal Foch (organic)

Non-VQA wines white—Mission Hill Private Reserve Chardonnay, Vintners Chablis, Vintners Chenin Blanc, Proprietors' Select White, Vintners Harvest Riesling, Vintners Riesling, Vintners Semillon/Sauvignon, Vintners Traminer/Riesling, Winemakers Reserve White, Mission Ridge Light White, Mission Ridge Premium Dry White

Non-VQA wines red—Mission Hill Private Reserve Cabernet Sauvignon, Private Reserve Cabernet Sauvignon/Merlot, Private Reserve Merlot; Mission Hill Vintners Burgundy, Proprietors' Select Red, Vintners Kuhlmann Cabernet;

Mission Ridge Premium Dry Red

Rosé—Mission Hill Winemakers Reserve Blush

Own stores: *White*—Grand Reserve Chardonnay, Grand Reserve Riesling, Grand Reserve Gewürztraminer, Grand Reserve Riesling Icewine; Private Reserve Muscat of Alexandria

Fortified—Private Reserve Dry Sherry, Mark Anthony Aperitif

Stores: Vancouver: Mark Anthony Wine Merchants, 962 West King Edwards Ave., Vancouver (604) 739-9463

Saanich: Mark Anthony Wine Merchants, 2560 A Sinclair Road, Saanich (250) 721-5222

White Rock: Mark Anthony Wine Merchants, 15220 North Bluff Road, White Rock (604) 538-9463

Store hours: Daily 9 am — 5 pm (9 am — 7 pm *July and August*)
Winery tours: Call for tour times (Hourly from 10 am — 5 pm, July and August)
Public tastings: Available during Boutique Hours

Recommended wines: Grand Reserve Chardonnay, Private Reserve Chardonnay, Grand Reserve Pinot Noir, Grand Reserve Merlot, Grand Reserve Cabernet Sauvignon, Riesling Icewine

Nichol Vineyard & Farm Winery

1285 Smethurst Road
Naramata, B.C.
V0H 1N0
Telephone:
(250) 496-5962
Fax: (250) 496-4275

Alex Nichol, a former symphony double bassist, has long been the conscience of the Okanagan. As a writer he has documented its history in *Wine and Vines of British Columbia* and has worked tirelessly to improve its wines. In 1989, he began to practice what he preached when he bought an alfalfa field and a year later set about turning it into a vineyard. It took three years for him and his wife Kathleen to complete. The vineyard is located under a granite cliff across the water from the Summerland Research Station. The sun's reflection off the 300-foot rock face and the heat that it holds allows Alex to ripen such warm-climate grape varieties as Syrah (B.C.'s first barrel-aged Syrah). He now makes some of the most powerful, flavourful and majestic wines of the region. His split canopy "Open Lyre" trellising system is unique in the valley. The wines are aged in "reworked" French *barriques*.

Winemaker: Alex and Kathleen Nichol

Acreage: 4.5

Soil: Clay-rich yet stony soil of glacial till

Grape varieties: Pinot Gris, Pinot Noir, Syrah, Cabernet Franc, St. Laurent

Production: 1,200 - 1,500 cases

Average tonnage crushed: 16 tonnes

Winemaking philosophy: "We are dedicated to the production of premium barrel-aged red wines and barrel-fermented and/or *sur lie* white wines. The wines are made as natural as possible. Red wines from the barrel are unfiltered."

Wines: Own store: *White*—Pinot Gris

Red—Pinot Noir, Syrah, Cabernet Franc

Specialty—Ehrenfelser Select Late Harvest

Store hours: *Spring to Thanksgiving:* Tuesday to Sunday, 11 am — 5 pm; call to check other times of year; anytime by appointment

Public tastings: During store hours

Recommended wines: Pinot Gris, Syrah, Pinot Noir, Cabernet Franc

---

Pinot Reach Cellars

1670 Dehart Road
Kelowna, B.C.
V1W 4N6
Telephone: (250) 764-0078
Fax: (250) 764-0771
e-mail: pinot@direct.ca

Susan Dulick, whose family has been growing grapes for over 50 years, created the farmgate winery in 1996 on the Kelowna vineyard her grandfather bought. The name is a homage to the Pinot family of grapes, especially the reds, which are cultivated on the property. Though the initial releases were white varietals, a sparkling Riesling was produced. The 1997 crush saw red varietals, Pinot Noir and Pinot Meunier added to the portfolio and Cabernet Sauvignon the following vintage. American oak is used for Chardonnay and the reds.

Winemaker: Eric von Krosigk

Acreage: 35

Grape varieties: Riesling, Bacchus, Optima, Pinot Blanc, Chardonnay, Gewürztraminer, Pinot Noir, Pinot Meunier, Cabernet Sauvignon

Production: 4000 cases

Average tonnage crushed: 60 tonnes

Winemaking philosophy: "To continue the family tradition of growing the finest grapes to produce the finest wines, true to their varietal characteristics."

Wines: *White*—Bacchus, Optima Dry (and Botrytis Affected), Riesling, Chardonnay, Pinot Blanc, Reserve Gewürztraminer, Riesling Icewine

Red—Pinot Noir, Pinot Meunier, Cabernet Sauvignon

Sparkling (champagne method)—Riesling Brut, Classic Cuvée, Pinot Noir Brut

Store hours: *Mid May to mid October:* Tuesday to Saturday, noon — 5 pm

Winery tours: No

Public tastings: Free

Recommended wines: Pinot Meunier, Late Harvest Optima

Poplar Grove Farm Winery

1060 Poplar Grove Road
RR #1
Penticton, B.C.
V2A 8T6
Telephone: (250) 492-2352
Fax: (250) 492-9162

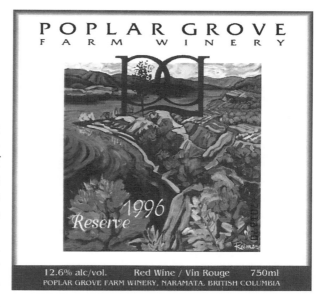

Ian Sutherland's love of claret led him to fly in the face of tradition and plant two and a half acres of Merlot and Cabernet Franc — instead of white varieties — on the eight-acre property he and his wife Gitta bought outside Penticton in 1992. Inspired then by his winery-owning neighbours, Bohumir and Vera Klokocka of Hillside Cellars, Ian pulled out apple trees to make way for his red grapes and planted in clay loam soil not unlike that of St. Emilion where the Merlot grape flourishes.

In 1997 Ian was invited by Seresin Estate in Marlborough, New Zealand, to be assistant winemaker for that winery's first crush. The experience helped to make Popular Grove's 1997 Chardonnay a critical success.

Winemaker: Ian Sutherland

Acreage: 7

Production (by 2002) 1,500 cases — 2/3 red, 1/3 white

Grape varieties: Merlot, Cabernet Franc, Chardonnay, Pinot Gris

Winemaking philosophy: "Stay small enough to control everything. The crop load is kept below four tonnes per acre and our wines are barrel-fermented and barrel-aged for up to 24 months. We build our red wines in Bordeaux style, with a hot fermentation followed by 12-18 months maturation in French oak barrels."

***

Recommended wines: Cabernet Franc, Merlot, Chardonnay

Prpich Vineyards

RR #1, S30, C8
Okanagan Falls, B.C.
V0H 1R0
Telephone: (250) 497-8246

Dan Prpich (pronounced Pur-pitch) began his winemaking as an amateur in Hamilton, Ontario, in 1959 using *labrusca* grapes. When he and his family moved to the Okanagan in 1973 he bought his 60 acre farm and pulled out some of the orchards to plant Okanagan Riesling and Maréchal Foch as well as some Chardonnay and Cabernet Sauvignon from Washington State, and then some Verdelet. He ripped out 20 acres of the hybrids during the pull out program and then replanted, concentrating on varietals such as Chasselas, Pinot Noir, Merlot as well as preferred hybrids such as Vidal and Seyval Blanc. Further replanting will include Cabernets, Ehrenfelser and Lemberger.

***

Recommended Wines: Pinot Blanc, Lemberger

Quails' Gate Estate Winery

3303 Boucherie Road
Kelowna, B.C.
V1Z 2H3
Telephone: (250) 769-4451
Toll free: 1-800-420-WINE
Fax: (250) 769-3451
e-mail: quails@direct.ca
web site:www.quailsgate.com

It was 1989 when, after years of planting and experimenting, Dick Stewart and his son Ben opened Quails' Gate Estate Winery in Kelowna. For the Stewart family the venture was a once in a lifetime opportunity to pursue a shared passion for Pinot Noir, and to realize a dream of producing it, and other varieties of wines, with a superior level of quality. At the time, many in the industry weren't convinced that it could be done, especially when it came to red wines. Dick and Ben Stewart set out to prove them wrong.

In the beginning, Quails' Gate employed a handful of people and produced less than 1,500 cases annually. Today, Quails' Gate employs more than 30 people. In August of 1998, a new $2-million production facility was officially opened by Prime Minister Jean Chrétien, increasing production ability to 60,000 cases and barrel storage ability to 1,500 French oak barriques.

Winemaker Peter Draper brought a depth of viticultural as well as oenological experience and training from Australia to Quails' Gate following a tradition of quality sets by winemaker Jeff Martin, also an Australian. After completing his studies at Roseworthy, Australia's renown wine school, he developed his winemaking skills at three of Australia's most highly rated wineries — Petaluma (under Brian Croser), Henshke in the Barossa Valley and Mount Mary in the Yarra Valley. Peter's main area of interest is Pinot Noir.

The product range includes over a dozen different varieties from Merlot, Cabernet Sauvignon, Chasselas and Chenin Blanc to specialty items such as Late Harvest Optima and Riesling Icewine. Of all its wines, Quails' Gate is perhaps best known for its Family Reserve Pinot Noir and Chardonnay.

The wine shop is situated in a carefully restored log cabin which was the original home of Okanagan Valley pioneers John and Susan Allison, who settled on the site in 1873.

Proprietor: Ben Stewart

Winemaker: Peter Draper

Acreage: 115

Soil: The vineyard is situated on the favourable south facing slope above Lake Okanagan and below the extinct volcano Mount Boucherie. The vineyards are planted between 1,123 feet (lake level bottom of vineyard) to 1,500 feet (top of vineyard) above sea level in a mixture of volcanic rock and clay (glacial/glaciolacustrine). Although difficult to farm, Quails' Gate believes that this unique site is partially why their wines are so rich, concentrated and interesting in character.

Grape varieties: Pinot Noir, Chardonnay, Riesling, Chasselas, Pinot Blanc, Optima, Chenin Blanc, Gamay, Cabernet Sauvignon, Foch, Merlot, Sauvignon Blanc, Cabernet Franc

Production: 60,000 cases

Average tonnage crushed: 675 tonnes

Annual tonnage purchased: 30 per cent

Winemaking philosophy: "Through the careful management of our vineyards, and the use of both new and old world winemaking techniques, we aim to make varietal wines distinctly different to each other, with an emphasis on producing world-class Pinot Noir and Chardonnay."

Wines: *Family Reserve Range*—Pinot Noir, Chardonnay

Limited Release Range—Chardonnay, Pinot Noir, Chenin Blanc, Dry Riesling, Merlot/Cabernet Sauvignon, Old Vines Foch, Gamay

Dessert Wine Range—Riesling Icewine, N.V. Select Tawny, Late Harvest Optima B.A.

Proprietor's Selection Range—Chasselas, Gewürztraminer

Store hours: 10 am — 7 pm during peak season; 10 am — 5 pm during shoulder season

Winery tours: *April 29 to June 25:* Daily, 11 am, 1 pm, 3 pm; *June 26 to September 6:* Daily, Conducted hourly from 11 am to 4 pm; *September 7 to October 11:* Daily, 11 am, 1 pm, 3 pm

Public tastings: All throughout the day during wine shop hours

————

Recommended wines: Limited Release Dry Riesling, Limited Release Chardonnay, Family Reserve Pinot Noir, Old Vines Foch, Botrytis Affected Optima

Recline Ridge Vineyards & Winery

2640 Skimikin Road,
RR1 S12 C16,
Tappen, B.C.
V0E 2X0
Telephone: (250) 835-2212
Fax: (250) 835-2228
e-mail: inquiry@recline-ridge.bc.ca
web site: www.recline-ridge.ba.ca

Mike and Sue Smith have been making wine for over two decades, expanding a hobby into a productive business. As award-winning amateurs they experimented with locally grown Ortega, Optima, Siegrrebe, Madeleine Angevine, Madeleine Sylvaner, Gewürztraminer, Pinot Auxerrois, Agria and Maréchal Foch. Many of these varieties now grace their five-acre vineyard. In the spring of 1998, the Smiths began construction of an expanded winery — a post and beam log building overlooking the vineyard and framed by Tappen Mountain and the Tappen and Skimikin Valleys. The wine-making facility, wine shop and tasting facility occupy a 3,300 square foot building on three levels. There is also a vineyard and farm walking trail.

Winemaker: Michael Smith

Acreage: 10 (5 in production)

Soil: clay loam

Grape varieties: Ortega, Madeleine Sylvaner, Madeleine Angevine, Siegerrebe, Optima, Gewürztraminer, Maréchal Foch, Agria

Production: 850 cases

Averages tonnage crushed: 14 tonnes

Average tonnage purchased: 6 tonnes

Winemaking philosophy: "Germanic style whites — crisp, fruity, not too dry — cool ferment Reds — full body, malolactic, oaked."

Wines: *White*— Ortega, Madeleine Angevine, Festival White (house blend), Optima, Siegerrebe, Gewürztraminer, Botrytis Affected Madeleine Sylvaner

Red: Northern Melody (house red), Maréchal Foch, Agria

Store hours: May to October, daily: noon — 6pm

Winery tours: yes, self-guided or by demand

Public tastings: free (except for Ice products)

Red Rooster Winery

910 De Beck Road
Naramata, B.C.
V0H 1NO
Telephone:(250) 496-4041
Fax: (250) 496-5674
e-mail: redrooster@img.net

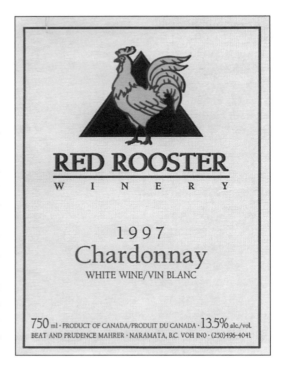

Beat and Prudence Mahrer opened their winery near Naramata (located above their vineyards) overlooking Okanagan Lake in 1997. Their first release was the 1997 vintage in which they produced Riesling, Gewürztraminer, Chardonnay, a blush wine and Merlot. Thanks to their experienced winemaker, Eric von Krosigk — a Geisenheim student who has made a specialty of sparkling wine at Sumac Ridge, Summerhill and the former LeComte — they also launched a sparkling wine made by the champagne method using Pinot Noir, Chardonnay and Riesling.

A unique aspect of Red Rooster is its line of five vineyard designated Icewines grown at nearby Paradise Vineyards, from Chardonnay, Riesling, Vidal, Verdelet and Viognier.

Winemaker: Eric von Krosigk
Acreage: 12
Grape varieties: Merlot, Chardonnay, Gewürztraminer, Pinot Gris
Production: 8,000 cases
Winemaking philosophy: "Quality before quantity."
Wines: *White*—Chardonnay, Pinot Gris, Gewürztraminer, Riesling, Late Harvest
    Riesling, Icewines
Red—Merlot, Pinot Noir
Sparkling—'Champagne Brut'
Store hours: *April to October:* Daily, 10 am — 6 pm
Public tastings: Free

Recommended wines: Brut sparkling, Riesling, Gewürztraminer,
Pinot Noir, Chardonnay, Merlot

St. Hubertus Vineyard

5225 Lakeshore Road
Kelowna, B.C.
V1W 4J1
Telephone: (250) 764-7888
Toll free: 1-800-989-WINE
Fax: (250) 764-0499
e-mail: st.hubertus@wrkpowerlink.com
web site:www.st.hubertus.bc.ca

St. Hubertus Estate Winery is named after the Gebert's family lodge in Switzerland. St. Hubertus Vineyard owned by Leo Gebert and Oak Bay Vineyard owned by brother Andy are located just opposite a 14-acre public park and beach. Established in the 1920s (one of the oldest in B.C.), the Geberts purchased the vineyards in 1984. The winery license was issued in 1992 and the Geberts changed its status to an estate winery in 1994. Wines produced under the St. Hubertus label see no oak: under the Oak Bay label are all barrel-fermented and/or aged in French and American oak.

Visitors arriving at the winery are greeted by an historic entrance sign, hand carved in the 1960s and several pieces of antiques (running) farm equipment once used to work the soil and transport the fruit to market. Many original buildings from the 1930s include the rustic winery with its cozy wine shop. Picnic tables are set in the vineyard and under the marquee.

Winemaker: Cherrie Mirco Johnes

Acreage: 52 planted (3 vacant)

Soil: Sandy, rocky, clay

Grape varieties: Pinot Noir, Gamay Noir, Pinot Meunier, Merlot, Riesling, Pinot Blanc, Bacchus, Gewürztraminer, Chasselas

Production: 10,000 cases

Average tonnage crushed: 120 tonnes

Winemaking philosophy: "The Okanagan has an excellent and unique microclimate for growing grapes. We don't have to compete with other wine regions; we simply have to promote our own distinct taste. Since we operate a small cottage winery we know and understand the needs of our customers and are able to give them the wine which matches the wine lover's taste."

Wines: Own store: *White*—Riesling, Verdelet, Bacchus, Pinot Blanc

Red—Gamay Noir, Maréchal Foch

Specialty—Bacchus Icewine, Riesling Icewine

Store hours: *May long weekend to October 15:* Daily, 10 am — 5:30 pm; *October 15 to December 31:* Tuesday to Saturday, noon — 5 pm; *January 1 to May long weekend:* Hours vary (call ahead)

Winery tours: Daily, June to October

Public tastings: During store hours

Recommended wines: Pinot Blanc, Riesling, Merlot

St. Laszlo Vineyards

RR #1, S95, L8   Telephone: (250) 499-2856
Keremeos, B.C.
V0X 1N0

Joe Ritlop and his family made the first crush at St. Laszlo in 1978 (Joe named the winery after his birthplace in Yugoslavia). They had already planted vineyards in the early 1970s, south of Keremeos on slopes above the Similkameen River, experimenting with a range of hybrid and *vinifera* vines. Joe is considered something of a maverick in the B.C. industry and has followed an independent path from the beginning. He makes his wine organically, using no chemicals in the vineyard and no sulphides, sorbates or preservatives in the cellar. The grapes are fermented on their own yeasts. The St. Laszlo style is full-bodied. Joe's late harvest wines such as Tokay Aszu and Golden Nectar are well worth trying, though costly. He has made Icewine since 1982.

Winemaker: Joe Ritlop

Grape varieties: Tokay, Riesling, Perle of Csaba, Pinot Auxerrois, Chardonnay, Semillon, Sovereign Royal, Verdelet; Maréchal Foch, Rougeon, De Chaunac, Cabernet Franc

Winemaking philosophy: "I will create my wine in my own fashion. I cannot do anything else. We can make as good or better white wines here than any of the European countries."

Recommended wines: Riesling, Tokai Aszu, vintage dessert wines

Saturna Vineyard

Saturna Island, B.C.   Telephone: (250) 539-2254
                           Toll free: 1-888-539-8800
                           web site:www.saturna-island.bc.ca

In June 1997, Lawrence and Robyn Page, owners of Saturna Lodge and Restaurant, officially opened their winery — the first such enterprise in B.C.'s Gulf Islands. The vineyards were prepared in the spring of 1995 on the 87-acre farm adjacent to

Saturna Beach. The first six acres of vines were planted year later with Pinot Noir and Gewürztraminer. This block was christened the Rebecca Vineyard in honour of the couple's daughter. Her mother was duly honoured a year later with the Robyn Vineyard, eight acres planted with Chardonnay, Merlot and Pinot Noir. Plans for the construction of a 3,000 square foot, split-level log frame winery and tasting room are currently underway.

Winemaker: Steve Cozine and Eric von Krosigk
Acreage: (eventually) 50
Grape varieties: Chardonnay, Pinot Gris, Gewürztraminer, Pinot Noir, Merlot
Production: 4,400 cases
Wines: *White*—Chardonnay, Semillon, Chardonnay/Semillon blend, Gewürztraminer
Red—Pinot Noir

Scherzinger Vineyards

7311 Fiske Street
Summerland, B.C.
V0H 1Z0
Telephone/fax: (250) 494-8815

Edgar Scherzinger's first love is wood carving, a passion he inherited from his father in the Black Forest. Evidence of his talent can be seen all around the winery's tasting room. In 1974, he and his wife Elizabeth bought a cherry orchard overlooking Summerland. Cherries were a losing proposition, so they planted *labrusca* grapes which produced wines Edgar hesitated to sell to the public. He understood that only *vinifera* would work and took a gamble by planting Gewürztraminer in 1978, at a time

when the accepted wisdom was that noble European varieties could not live long in the Okanagan. He sold the fruit to Sumac Ridge and eventually added Chardonnay and Pinot Noir to the vineyard. In 1994 he decided to make the leap from grower to winemaker.

Winemaker: Edgar Scherzinger
Acreage: 6.6 (no pesticides or herbicides, minimal sulphur)

Soil: Coarse sandy soils

Grape varieties: Gewürztraminer, Chardonnay, Pinot Noir

Production: 460 cases (1995), 900 cases (1996)

Average tonnage crushed: 30 tonnes

Winemaking philosophy: "Quality in wines."

Wines: Own store: *White*—Gewürztraminer, Gewürztraminer Caroline (sweet), Chardonnay

Red—Pinot Noir

Store hours: 10 am — 6 pm

Winery tours: Yes

Public tastings: 10 am — 6 pm

Recommended wines: Gewürztraminer

Slamka Cellars

2815 Ourtoland Road
Kelowna, B.C.
V1Z 2H5
Telephone: (250) 769-0404
Fax: (250) 763-8168
e-mail: slamka@silk.net

Thirty years ago the Slamka family (Joseph, Freya and their sons Peter, Richard and Tim) planted their first vines on the south-east slope of Boucherie Mountain at Lakeview Heights west of Kelowna in preparation for a vineyard. Now it extends to eight acres. The doors opened officially for Slamka Cellars in the fall of 1996.

Today the three brothers have taken the vineyard to another level and created Slamka Cellars Winery. A blend of traditional growing techniques, modern wine making practices and 25 year-old vines all combine to create the unique and fresh taste of their wines. Ageing is done in various French and American oak and stainless steel.

Winemaker: Peter Slamka
Acreage: 6.5 planted (9.5 site)
Soil: Volcanic ash, sandy, gravel mixture

Grape varieties: Pinot Noir, Auxerrois, Riesling, Lemberger, Merlot, Siegerrebe

Production: 1,500 cases

Average tonnage crushed: 25+ tonnes

Winemaking philosophy: "Good wine starts in the vineyard."

Wines: *White*—Pinot Auxerrois, Riesling, Tapestry (blend), Auxerrois Icewine
Red—Pinot Noir, Rosé

Store hours: Daily, 11 am — 5 pm

Winery tours: By appointment only

Public tastings: Free

Recommended wines: Auxerrois

Stag's Hollow Winery & Vineyard

RR1, Site 3, Comp 36
12 Sunvalley Way
Okanagan Falls, B.C.
V0H 1R0
Telephone/Fax: (250) 497-6162
e-mail: stagwine@vip.net

Owning a vineyard and making wine has been Larry Gerelus' dream since the early 1980s. In 1992 the former actuary and his accountant wife Linda Pruegger visited the Okanagan to look for a property. They found a vineyard near Okanagan Falls on a bench surrounded by mountains and vineyards. They purchased the seven acre vineyard in June and commuted from Calgary for over three years to look after it. They started building the winery in 1995 and moved to the valley the following spring. By late July the wine shop was open, selling three white wines from the 1995 vintage, custom-made at Sumac Ridge. Their first official crush at the new facility was in the fall of 1996.

The couple's house, wine shop and cellar are all one building which looks like a cross between a railway station and a miniature French château. While they made their initial mark with whites they are now predominantly red in their mix of wines.

Winemaker: Larry Gerelus
Acreage: 7

Soil: Variable: Merlot primarily gravel; Pinot Noir, gravel with clay seams; Chardonnay and Vidal on rocky silt

Grape varieties: Merlot, Pinot Noir, Chardonnay, Vidal

Production: 1,300 cases

Average tonnage crushed: 20 tonnes

Winemaking philosophy: "Foremost we believe quality wine is made in the vineyard. To the degree possible we minimize the manipulation of wine and let the grapes express themselves in the bottle."

Wines: *White*—Chardonnay, Late Harvest Vidal, Vidal/Ehrenfelser

Red—Merlot, Pinot Noir, Clarete, Serenata

Store hours: Daily, 10 am — 5 pm

Winery tours: By appointment

Recommended wines: Vidal, Chardonnay, Pinot Blanc/Chardonnay, Merlot

---

Sumac Ridge Estate Winery

17403 Highway 97, P.O. Box 307
Summerland, B.C.
V0H 1Z0
Telephone: (250) 494-0451
Fax: (250) 494-3456
e-mail: sumac@vip.net
web site: www.sumacridge.com

Sumac Ridge Estate Winery became British Columbia's first Estate winery when it was established in 1979, and has been a leading force in British Columbia's wine industry since then. Harry McWatters has been the company's President since its inception; partner Bob Wareham joined the operation in 1991. Harry, founding President of the British Columbia Wine Institute, founding Chairman of the Okanagan Wine Festival board, and founding Chairman of VQA Canada, has helped forged the way for the country's home grown wine industry for over 20 years.

The winery property in Summerland is comprised of the winery buildings, a large warehouse facility, and seven acres of vines. Picnic facilities and a reception/board room are available on-site, and The Cellar Door Bistro is located within the winery. The majority of the winery's grapes are grown at the 115-acre Black Sage Vineyards site in the extreme south part of the Okanagan Valley, where red grape varieties, in particular, flourish amid the hot, dry weather conditions and the sandy soil.

Sumac Ridge Estate Winery's barrel program has always been important to the winery, and today, an ever-growing collection of French and American oak barrels are joined by the country's first ever purchase of Chinese-made oak barrels.

Sumac Ridge Estate Winery was the first British Columbia producer to make *Méthode classique* sparkling wines. In addition to sparkling wines, the winery produces premium red and white table wines and dessert wines, including a port-style wine called "Pipe" and the rare Pinot Blanc Icewine.

Winemaker: Mark Wendenberg

Acreage: 132

Grape varieties: Chardonnay, Pinot Blanc, Sauvignon Blanc, Gewürztraminer, Riesling, Merlot, Pinot Noir, Cabernet Sauvignon, Cabernet Franc

Production: 50,000 cases

Average tonnage crushed: 800 tonnes

Winemaking philosophy: "We are dedicated to the marriage of food and wine and produce distinctive wines to complement distinctive food flavours."

Wines: LDB: Chardonnay, Pinot Blanc, Private Reserve Gewürztraminer, Riesling, Sauvignon Blanc, Merlot, Cabernet Franc, Cabernet Sauvignon, Private Reserve Pinot Noir, Steller's Jay Brut

Own store: Chardonnay, Private Reserve Chardonnay, Pinot Blanc, Private Reserve Pinot Blanc, Private Reserve Gewürztraminer, Riesling, Sauvignon Blanc, Meritage (White), Merlot, Private Reserve Pinot Noir, Cabernet Sauvignon, Cabernet Franc, Meritage (red), Elegance (sweet Muscat), Pinot Blanc Icewine, Pipe, Steller's Jay Brut, Blanc de Noir

Store hours: *Winter:* Monday to Friday, 9 am — 5 pm; weekends, 10 am — 5 pm; *Summer:* Daily, 9 am — 7 pm

Winery tours: *Summer:* Daily, hourly between 10 am and 4 pm; *Winter:* on request

Public tastings: During store hours

Recommended wines: Gewürztraminer, Chardonnay, Pinot Blanc, Sauvignon Blanc, White Meritage, Cabernet Sauvignon, Merlot, Red Meritage, Steller's Jay Brut, Pinot Blanc Icewine

Summerhill Estate Winery

4870 Chute Lake Road
Kelowna, B.C.
V1W 4M3
Telephone: (250) 764-8000
Toll free: 1-800-667-3538
Fax: (250) 764-2598

When New Yorker Steve Cipes found-ed his sparkling wine operation in 1991 at Summerhill Vineyards, south of Kelowna in Okanagan Mission he orig-inally called it Pyramid Cellars after the thirty-foot-high pyramid he had built by the vineyard. (His belief is that the perfect shape of the structure adds a dynamic component to the ageing process.) Steve, an indefatigable pro-moter, chose as his first winemaker a native of the Okanagan, Eric von Krosigk, who had made still and sparkling wines at the German grape research station at Geilweilerhof in the Rheinpfalz and at estates in the Rheingau and Mosel. The cur-rent winemaker, Alan Marks, came from the Hermannhof Winery in Missouri.

In its first year of operation Summerhill made 15,000 gallons of base wine from Pinot Noir, Chardonnay and Riesling for their sparkling wines. Small lots of 1,200 to 2,500 gal-lons are fermented and aged as reserves for the final blends. Apart from award-winning sparkling wine, Summerhill also makes table wine and Icewine from Riesling and Pinot Noir. Over 40 per cent of its production is champagne-method sparkling wine.

Winemaker: Alan Marks

Acreage: 60 (36 planted)

Soil: A cross-section, sandy loam and chalk; "We use rock dust (glacial) and organic fertilizers."

Grape varieties: Riesling, Ehrenfelser, Chardonnay, Verdelet, Pinot Meunier, Pinot Noir, Gewürztraminer

Production: 20,000 cases

Average tonnage crushed: 225 tonnes

Annual tonnage purchased: 50 per cent

Winemaking philosophy: "Our wines are made from 100 per cent B.C.-grown grapes with selected lots from our vineyard bottled separately and identified as made from 100 per cent estate organically grown grapes. Sparkling wines are produced by the *mèthode traditionelle* process and aged in a recently completed replica of the Cheops pyramid. The Cipes line of sparkling wines is produced with no sulfites added. Traditional winemaking techniques are utilised along with recent developments in viticulture and cellar practices, emphasizing minimal processing at all steps."

Wines: LDB: *White*—Nordique Blanc Ehrenfelser, Nordique Riesling

Own store: *White*—Pinot Blanc, Gewürztraminer, Chardonnay, Chardonnay Reserve, Riesling, Late Harvest Riesling, Ehrenfelser, Riesling Icewine, Pinot Noir Icewine

Red—Pinot Noir, Merlot, Gamay Noir, Pinot Noir Estate Reserve

Sparkling—Summerhill Brut, Cipes Brut, Cipes Brut de Brut, Cipes Aurora

Specialty—Gewürztraminer Reserve

Store hours: 10 am — 7 pm

Winery tours: Yes, "champagne" making and Pyramid tours

Public tastings: Daily, during store hours, year round

Veranda Restaurant: 11 am — 3 pm

Recommended wines: Platinum Series Pinot Noir, Gamay Noir,
Cipes Aurora Blanc de Blanc

Sunset Vineyards

c/o International Bag Manufacturers Ltd.   **Telephone:** (604) 941-4666
#104-1650 Broadway
Port Coquitlam, B.C.
V3C 2M8

Rob Milne, an accountant and co-owner of a company that manufactures plastic wrapping for industry, purchased 92 acres south of Oliver — a former terraced vineyard then planted with alfalfa. In 1994, he planted 20 acres of Cabernet Sauvignon, Pinot Noir, Merlot and Chardonnay. The winery was operational in 1996.

Tinhorn Creek Vineyards

RR #1, S58, C10
Oliver, B.C.
V0H 1T0
Telephone: (250) 498-3743
Toll free: 1-888-4Tinhorn
Fax: (250) 498-3228
e-mail: winery@tinhorn.com
web site: www.tinhorn.com

Calgary oilman Robert Shaunessy took a businessman's approach to wine and hit the ground running when he bought vast tracts of established vineyard land in 1993, at a time local growers were still smarting from the pull-out program of 1988. Inspired by the Napa and Sonoma Valley experience, he and his wife Barbara envision the same success for the Okanagan.

With partners Kenn and Sandra Oldfield, the Shaunessys created one of the largest and most impressive estate wineries in the region. Kenn, an Ontario-born chemical engineer, trained in viticulture at UC Davis where he met Tinhorn Creek winemaker, Sandra, also a UC Davis grad. In four short years, Tinhorn Creek has completed its aggressive planting program, opened its majestic winemaking and touring facility, and has amassed a long list of awards for its early vintages. Production is 65 per cent red and 40 per cent white and is dedicated to only a few select *vinifera* varieties. All the wines, apart from Gewürztraminer, spend time in American oak. Tinhorn Creek production will reach 43,000 cases by the 2001 harvest. A 2,500-square-feet climate-controlled barrel cellar and a 300-seat natural amphitheatre are current projects that will ensure Tinhorn Creek is a must-see destination for Okanagan wine country travellers.

Winemaker: Sandra Oldfield

Acreage: 165 (fully planted)

Soil: 35 are within the "Golden Mile," South Okanagan West, side bench lands on rocky slopes; 130 acres on South East Bench, predominantly sand

Grape varieties: Pinot Gris, Chardonnay, Merlot, Pinot Noir, Kerner, Gewürztraminer, Cabernet Franc

Production: 17,000 cases (1998); 43,000 (2001)

Winemaking philosophy: "To produce only premium *vinifera*-based red and white table wines by focusing on tightly controlled, low cropping, viticultural practices."

Wines: *White*—Pinot Gris, Chardonny, Kerner Icewine, Gewürztraminer

Red—Merlot, Pinot Noir, Cabernet Franc

Store hours: Daily, 10 am — 5:30 pm
Winery tours: Yes
Public tastings: During store hours

Recommended wines: Pinot Gris, Chardonnay, Pinot Noir, Merlot, Kerner Icewine

---

Venturi-Schulze Vineyards

4235 Trans Canada Highway
Cobble Hill, B.C.
V0R 1L0
Telephone: (205) 743-5630
Fax: (250) 743-5638
e-mail:
vsvineyard@coastnet.com

Giordano Venturi, a former electronics instructor from Italy and his wife Marilyn Schulze, an Australian-born microbiologist and French teacher, decided to move to the tranquility of Vancouver Island in 1988. They purchased a 100-year-old farm near Cowichan Bay and immediately planted a test block of 25 grape varieties which they have now narrowed down to 12. A system of netting and electrified wires protect the small, organically farmed acreage against marauding wildlife. They got their licence in 1993 and began producing wines that are truly hand-crafted, beginning with careful attention to the vineyard. Some French and Slovenian oak are used.

Apart from home-winemaking Giordano has been producing balsamic vinegar for 25 years, a nod towards his heritage (he grew up near Modena) and his production is kept well away from the winery in a separate facility. Production has expanded and the vinegary increased to 108 barrels of cherry, chesnut, acacia, ash and oak. In addition to wine and aged balsamic vinegar bottle-fermented sparkling wine is also produced. Giordano designed and built the riddling machine.

Every V-S bottle carries a tiny pamphlet describing how the wine was made and a profile of the operation. The couple also write an engaging newsletter and offer "special food and wine functions for small groups."

Winemakers: Giordano Venturi and Marilyn Schulze
Acreage: 20
Soil: Clay, heavy in part, over deep sand and gravel; south-facing slope cooled by the ocean influence

Grape varieties: Pinot Noir, Pinot Auxerrois, Pinot Gris, Schönburger, Madeleine Sylvaner, Siegerrebe, Ortega, small plantings of Kerner, Chasselas, Gewüztraminer, Madeleine Angevine

Production: Over 500 cases

Average tonnage crushed: 9 tonnes

Winemaking philosophy: "We grow the grapes that we use in our wines without the use of pesticides and herbicides. We take great pride in being personally accountable for every aspect of our operation. The winery philosophy is simple — ensure that the quality of the grapes is reflected in the purity of the wine. We aim for intensity of flavour and cautiously use oak on occasion for added dimension, but not as a condiment. Our techniques vary depending on our focus for each wine; some varieties benefit from extended lees contact, others do not. In our whites, we generally avoid skin contact and press very lightly. Our reds are destemmed manually to avoid incorporating green stem tannins into the wine."

Wines: Own store: *White*—Madeleine Sylvaner, Schönburger, Kerner, Siegerrebe, Millefiori (Madeleine Angevine/Siegerrebe), Pignoletto Aromatico (Schönburger, Ortega, Gewürztraminer), Terracotta

Red—Pinot Noir

Sparkling—Brut Naturel Black Label (Pinot Auxerrois, Chasselas, Pinot Gris), Brut Naturel White Label (100% Müller-Thurgau), Brut Naturel Old Cuvée (Black Label blend)

Store hours: By appointment only

Tours and tastings: "Welcomed for individuals and small groups when product is available, but strictly by appointment."

––––––––––

Recommended wines: Brut Naturel, Millefiori, Madeleine Sylvaner Sur Lie

Vigneti Zanatta

5039 Marshall Road
RR #3
Duncan, B.C.
V9L 2X1
Telephone: (250) 748-2338
Fax: (250) 746-2347
e-mail: zanatta@seaside.net

Dennis Zanatta, a native of Treviso in northern Italy, and his wife Claudia bought a dairy farm in the Cowichan Valley on Vancouver Island in 1959 and began planting experimental vines. In 1983, he took part in a government-sponsored trial program to

see what varieties were sustainable on the island. Among the grapes planted were five acres of Ortega and Cayuga which flourished. Now the Zanatta family operates a 25-acre vineyard and winery (the oldest on the island) which is under the guiding hand of daughter Loretta, who studied oenology in Italy. The historic family home, built in 1903, houses the wine shop.

Winemaker: Loretta Zanatta

Acreage: 30

Soil: Sandy loam, south facing rolling slope

Grape varieties: Ortega, Auxerrois, Pinot Grigio, Pinot Nero, Muscat

Production: 4,000 cases

Winemaking philosophy: "Our quality wine begins in the vineyard. We use 100 per cent our own grapes, grown and vinified to bring out our own regional character."

Wines: *White*—Ortega, Pinot Grigio, Damasco, Muscat, Madeleine

Red—Pinot Nero

Sparkling—(champagne method) Glenora Fantasia Brut, Allegria

Store hours: *May to December:* Wednesday to Sunday, 12 noon — 5 pm; *February to April:* Friday to Sunday, 12 noon — 5 pm

Winery tours: No

Vinoteca Restaurant: *May to October:* 12 noon — 5 pm; Dinners Thursday, Friday, Saturday

---

Recommended wines: Auxerrois, Glenora Fantasia Brut

Vincor International (Jackson-Triggs)

38691 Highway 97
North Oliver, B.C.
V0H 1T0
Telephone: (250) 498-4981
Fax: (250) 498-6505
web site: www.atlaswine.com

Vincor's contemporary-rustic 45,000-sq.ft. building stands in splendid solitude in a wilderness of pine-clad granite mountains and arid plains in southern B.C. On the wall by the entrance hangs a framed photograph

Red Wine   *Vin Rouge*

JACKSON-TRIGGS
PROPRIETORS' SELECTION
Cabernet Sauvignon

PRODUCT OF CANADA/PRODUIT DU CANADA
750 ml JACKSON-TRIGGS VINTNERS, OLIVER, CANADA 11.5% alc./vol.

showing the chief of the Osoyoos Indian Band, Sam Baptiste, shaking hands with the then managing director of Brights, Ed Arnold. It is dated May 14, 1982, the official opening date of the winery (although the company had 1981 wines on the market, produced at the winery before the roof was on.)

The Indian Band farms the Inkameep vineyard adjacent to the winery. This vineyard is the largest in the Okanagan, 200 acres of which are contracted to Vincor. Lynn Bremmer, B.C.'s first female winemaker, presided over the winemaking for eleven years until 1992, when Frank Supernak became head winemaker. Now Bruce Nicholson is in charge of the Jackson Triggs wines.

Winemaker: Bruce Nicholson

Acreage: 200 acres

Soil: Ranges from sandy to clay; contract vineyards: rocky upper, gravelly loam lower

Production: 30,000 cases

Average tonnage crushed: 500 tonnes

Annual tonnage purchased: 500 tonnes

Winemaking philosophy: "To have each grape variety that enters the winery reach its maximum potential and never add to or handle the wine more than is necessary."

Wines: *White*—Chardonnay, Pinot Blanc, Gewürztraminer, Dry Riesling, Riesling Icewine

Red—Merlot, Cabernet Sauvignon, Pinot Noir

Store hours: Monday to Friday, 9 am — 4 pm

Winery tours: 10 am, 2 pm

Public tastings: Free

_____

Recommended wines: Jackson-Triggs Riesling, Pinot Blanc, Chardonnay, Merlot, Riesling Icewine

The Vineyard at Bowen Island

P.O. Box 135   Telephone: (604) 947-0028
Bowen Island, B.C.   Fax: (604) 947-0693
N0N 1G0   e-mail: staff@vineyard.bc.ca

Larry and Elena Wildman have an acre and a half of vineyards on Bowen Island off Horseshoe Bay planted with the three Pinots. Other plots totalling four and a half acres include Gewürztraminer, more Pinot Noir, Ortega and Siegerrebe. The plan for the Waldmans and their neighbours is to have 20 acres by the turn of the century. The winery constructed in 1997 is a "business only" operation — 2,000 square feet contained in concrete walls with 12 foot ceilings.

More glamorous are the luxurious guest rooms with adjacent professional croquet lawn as well as pool and billiard room.

Winemaker: Eric von Krosigk

Acreage: 6

Soil: Clay

Grape varieties: Pinot Gris, Pinot Blanc, Gewürztraminer, Ortega, Siegerrebe, Pinot Noir, Gamay

Production: 4,000 cases

Average tonnage crushed: 1 tonne

Average tonnage purchased: 12 tonnes

Winemaking philosophy: "Simple, straightforward fruity wines, organically grown with no pesticides or additives."

Wines: *White*—Pinot Blanc, Bacchus

Red—Pinot Noir, Gamay

Store hours: By appointment

Winery tours: No

Recommended Wines: Bacchus, Pinot Blanc

Wild Goose Vineyards

RR #1, S3, C11
Okanagan Falls, B.C.
V0H 1R0
Telephone: (250) 497-8919
Fax: (250) 497-6853
e-mail: wildgoose@img.net

Along with Guenther Lang and the Klokockas, Adolf Kruger was one of the pioneers of the farm winery concept in B.C. A consulting engineer and talented amateur winemaker formerly from Kehrberg in the former East Germany, Adolf was forced to make his hobby a profession when a downturn in the economy left him without work in electrical engineering. With his sons Roland and Hagen, he opened Wild Goose Vineyards in June 1990, days after Lang Vineyards started up as the first farm winery in Canada. Adolf had realized his dream of turning his vineyard (planted in 1984) into a winery.

Winemaker: Hagen and Adolf Kruger

Acreage: 10 planted, 10 contracted

Soil: Riesling has a southern exposure on rocky soil which absorbs a lot of heat during the day and releases it in the evening. Gewürztraminer is planted in clay-like soil with scattered stones. Very hot summers.

Grape varieties: Riesling, Gewürztraminer, Pinot Noir, Pinot Gris, Merlot

Production: 5,000 cases

Average tonnage crushed: 60 tonnes

Annual tonnage purchased: 30 tonnes

Winemaking philosophy: "As a small family winery, we take much pride in the wines we vint. Minimal filtration is used and all production is done by the family unit. Trying to produce the best wines possible, no wine will be bottled or sold before it passes our strict tasting standards. People visiting our winery are given personal treatment and always are met by one of the smiling family members."

Wines: Own store: Riesling Autumn Gold (Riesling/Vidal), Autumn Blue (Riesling with Sweet Reserve), Gewürztraminer, Pinot Blanc, Maréchal Foch, Pinot Gris, Merlot, Pinot Noir, Cabernet Sauvignon

Store hours: 10 am — 5 pm

Winery tours: By appointment

Public tastings: During store hours

————

Recommended wines: Gewürztraminer, Pinot Blanc, Autumn Gold, Riesling, Maréchal Foch

QUÉBEC

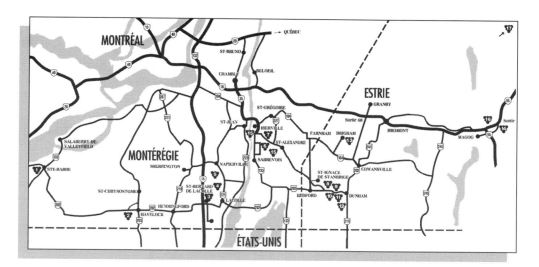

Wine Regions of Québec

W hen you think of Canadian wine, images of Ontario's Niagara Peninsula or B.C.'s Okanagan Valley spring readily to mind. With a little imagination, perhaps you might conjure up Nova Scotia's Annapolis Valley or the Northumberland Strait.

But wine made from grapes in Dunham, Québec?

The idea that they actually grow wine in the Eastern Townships 80 km southeast of Montreal is not only a revelation to most Canadians, but an ongoing source of amazement to virtually all the 3,108 inhabitants of this old Loyalist village.

Dunham is to Québec what Bordeaux is to France — in microcosm: the epicentre of the province's wine industry, accounting for nearly half of all bottles bearing Québec labels. Since 1985, a number of licensed cottage wineries have mushroomed along the Vermont-New York State border from Ste-Barbe to Sherbrooke.

Although some wineries have just opened, some closed, and others have merely changed hands, the number of enterprises seems to have momentarily stabilized at 17, of which 15 are members of l'Association des Vignerons du Québec. The association, which brings the vignerons together to share knowledge on growing vines and making wine in Québec's "special" climate, also makes volume equipment purchases to save money for its members. As well, the association publishes a pamphlet outlining Québec's wine route, on which most of the wineries figure.

A few more wineries were expected to have come on-line by now, but viticultural problems have slowed things up. For example: one winery that had — rather naively — planted the tender Muscadet/Melon de Bourgogne *vinifera* as their sole grape variety, lost over 75 per cent of the young plantation to the horrible winter of 1993-94.

It's stories like these — of which there are many — that remind us that these men and women are heroic pioneers. These are the people with the vision that turned this rolling landscape of farms and orchards into vineyards, produce some 250,000 bottles a year, roughly the annual output of Château Mouton-Rothschild in the Médoc. But Québec makes 90 per cent white wine, mostly from the hybrid Seyval Blanc grape, and its vignerons accomplish the feat against horrendous odds, not the least of which is the bureaucratic indifference of the provincial liquor board — but more of that later.

The winemakers themselves speak lovingly yet defensively about their magnificent obsession — an obsession that the *Montreal Gazette's* wine columnist, Malcolm Anderson, affectionately calls "a fine madness." The terms "artisanal" and "marginal" are often used when they refer to the wines and the *terroir* that provides them, because there is something Quixotic about the compulsion to make wine in Québec, a place of snow and polar temperatures where winter's only harvest used to be maple syrup. But soon the winter harvest may be Icewine if the dreams of Jacques Breault and his highly motivated colleagues are realized. Icewine could be the saviour of the Québec wine industry which currently exists from vintage to vintage on its novelty value rather than the quality and price of its products. Nine dollars or more for a fresh, young wine similar in style to a Muscadet is a hefty charge for a domestic Seyval, especially when a Sauvignon Blanc or Chardonnay from Chile, Southern

France or South Africa can be had for a similar amount. But Montrealers are showing the flag by taking the bridge south for a day in the country and bringing back a few bottles as souvenirs.

Winemaking in Québec is not a twentieth-century phenomenon. In 1535, when Jacques Cartier sailed down the St. Lawrence on his second voyage to New France, he anchored off "a great island" where he found wild *labrusca* grape vines growing up the trees.

Various attempts at establishing a wine industry in Lower Canada were tried during the eighteenth and nineteenth centuries, but these were abandoned because of the severity of the climate. Ice can split the trunk of a vine stock and even the hardiest *labrusca* plants are susceptible to winter kill. A vine will only grow in temperatures of ten degrees Celsius or higher and it requires a certain number of sunshine hours during the growing season to ripen the fruit. The average Québec sunshine hours during this season are approximately 930, but in Dunham and Magog the figure rises to 1150 (in Bordeaux the average sunshine hours are 2069). Dunham's secret, along with the other growing regions in Québec, is microclimate — highly localised topographical features that create warm spots and allow a vine to thrive. These features could be a body of water near a vineyard that stores up heat during the summer and acts like a hot water bottle during the winter as well as reflecting the sun's rays onto the vines, or it could be a warm wind that blows down the valley from Montreal, or a well-protected south-facing slope.

But the problem of winter and frozen vines remains. The most radical measure to safeguard the plants is burial — to cut them back after the harvest and cover them with earth until the spring. The operation is called "hilling"; that is, banking earth over the roots by back-ploughing between the rows of vines, an exercise that costs the grower at least four cents a plant to cover and another four cents to uncover.

The concept of hilling was brought to Québec by an oenologist from the South of France, Hervé Durand, who had learned of it in Russia and China. In 1980, he purchased a farm in Dunham and two years later planted a vineyard. His neighbour Frank Furtado was so intrigued that he bought into the dream and with winemaker Charles-Henri de Coussergues (and later Pierre Rodrigue) founded what has become Québec's most successful winery. The enterprise owes it name to the province's renowned singer-poet, Gilles Vigneault, who told Durand, "To make wine in Québec is like panning for gold."

L'orpailleur is the French term for those who search for gold by panning (literally, "gold washer"), an apt metaphor for the time, patience and skill it takes to extract wine from the soil of *la belle province*.

Literally next door, Pierre Genesse and his wife Marie-Claude own Les Blancs Coteaux, a *bijou* winery with a production of 18,000 bottles. Pierre, another Ste-Hyacinthe graduate, learned his winemaking in Burgundy while picking grapes in the Mâconnais. All his products are hand labelled, including the vinegar, jams and jellies, dried flowers and herbs he and his wife sell from their beautiful old farmhouse. In addition, they offer picnic tables for those guests who want to spend a pleasant moment outdoors with a glass of wine and some gourmet products from their *boutique champêtre*.

Further east on Route 202 towards the town of Dunham is Domaines de Côtes d'Ardoise, a name that speaks to the slaty soil in the eight-hectare vineyard shaped like an amphitheatre. This unique landscape configuration, Dr. Jacques Papillon will assure you, permits an extra two weeks of growing season over his competitors.

The vineyard was originally planted by Papillon and Christian Barthomeuf, a self-taught winemaker from Arles in southern France, whose former career was as a film producer. He came to Québec on sabbatical in 1974 and stayed. He planted the Domaine in 1977, remaining with Papillon as winemaker until the early 1990s.

Incidentally, Barthomeuf, after his split with the Domaine de Côtes d'Ardoise, tried working with a couple of apple producers (Dunham is a region carpeted with orchards) and has settled in at La Pommelière which is, ironically, just a kilometre down the road from Les Côtes d'Ardoise. There he makes what may just be the world's first "ice wine" made from apples. Although reviewing all of Québec's mead, fruit wine and cider producers is beyond the scope of this book, it should be noted that Barthomeuf's apple "ice-wine," selling at $9.90 for a Niagara look-alike half-bottle, is a delicious, rich, glycerine-laden nectar, with a warm, spiced butter and cream finish.

Another kilometre east and you can stop into Dunham's newest vineyard, Les Trois Clochers, a name which refers to the bell towers of the three churches of Dunham. Here, Claude Rhéaume and Réal Normandeau offer a crisp Seyval, as well as a fragrant, yeasty strawberry wine.

Once in the town of Dunham, head up the hill to the Vignoble Les Arpents de Neige, a name that resonates with French history ("a few acres of snow" were not worth fighting for, according to French King Louis XIV's advisors.) Originally planted by Jacques Breault, who once worked for l'Orpailleur, Les Arpents de Neige went into bankruptcy and was bought in 1992 by Gilles Séguin, a restaurateur who, with the help of his French winemaker, Jean Paul Martin, made a very good Seyval in 1994. As well, Séguin offers — naturally — meals for groups who book ahead.

Just north of Dunham you can visit Vignoble La Bauge, where wine is a passionate sideline for Alcide and Ghislaine Naud, whose main occupation is raising *sanglier* (wild boar), as well as llamas, highland cattle and many other exotic farm animals, including a chicken with fur!

The most northerly vineyard in the Eastern Townships (Cantons de l'Est) is the Cep d'Argent in the Magog/Sherbrooke vicinity, where French (Champagne) know-how combines with Québecer ingenuity to make a solid range of wines.

The Montérégie

The Montérégie is emerging as a separate wine region in its own right; it already has eight vineyards to the Townships' eight! The Montérégie are a series of extinct volcanos (Mont-Royal, which forms the Island of Montreal, is the best known) that jut suddenly and impressively out of the vast, flat plains that run from Montreal south to the U.S. border. Essentially a region of market "salad bowl" gardens and grain farmers (unlike the dairy country of the Eastern Townships), Le Montérégie is hardly somewhere you drive through on the way to "cottage country," yet thousands of Montrealers are nevertheless slowly discovering the vinous riches of the region.

Although the soil is made up largely of black earth and heavy clay, hardly ideal for winemaking, if the viticultural property is well chosen, there are soils that include deposits of sand and small stones in their makeup, debris left behind by the receding waters of Lake Champlain and the St. Lawrence River, both of which entirely covered the Montérégie some 60,000 years ago.

Now, while it is an established fact that almost every vigneron will tell you that they have the warmest microclimate in Québec, it is becoming clear — even at this early stage in the young wineries' history — that the Montérégie is marginally warmer than the Dunham region. What remains unclear is whether this is due to the more southerly location, or to the fact that air currents are warmed as they pass over Montreal.

This does not necessarily mean that the wines produced here are better than those in Dunham, but only that some different characteristics are beginning to emerge in the wines. The Montérégie's Seyvals, for instance, seem to be somewhat rounder and fuller, while those of Dunham have more intense, mineral and white pepper bouquets. Another of the distinguishing features of the Montérégie is that grapes such as Cayuga and Vidal — as well as two Geisenheim clones from Germany — are beginning to be grown here while they are virtually ignored in Dunham.

One of the Montérégie's best wineries is Vignoble Dietrich-Jooss. Victor Dietrich and Christiane Jooss hail from Ingersheim, in Alsace, where they learned the family business — making wine. Their Québec wines are typically Alsatian, with just a kiss of residual sugar to balance perfectly the naturally high acidity of the grapes. In their beautiful France-meets-North-America-styled winery, just a kilometre or two from the wide Richelieu River, they make six elegant wines that set the standard for their neighbours. The Cuvée Stephanie, named after their winemaker-to-be daughter, is a light but luscious Vendange Tardive wine that falls somewhere between a Late-Harvest Wine and an Icewine in style.

Nearby neighbour, the Piedmont-born Domenic Agarla, runs Vignoble St. Alexandre, which specializes in red wine from the hybrid De Chaunac grape. A few kilometres away, Gilles Benoit runs Vignoble des Pins, where he makes some fine Seyval and Méthode Champenoise Sec sparkler on his small, but extremely well-cared-for, property.

Further south, across the Richelieu River, Vignobles Le Royer-St. Pierre are turning out a lovely, scented wine from the Cayuga grape, while Étienne Héroux at Vignoble Morou is making whites with finesse and elegance rare in Québec, as well as some light but sensuous reds.

Even further south, near Lacolle (the "Glue"), a town that is practically soldered to the U.S. border, hard-working Jean-Guy Angell and his son Guy are also turning some good wines.

At Le Marathonien (the Marathon-runner), smack in the middle of apple country near Havelock and Hemmingford, Jean and Line Joly are making nice wines that rival the quality of those of their mentor, Victor Dietrich. Réjean Gagnon has taken over La Vitacée, which remains Québec's only vineyard dedicated to finding grape varieties that do not need to be "hilled." With the help of Luc Rolland, who also vinifies at Le Bauge, he turns out Québec's deepest-coloured red, the Rhône-style(!) Barbe-Rouge.

A Note on Hybrids

Québec's difficulty in bringing grapes to full maturity (i.e., without the need to chaptalise; that is, to add sugar during fermentation to bring up the alcohol level) is proving something of a boon; vignerons are noticing that wines from varieties such as the American-bred Cayuga are not showing any musky, foxy, *labrusca* characteristics that appear when they are fully ripe or overripe, as they would be in Niagara, Ontario, British Columbia, or even the New York Finger Lakes regions. Maréchal Foch, De Chaunac, Seyval and other hybrids also show pure fruit flavours in Québec.

The wines of Québec are improving steadily. While Québec's punishing climate makes it an easy target for those who would dismiss its wines, the fact remains that you cannot judge an upstart region like this by the wines it was producing a few years ago. There have been many additions to the wine scene here since the last edition of this book, and the vines of the already-existing wineries are that much older, producing more concentrated, better-balanced grapes. As well, Québec has been recently blessed with a string of warm autumns, providing winemakers with some comparatively ripe raw material.

Don't make the mistake of underestimating the passion and resourcefulness of Québec winemakers, who are ceaseless in their quest to find better ways to make better wines. Despite a recent ruling that allows Québec wineries to blend up to 15 per cent of (usually more ripe) Ontario musts into their blends, in a recent initiative, the Québec Association of Vignerons has recently approached the Ontario VQA (Vintners Quality Alliance) with the hopes of affiliating with them.

Time will tell if Ontario and British Columbia accept Québec into the fold, but a VQA designation would allow Québec's more serious winemakers the chance to proudly put a 100 per cent Québec product on the market. How else will we get to know the different terroirs of Québec wine regions?

Unfortunately, many of the wineries are being forced to charge for their tasting wines, tired of receiving car loads of people who taste through the winery's entire range consuming two or three bottles in the process, buying only one bottle as they leave. Some do so much of this sort of thing, that they have made a negative into a positive, actually courting the tour buses, and end up selling most of their wine to be drunk on the premises in tastings!

One new trend since the last edition of this book: more wineries seem to be planting the German Geisenheim crossing (there are actually two different numbered Geisenheim clones), a grape which brings a fruity, Riesling-like component to many of the wines. This is a welcome change after years of the sameness of Seyval. Cayuga, too, seems to be increasingly-planted. On the red side of things, Maréchal Foch is showing up more and more.

For those who don't want to "hill up" their vines and prefer to have them up on a trellis à l'Europe, two hardy American crosses, Cliche-Vandal (white) and Ste. Croix (red) are increasingly planted, especially in the cooler, northern sites.

Although Québec has a tough time ripening grapes, there is a silver-lining: because of this, Québec vignerons make more elegant wines than many warmer wine regions from the cold-hardy, so-called "foxier" hybrids, for their underripeness prevents them from (mercifully) fully expressing their worst qualities.

When planning to visit Québec wineries, bear in mind that most of them are small family concerns. No matter what the season, call first to make sure they are at home, and not out in the fields.

Québec may have quite a long history of buying and drinking wines, but buying from small growers is, perhaps, still quite a new thing for many winery visitors, who have obviously not yet grasped the etiquette. It is not recommended behaviour, whether in a group of three or 13, to show up "en masse" and taste all a winery's offerings without buying.

Oh, and one more thing. In a harsh climate like this one, you do a lot of research before you buy your farm. Everybody believes they have stumbled across "the" best microclimate in Québec, and who's to argue? Visit a few of these dedicated winemakers, and decide for yourself.

Where the Wines May Be Sold

Given the miniscule quantities produced, most wines are sold at the farm gate only, with just a couple of the best-known wineries placing products in Québec's SAQ stores. Some wines are also available at "La Maison des Vins, Boissons artisanales et produits fins de Québec" at the Marché Maisonneuve (4445, rue Ontario est, C.P. 14, Montréal, Québec, Telephone (514) 255-5999, Fax 256-5999). As well, wineries are allowed to directly deliver their wines under certain conditions.

QUÉBEC WINERIES

*Don't miss the opportunity to visit the wineries of Québec —
even if you don't speak French. All Québec winemakers and their
colleagues enjoy receiving English-speaking visitors whether
their command of the language varies from the tentative to the
flawlessly fluent. The language of wine, after all, is universal.*

Clos St. Denis

1149, Chemin des Patriotes
St. Denis sur Richelieu, Québec
J0H 1K0
Telephone/Fax: (450) 787-3766

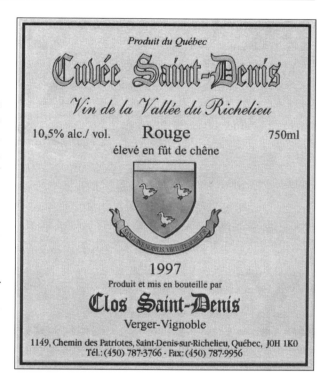

Guy Tardif and Ghislaine Meunier are the owners of this beautiful vineyard/apple orchard overlooking the Richelieu River. They are one of the few vineyards in Québec to refuse to hill-up (fr. *butter*) their vines for the winter. Because of this, they have chosen to plant native vines that can withstand the -40°C winters this region sees every year. Guy Tardif does all the vineyard work himself, overseen by his son François Tardif, an *agronôme* who is their *maître de champ*. Christian Donaldson, their *maître de Chai*, is a Burgundy-trained winemaker who never ceases to reinvent himself with each passing vintage. As a result, their wines have improved enormously over the past few years, and can now number themselves among the best wineries in Québec.

Winemaker: Christian Donaldson
Acreage: 18.5
Soil: Mostly clay with more sand as the ground rises away from the river
Grape Varieties: Éona, Cliche 8414, Ste. Croix, Cayuga, Seyval
Production: 400 cases wine, 400 cases Apple Ice Wine (*Pomme de Glâce*)

Annual tonnage purchased (tonnes): A small percentage of the total is bought in from other vineyards nearby

Winemaking philosophy: "To continue to undertake research for new ways to make fine wine in Québec, to never stop looking for ways to improve our wine."

Wines: *White*—La Cuvée St. Denis (Éona 100%); La Cuvée Montérégienne

Red—La Cuvée St. Denis (Ste. Croix)

Speciality—Le Cidre du Bourg Saint-Denis; la Pomme de Glâce (Icewine-style sweet cider from frozen apples)

Store: Like all Québec wineries, at the winery only for the moment; eventually at public markets that will sell "produits du terroir."

Store hours: Open all *summer*, *winter* by appointment

Winery tours: Guided, by appointment

Recommended wine: Le Clos St. Denis

Coop des Producteurs Viticole Bourg-Royal

1910, rue des Érables   Telephone: (418) 622-2230
Charlesbourg, Québec   e-mail: VITISQC@globetrooter.qc.ca
G2L 1R8

The Bourg-Royal Cooperative functions a little differently from the classic cooperatives in France, wherein many different vignerons bring their produce to a communal winery to be vinified. In this case, you have one vineyard, and many different owners who buy-in, investing in both the winery and the vineyard (50 plants minimum per investor).

Gilles Tremblay, winemaker of the Coop des Producteurs, says that his is one of the oldest vineyards in modern Québec viticulture: the first plantation dates to 1982. The Coop has or is testing some 350 different varieties of hardy vines, most of which are a legacy of the research work of the late Joseph O. Vandal of the University of Laval.

Winemaker: Gilles Tremblay

Acreage: 25

Soil: Sandy loam topsoil with a high percentage of clay in the subsoil, some amelioration of the soil has been effected in the north part of the vineyard

Grape varieties: Éona, Vandal Blanc (white), Maréchal Foch, and Minnesota, for rosé and red wine. The Ste. Croix grape, making a full-bodied red, is a recent addition to the vineyard.

Production: 1200 cases

Average tonnage crushed: 11 tonnes

Winemaking philosophy: Gilles believes in a classic white wine fermentation with a bit of *pelliculaire maceration* (skin contact), and, for the reds, he prefers a *maceration carbonique* (Beaujolais-style) approach. In a hot year, he will include a little Leon Millot and Michurinetz in the red blend.

Wines: *White*—Le Bourg-Royal Blanc

Red—Le Bourg-Royal Rouge

Speciality—La Rosélin, a Rosé, made from just-pressed red grapes

Store: Like all Québec wineries, at the winery only for the moment.

Store hours: *May to December:* Monday to Sunday; *Winters:* weekends only, 10 am — 6 pm

Winery tours: Guided at 11 am, 2 pm, and also by appointment

Tastings: $0.50 each; 2 tastings free in the guided $5 tour

Additional features: Boutique, picnic site, catered events on request, reception hall available

Special tasting event: *"Québec's wines and cheeses,"* by appointment: wines from five Québec vineyards tasted with local cheeses

---

Recommended wine: Le Bourg-Royal Blanc

Domaine des Côtes d'Ardoise

879, Route 202
C.P. 189
Dunham, Québec
J0E 1M0
Telephone: (450) 295-2020
Fax: (450) 845-6307

Ardoise means slate, which speaks to the soil of Dr. Jacques Papillon's horseshoe-shaped vineyard behind the weathered old barn that acts as winery and tasting room. Christian Bartomeuf, a film producer from Arles, came to Québec in 1974 on sabbatical and stayed. He bought the farm in 1977. In 1980 he planted what is considered now to be the first vineyard in Québec province.

Jacques Papillon bought from Barthomeuf in 1984 and is still the owner.

The very special microclimate allows him to grow *vitis viniferas* (Riesling and Gamay) as well as hybrids (Seyval, Aurore, De Chaunac, Maréchal Foch, Vidal).

The winery offers an unusually large number of products for a Québec enterprise of this nature. The winemakers are Vera Klokocka and John Fletcher, former owners of Hillside Estate Vineyard in British Columbia, who took over from Patrick Barrelet.

Winemaker: Vera Klokocka and John Fletcher

Acreage: 20

Soil: Slatey, north-facing slope in a natural amphitheatre

Grape varieties: Aurore, Seyval Blanc, De Chaunac, Maréchal Foch, Riesling, Gamay, Vidal

Production: Approximately 1,600 cases

Average tonnage crushed: 25 tonnes

Winemaking philosophy: In the vineyard is a printed sign: "*The only thing on earth that I know is serious is the culture of the vine* (Voltaire)."

Wines: *White*—La Maredoise (Aurore with Seyval, Gamay or Riesling), Carte d'Or Seyval (oak-aged), Riesling

Red—Haute Combe (Maréchal Foch/De Chaunac), Côte d'Ardoise (Maréchal Foch/Gamay oak-aged), Estafette (fortified vin doux naturel from five varieties)

Specialty—Vidal Icewine

Store: Yes (restaurant open June to September)

Winery tours: Group reservations (four or more) from *May 15 to October 15*. Wine and cheese visits, tours with meals etc. by reservation

Public tastings: Yes

Recommended wines: Not yet tasted

Domaine Félibre

740, Chemin Bean
Stanstead, Québec
J0B 3E0
Telephone/Fax: (819) 876-7900

Like finding little gems off the beaten track? The Domaine Félibre, owned and operated by Gilles Desjardins and Catherine Hébert, is located in a hidden corner of Québec's Eastern Townships, some 20 minutes east of Stanstead, towards Coaticook. Situated high in the hills some 425 metres above sea level, the panoramic view includes both Mount Orford to the Northwest, and Vermont's Green Appalachian Mountains directly to the south. Here, the grapes have to be hardy American crossings to withstand the severe winters, late springs and early autumns. Domaine Félibre is also justly proud of their cidre, of which they make two types, a "strong" and a "perlant."

Domaine Félibre

Cru des Vallons
1996
Vin blanc / White wine

Mis en bouteille au domaine
740 chemin Bean, Stanstead (Québec)

Produit du Québec / Product of Québec
9 % alc. / vol.

500 ml

Winemaker: Gilles Desjardins

Acreage: vines: 5; orchard: 2.5

Soil: Schist

Grape varieties: Éona

Production: 400 cases (increasing to 800 cases within the next two years)

Winemaking philosophy: Domaine Félibre strives to offer wine and cider that are innovative in both their taste and in their presentation.

Wines: *White*—Cru des Vallons (100% Éona)

Speciality—two Apple Ciders vinified as white wines: Pommé (dry, still) and Fruit Défendu (off-dry and perlant)

Store: Like all Québec wineries, at the winery only for the moment; eventually at public markets that will sell "produits du terroir"

Store hours: Open all *summer*; *winter* by appointment

Winery tours: Guided, by appointment

Public tastings: Free, but wine sells out quickly

Domaine Royarnois

146, Chemin du Cap
Tourmente
St. Joachin
(Montmorency), Québec
G0A 3X0
Telephone: (418) 827-4465
Fax: (418) 827-5002

Domaine Royarnois is located on a massive piece of
land near the St. Laurent
River in Montmorency,
Québec. It is close to the
Cap Tourmente wildlife
reserve where tourists can
seek out the past while revelling in the present and partaking in the grandiose scenery
and wildlife (Snow Geese). Like many of Québec's more northern wineries, as well
as those southern wineries that are loathe to bury their vines, Domaine Royarnois
uses the Mario Cliche-Vandal and Ste. Croix grapes, and trains them above ground
at full height. A practice not unlike, says Roland Harnois, the vine training systems
of Niagara.

Winemaker: R.A. Harnois, Eng.

Acreage: 30

Soil: Located right on the St. Laurent in a microclimate, on a soil that is 50%
sandy loam and 50% medium loam, high-quality agricultural land

Grape varieties: Cliche-Vandal 85%, Ste. Croix 15%

Production: 1000 cases minimum

Average tonnage crushed: 15 tonnes

Winemaking philosophy: Making a high-quality wine is the reward of good grapes
and exacting quality control. Unhurried winemaking is another tenet here, they
bottle their whites a little later than some other Québec wineries.

Wines: *White*—Cru du Domaine (dry), Petit Cap (off-dry)

Red—Montmorency

Store: At the winery only for the moment, but also available in some local restaurants

Store hours: Tuesday to Sunday, 9 am — 5 pm

Winery tours: Guided, by appointment

Public tastings: Small charge

Recommended wine: Cru du Domaine

La Vitacée

816 Chemin de l'Eglise
Sainte-Barbe, Québec
V0S 1P0
Telephone: (514) 373-8429

Two biochemists from the Université de Montréal, Robert Cedergren and the late Roger Morazain, created this bijou operation in 1979 when they planted their original vineyard. In spite of the size of their winery, they have done much to increase the knowledge of what varieties will thrive in Québec's difficult growing conditions with their experimental plantings of esoteric hybrids. Réjean Gagnon — a former customer of the winery — and Alain Loiselle are the new owners. Réjean has continued Roger's work of experimentation in the vineyard, growing hybrids high on a trellis without hilling in winter. The buds are kept from freezing by the heat of a string of sixty-watt bulbs suspended from the top wire. They have plans to enlarge the vineyard to four times its current size as well as provide visitors with a self-guided tour and shaded picnic spots for hot summer days.

The red wines are aged in Missouri oak.

Winemakers: Réjean Gagnon and Alain Loiselle (with oenologist Luc Rolland)

Acreage: 10

Soil: Situated near Lac Saint-François in the warmest region of Québec; gravelly soil with some clay; lightly sloped Montérégie vineyard

Grape varieties: De Chaunac, St. Croix, Kay Gray, Saint-Pépin, Lacrosse

Production: 2,500 bottles

Winemaking philosophy: "Since La Vitacée's foundation, our principal activity has been to concentrate on evaluating new hybrid varieties that don't need winter protection and have the potential to produce good wines. While continuing to evaluate these new varieties, we have begun planting larger quantities of those grapes we have kept and production ought to increase in the coming years."

Wines: Barbe-Rouge, Barbe-Blanc, Barbe-Rosé

Store hours: *April to December:* Tuesday to Sunday, 12 am — 5 pm

Winery tours: Yes

Public tastings: During store hours

Le Vignoble Angile

267, 2e. Rang Ouest (Route 218)
Saint-Michel-de-Bellechasse, Québec
G0R 3S0
Telephone/fax: (418) 884-2327

Since 1985, the vineyard has made fruit wines from 20 acres of strawberries and raspberries as well as blended table wines from winter hardy varieties. The winery is a 35-minute drive east of Québec City.

All the wines are made in stainless steel.

Winemaker: Nick Raymond and
    Manon Boulet
Acreage: vines: 5.5; soft fruit: 20
Soil: Gravelly, south facing slope
Grape varieties: Éona, Minnesota, Michurinetz, Vandal
Production: 6,000 bottles wine; 2,000 bottles fruit wine
Average tonnage crushed: 3 tonnes
Winemaking philosophy: "We welcome many people to the vineyard and offer
    them wines of quality."
Wines: Own store: Cuvée d'Angile Blanc (Sec), Cuvée d'Angile Rosé (Sec)
Sparkling—Cuvée d'Angile (champagne method)
Fruit wines—Picoline (14% alcohol, strawberry), Ambrosia (14% alcohol, strawberry and raspberry with maple syrup), Grand Frisson (14% alcohol, raspberry)
Store hours: Daily, 9 am — 6 pm
Winery tours: By reservation, $3 per person (reserve for large groups)
Public tastings: During store hours

Recommended wines: Cuvée d'Angile Blanc

Vignoble Angell

134 Rang St-Georges
St-Bernard de Lacolle, Québec
J0J 1V0
Telephone
Montreal: (450) 522-1012
Vineyard: (450) 246-4219

Jean-Guy Angell is one of the original Québec vignerons. He planted 200 vines in 1978 and opened his doors in 1985 with the requisite 5,000 vines. He now has 32,000 in the ground with 15,000 more currently being planted. This is the largest family-owned vineyard in Québec. Guy, Jean Guy's son, has taken over the winemaking duties from his father. Jean-Guy swears that their New York-border vineyard in Montérégie gives them a three-week advantage over Dunham, and certainly their 1992 white won a signal honour: it was chosen to be served in the Québec legislature. In 1995, the ever-industrious Jean-Guy (who also owns a string of karate schools across Canada) has expanded the barrel-aging room in the rock-floored cellar of his traditional Québecois stone house, as well as adding a banquet room where he serves Méchoui (spit-roasted marinated lamb.)

Winemaker: Guy Angell

Acreage: 18 (9 in production)

Soil: A mixture of sand, black earth and clay; typically flat Montérégie vineyard

Grape varieties: Seyval Blanc, Vidal, Chardonnay, De Chaunac, Merlot, Pinot Noir (currently on trial)

Production: 20,000 - 25,000 bottles

Wines: Own store: Vignoble Angell Blanc, Vignoble Angell Rouge

Winery tours: Yes

Additional Features: Picnic facilities, wine and cheese tasting

---

Recommended wines: Vignoble Angell Blanc

Vignoble Cappabianca

586 St. Jean-Baptiste   Telephone: (450) 691-1515
Mercier, Québec (near Châteauguay)   Fax: (450) 691-4212
J6R 2A7

Before emigration to Canada, Francesco Lapenna's family had a vineyard in Italy, although they lost it in World War II. The loss of the Italian vineyard never sat well with Francesco, and so, 15 years after hearing about hybrid grapes (he was in the nursery business), he finally decided to "go for it" in 1993, and planted his current vineyard. One of Vignoble Cappabianca's claims to fame is that it is the closest winery to Montréal: being just 20-25 minutes from downtown. The vineyard – Cappabianca – is named after his mother's family.

Winemaker: Francesco Lapenna
Acreage: 8
Soil: Mostly sandy loam
Grape varieties: Seyval Blanc, Maréchal Foch, Lucie Kuhlmann
Production: 400 cases
Winemaking philosophy: "To produce the best quality possible out of grapes produced entirely by our vineyards."
Wines: *White*—Cappabianca White
Red—Cappabianca Red
Store: Like all Québec wineries, at the winery only for the moment; eventually at public markets that will sell "produits du terroir"
Store hours: Open all *summer, winter* by appointment
Winery tours: Self-guided visit of the vineyards, or by appointment
Public tastings: Charge

Recommended wines: Cappabianca White

Vignoble Clos de la Montagne

330, de la Montagne
Mont St-Grégoire, Québec
J0J 1K0
e-mail:
Aryden@mtl.mdigital.qc.ca
Telephone: (450) 358-4868
Fax: (450) 358-5628

Vin Blanc   White Wine

SAINT GRÉGOIRE
1997
ÉLEVÉ ET MIS EN BOUTEILLE AU
VIGNOBLE CLOS DE LA MONTAGNE
330, De La Montagne.
MONT St.GRÉGOIRE, Québec, CANADA

11% alc./vol.   Nº 1004   750 ml

Produit du Québec   Product of Québec

For those living in or leaving Montréal to visit Québec's vineyards, Le Clos de la Montagne, at just 30 minutes from the Champlain Bridge, runs a close second to Vignoble Cappabianca as being the nearest winery to the urban centre. Le Clos de la Montagne also is one of the most diversified wineries, which, aside from offering several wines and apple ciders, also offers apple picking, apple products, a stained glass studio, llamas, hens, and exotic birds! The winery is a stop on the "Route des cidres de la Montérégie," of the "Route des Vins," the "Route des Cabanes à sucre" (maple syrup), and the "Route des Vergers" in the autumn (u-pick route).

Winemaker: J. Paul Martin

Acreage: 6.5

Soil: Gravelly

Grape varieties: *White*—Geisenheim, Cayuga, Seyval Blanc
    Red— DeChaunac, Maréchal Foch, Seyval Noir, Chancellor, Gamay

Production: 800 cases

Average tonnage crushed: 9 tonnes

Winemaking philosophy: "We always strive to make the best wine possible out of the grapes from our property."

Wines: *White*—St. Grégoire, Cuvée Joffrey

Red—St. Grégoire, Cuvée Versailles

Sparkling—Méthode Champenoise Apple Cider 8%

Speciality—two apple cider-based apéritifs and one table apple cidre

Store: Like all Québec wineries, at the winery only for the moment; eventually at public markets that will sell "produits du terroir"

Store hours: Daily, 9 am — 6 pm

Winery tours: Guided, at any time

Public tastings: Free

Additional features: Picnic sites, apple picking, stained-glass studio and curios for sale

––––––––––

Recommended wine: Cuvée Versailles

Vignoble de la Sablière

1050 Chemin Dutch
St. Armand, Québec
(roughly between Freligsburg and
Missisquoi Bay of Lake Champlain)
J0J 1T0
Telephone/Fax: (450) 248-2634

A new winery on the Québec scene that
is looking to make a name for itself with
a Vinho Verde-style wine — a bit pétil-
lant, at 8.5 per cent, low in alcohol, easy
to drink.

Winemakers: Irénée Belley and Sandra
    Moreau

Acreage: 8

Soil: Sandy, soil with some gravel

Grape varieties: Seyval, Geisenheim,
    Maréchal Foch, Vidal and St. Croix

Production: 350 cases

Winemaking philosophy: "To make the best products we can without chaptalisa-
    tion, without herbicides, without pesticides, if possible."

Wines: *White*—La Sablière Blanc (Seyval), Le St. Armand Blanc (more perfumed)

Red—Still to come

Speciality—"Vin de glâce" still to come

Store: Like all Québec wineries, at the winery only for the moment, eventually at
    public markets that will sell "produits du terroir"

Store hours: Open all *summer*, *winter* by appointment

Winery tours: Self-guided, or by appointment

Public tastings: Yes, no charge so far

Vignoble de l'Aurore Boréale

1421, rang Brodeur
St. Eugène de Grantham, Québec
J0C 1J0
Telephone/Fax: (819) 396-7349

A few years ago, in late August just before harvest, Guy Desrochers and Lucie Robitaille were admiring their just-planted vineyards, watching the Aurora Boréalis light show. It was a beautiful moment, and they decided then and there on the winery's name. Like so many other couples, to make their dream winery come true, they've had to support it by keeping one partner's day job. Guy Desrochers is the desk editor (chef de pupitre) of the "Arts et Spectacles" section of the *La Presse* daily in Montréal. His partner in life and in wine, Eugène Robitaille (formerly an *horticultrice*), has taken over the day-to-day running of the vineyards and winery.

Like many other wineries, they believe their microclimate to be one of the best; certainly warmer than that of Dunham (where many upstart Québec wineries were first concentrated).

Winemaker: Guy Desrochers and Eugène Robitaille

Acreage: 10

Soil: Loam, sandy-clay with some limestone; the vineyard is well-drained despite the absence of a slope

Grape varieties: Cayuga, Geisenheim, Seyval, Bacchus, Lucie Kuhlmann, Chancellor, Baco Noir

Production: 1,100 cases; 1,300 cases for 2002

Winemaking philosophy: "To make dry table wines from choice, well-ripened grapes."

Wines: *White*—l'Aurore Boréale Blanc; l'Aurore Boréale Séléction

Red—Rosé des Peupliers; l'Aurore Boréale Rouge Séléction; La Nuit Persëides

Speciality—Les Plëides — apéritif-style

Store: Like all Québec wineries, at the winery only for the moment; eventually at public markets that will sell *produits du terroir*

Store hours: Open all *summer*; *winter* by appointment

Winery tours: Self-guided, groups by appointment

Recommended wine: La Nuit Persëides

Vignoble de l'Ardennais

158 Ridge
Stanbridge est,
Québec
J0J 2H0
Telephone/Fax:
(450) 248-0597

Winemaker: François Samray

Acreage: 12

Soil: Slatey soil

Grape varieties: Seyval, Vidal, Cayuga, Riesling, 5247, Chancellor, Maréchal Foch, De Chaunac

Production: 1000+ cases

Winemaking philosophy: "Leave the wine the time it needs to evolve; wait patiently until the malolactic fermentation is completed, for the end result is a superior quality of wine."

Wines: *White*—Vignoble de l'Ardennais Seyval

Red—Vignoble de l'Ardennais Chancellor

Rosé—Côteau de Champlain

Store: Like all Québec wineries, at the winery only for the moment; eventually at public markets that will sell "produits du terroir"

Store hours: Daily, 9 am — 6 pm

Winery tours: Yes, guided, by appointment only

Public tastings: $.50 per glass, free with purchase

Recommended wine: Rosé (Côteau de Champlain)

Vignoble de l'Orpailleur

1086 Route 202
Dunham, Québec
J0E 1M0
Telephone: (514) 295-2763
Fax: (514) 295-3112
e-mail: int@orpailleur.ca
web site: www.orpailleur.ca

Hervé Durand, a winemaker from Avignon who studied in Dijon and taught oenology in Argentina, bought the Dunham farm in 1980 and planted his vineyard two years later. His neighbour, Frank Furtado, an impressario who puts on firework displays, was so intrigued by the notion that he became a partner. Later publisher Pierre Rodrigue bought in, and with French winemaker Charles-Henri de Coussergues the winery has become the commercial leader in the province. Gilles Vigneault inadvertently named the enterprise when he told Hervé, "making wine in Québec is like panning for gold." L'Orpailleur is a man who does just that.

A white woodframe farmhouse stands in front of a modern cedar-built winery with a magnificent terrace where you can dine on summer days. The store sells sweatshirts and other winery memorabilia. French and American oak barrels are used. Picnic tables are available.

Winemaker: Charles-Henri de Coussergues

Acreage: 24

Soil: Sand and gravel; the soil is very dry and warm; gentle slopes

Grape variety: Seyval Blanc, Vidal

Production: 6,500 cases

Average tonnage crushed: 85 tonnes

Winemaking philosophy: "Our wine is made exclusively from grapes grown in Québec. We will continue to do research to discover the best varieties to plant in our soil."

Wines: Own store: L'Orpailleur Vin Blanc, L'Orpailleur Élevé en Fût de Chêne, Apéri d'Or, La Mousse d'Or (méthode champenoise sparkling wine), l'Orpailleur Rosé, Icewine

Store hours: *April 15 to November 15:* Daily, 9 am—6 pm; *November 15 to April 15:*

Saturday and Sunday, 10 am — 12 noon and 1 pm — 5 pm (the rest of the week by appointment)

Winery tours: Wine path tours and tastings — *May 15 to October 15* (restaurant facilities)

Public tastings: During store hours

Additional facilities: Restaurant

Recommended wines: Orpailleur (vin blanc), Orpailleur Élevé en Fûr de Chêne, Mousse d'Or

---

Vignoble des Pins

136 Grand Sabrevois
Sabrevois, Québec
J0J 2G0
Telephone/Fax: (450) 347-1073
e-mail: vigdespins@aol.com

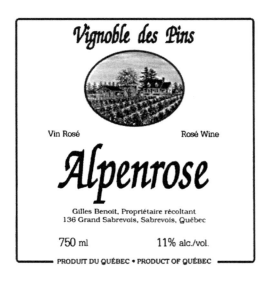

If you've ever dreamed of making wine, Gilles Benoit is the man you should visit. He has realized his dream: to plant a manageable five-acre vineyard, stay small and make wines the way he wants to make them. Being small, he can take the time to experiment, like laying straw on top of his hilled-up tender *vinifera* during winter months to lovingly making a *methode champenoise* sparkler by hand. Gilles' Vignoble des Pins opened in May 1990.

Situated in the plains, he named his winery after the stands of red and white pine around the property. His soil has more clay than the hillier region around Dunham, which gives more body to his red wines. The vineyard was first planted in 1986 with French hybrids and some *vinifera*. Production is half red, half white.

There are picnic and tasting facilities for 50 people.

Winemaker: Gilles Benoit

Acreage: 5

Soil: Clay-loam

Grape varieties: Seyval, Cayuga, Geisenheim 318 & 322, Bacchus, Vidal, Maréchal Foch, Gamay, Cabernet Franc, Lemberger

Production: 1,000 cases

Average tonnage crushed: 10 tonnes

Winemaking philosophy: "We are aiming for a light fruity style in our wines. The emphasis is on reds, blends of hybrids and *viniferas*. We also produce a blanc de blancs sparkler using Seyval grapes and the *méthode champenoise*."

Wines: Own store: *White*—Pin Blanc (85% Seyval, 15% Cayuga), Edelweiss (Geisenheim/Cayuga blend), Geisenheim Late Harvest, Icewine (Geisenheim)

Red—Maréchal (Maréchal Foch Primeur), Alpenrose (Gamay, Maréchal Foch and various *Vinifera*), Réserve (Maréchal Foch and various *vinifera*)

Sparkling—Mousse des Pins (Seyval Blanc)

Store hours: 10 am — 6 pm year round

Winery tours: Yes

Public tastings: Yes ($3.50 per person charge for bus tour and tasting)

Recommended wines: Geisenheim Late Harvest

Vignoble Dietrich-Jooss

407 Grande-Ligne
Iberville, Québec
J2X 4J2
Telephone: (450) 347-6857

Husband and wife Victor Dietrich and Christiane Jooss come from the Alsace village of Ingersheim where their respective families had been immersed in viticulture and winemaking for generations. The couple founded their company in 1986 and the following year planted the vineyard in the Richelieu Valley, east of Iberville. In order to find the best varieties for their microclimate, they have some 36 different plants in the ground, primarily white. An experimental plot includes vines from South Africa, Australia, the United States, South America and the noble varieties of Europe, including several Geisenheim clones which, says Victor, appear promising. These grapes go into his wines neck-labelled Cuvée Spéciale.

Their label bears a replica of the coat of arms that appeared on the bottles Victor made in his native Alsace. He believes that Chasselas, Gamay and certain Pinot varieties could do well in Québec. Much of the equipment comes from Alsace. American oak is used. The winery is located in a large wood barn and the enthusiastic reception of visitors won the couple three Québec tourism awards.

Victor is a past president of the Association des Vignerons, a man whose expertise and experience have inspired many young Québecois who have come into the profession. His daughter Stephanie (for whom the Late Harvest Cuvée is named) is studying oenology in Montpellier.

Winemaker: Victor Dietrich

Acreage: 12

Soil: Silty-sand, lightly pebbled; benefits from the proximity of two bodies of water, the Richelieu River and Lac Champlain

Grape varieties: French hybrids, including Seyval, Cayuga, Vidal and Vineland 50201, several Geisenheim clones. Reds include Maréchal Foch, De Chaunac, Chancellor and Villard Noir. Some *vinifera* is planted, including Chardonnay and Riesling.

Production: 2,700 cases (850 cases red and rosé)

Winemaking philosophy: "As a winemaker from Alsace in Québec, I want to use traditional Alsatian winemaking techniques to create that particular style in the wines we make here. My experiments in the vineyard are aimed at finding wines that resemble Riesling in character."

Wines: Own store: Vin Blanc, Vin Rosé, Vin Rouge, Vin Blanc Cuvée Spéciale, Storikengold (a wine made for fish and seafood)

Sparkling—Blanc de Blancs (champagne method)

Specialty—Cuvée Stephanie (Late Harvest/Sélection Imperiale Icewine)

Store hours: *Year-round:* Tuesday to Sunday, 9 am — 7 pm

Winery tours: Yes; guided tours for groups are $4 per person

Public tastings: Yes (group reservations necessary). Picnic tables available.

———

Recommended wines: Vin Blanc Cuvée Speciale, Vin Blanc Storikengold, Vin Rosé d'Iberville, Vin Rouge Réserve des Tounnellier

Vignoble du Marathonien

318 route 202
Havelock, Québec
J0S 2C0
Telephone vineyard:
(514) 826-0522
Telephone/Fax Montreal:
(514) 321-9347

If you drive along the orchard-studded route 202 between Hemmingford and Havelock, you'll be parallel to the U.S. border which lies a few kilometres to the south. Just east of Havelock, turn left into what is perhaps the quaintest vineyard in the province — and certainly one of the best for tourists. A pretty, well-kept, red-roofed white house and surrounding converted barn that sits at the end of a long gravel driveway is surrounded by vineyards and an apple orchard. Line and Jean Joly own and work the vineyard but it is Jean, a full-time engineer, whose determination and love of winemaking drives the place. Whether their endurance comes from running marathons or from parenting four children is another question, but there is no doubt that this picturesque young vineyard is making some really nice white wines. Icewine, called Vin de Glace, is something of a specialty here.

Winemaker: Jean Joly

Acreage: 3

Soil: Small rocks and gravel, black earth, little clay; flat vineyard

Grape varieties: Seyval, Cayuga, Vidal, SV 23512, Geisenheim 318; Maréchal Foch (experimental: Pinot Noir, Cabernet Franc, a little Merlot)

Production: 5,000 bottles

Average tonnage crushed: 7 tonnes

Winemaking philosophy: "In winemaking, we must never stop learning; and a good wine must begin with the careful pruning of the vine."

Wines: Own store: *White*—Vin Blanc, Cuvée Spéciale (Seyval, Cayuga, SV 23512), Vidal Vendange Tardive, Cuvée Fûr de Chêne (Seyval), Vidal Vin de Glace

Red—Vignoble du Marathonieu (Foch with other experimental varieties)

Winery tours: Self-guided; guided tours for busloads: small charge

Public tastings: *June to August:* Daily, *March to May and September to October;* Weekends; at other times by appointment

Recommended wines: Cuvée Spéciale, Vidal, Vin de Glace, Cuvée Fûr de Chêne

Vignoble La Bauge

155 des Erables
Brigham, Québec
J0E 1J0
Telephone: (514) 263-2149

The boar eating grapes on the label of the late Alcide Naud and Ghyslaine Poulin-Naud's *vin blanc* gives the game away. La Bauge actually means a "boar's den." Alcide had been a dairy farmer for 40 years in Brigham before he bought a herd of wild boar, deer, wild sheep and stags. He began growing wine in 1987 and reared his game menagerie for terrine and for the sport hunters who paid $120 each to bring their bow and arrow and hunt their own "Sanglier" in the woods. Most wine lovers will, perhaps, prefer looking at the boar from the other side of the fence and settle for taking away a jar of the Wild Boar terrine with a bottle of his son Simon's wine.

Besides Sanglier, the family also raises deer, faun, Picari (dwarf boar) and many types of wild pheasant and other exotic fowl, including a chicken with fur! Incidentally, their barrel-aged "Solitaire" is named after the lone male who heads a pack of several females: a "solitaire" because he permits no other male in his presence. Simon now makes a red from Chancellor and a Late Harvest Seyval Blanc.

Picnic tables are available.

Winemaker: Simon Naud
Acreage: 7
Soil: Gravelly
Grape varieties: Seyval Blanc, Chancellor
Production: 500 cases
Average tonnage crushed: 8 tonnes
Winemaking philosophy: "I hope that one of my five sons will follow in my footsteps, because it's a fascinating pursuit."
Wines: Seyval Blanc, Séléction Camille, Bête Rousse, Solitaire (Seyval oak-aged), L'Aube
Store hours: Daily, 9 am — 6 pm
Winery tours: Vineyard and animal reserve tour by car — $6 per person ($3 for children aged 5 to 12)
Public tastings: Yes

Vignoble le Cep d'Argent

1257 Chemin de la Rivière
Magog, Québec
J1X 3W5
Telephone: (819) 864-4441
Fax: (819) 864-7534

Le Cep d'Argent is Estrie's most easterly winery, situated between Magog and Sherbrooke. From eight grape varieties, winemaker François Scieur makes four different products to attract consumers to this small facility across the railway tracks from the banks of Petit Lac Magog. Here, perhaps more than anywhere else in Québec, the majestically sloping fields with their pine-topped hills and plots with vine rows set at varying angles to each other are vineyards reminiscent of the Grand Crus of France and Italy.

François and his brother Jean Paul are originally from the Champagne region which accounts for the presence of champagne-method sparkling wine, kir and ratafia on their product list. In fact, they were the first to produce sparkling wine from grapes grown in the province. The winery was founded in 1985 after research to find the right site for the vineyard was undertaken by Jacques Daniel and his son Marc. The other partner in the enterprise is Denis Drouin. The champagne cellar with its A-frames set up for riddling is well worth seeing.

The reception hall resembles a medieval armoury and accommodates 150 people, while upstairs the windowed, prettily designed dining room has the swank and elegance — as well as the sunset view across the water — to carry off a wedding reception or other special event.

Winemaker: François Scieur

Acreage: 30

Soil: Silty sandy-clay; south-south-east slope

Grape varieties: Seyval, Maréchal Foch, De Chaunac, Geisenheim, "Wiley White" from Niagara

Production: 4,500 cases

Average tonnage crushed: 65 tonnes

Winemaking philosophy: "Our philosophy is to ignore the ideas of people who say that the vine can't produce wines of quality in Québec."

Wines: Le Cep D'Argent Vin Blanc (Seyval Blanc), Délice du Chais, Réserve des

Chevaliers (barrel-aged), Fleur de Lys (white wine with cassis syrup), Mistral (Ratafia-style aperitif), L'Archer (digestif made from red wine, cognac and maple syrup), Cuvée 2000 (*méthode champenoise blanc de blancs*)

Store hours: Daily, 9 am — 5 pm

Winery tours: Hour-long bilingual tours with tasting: $4 per person (children 12 and under free; *May 1 to 29:* every hour; *June 30 to August 24:* every 45 minutes; *August 25 to November 2:* every hour; *November 3 to April 30:* Saturday and Sunday only. Groups of 25 or more by reservation.

Additional facilities: Restaurant facilities by reservation

———————

Recommended wines: Délice du Chais, le Cep D'Argent (vin blanc), Réserve des Chevaliers

———————————————————————

Vignoble Le Royer St-Pierre

182 route 221
St-Cyprien de Napierville, Québec
J0J 1L0
Telephone: (450) 245-0208
Fax: (450) 245-0388
e-mail: robertleroyer@sprint.ca

Robert Le Royer and Lucie St-Pierre founded their winery in 1990 and were determined to grow Chardonnay. They are currently studying different rootstocks for the 16 varieties they have planted. They are also experimenting in the vineyard with different trellising systems — all on the same vine. Vignoble Le Royer St. Pierre, a kilometre away from Morou, is a testimony to Robert's passion for the grape and his quest for their Holy Grail — the "right" variety for Québec. The wines themselves have intriguing names that involve local history, geography or geology.

The property is distinguished by a very solid-looking white silo that could, with a little imagination, become the subject of another quaint label.

The couple have four American oak barrels for ageing. They receive visitors enthusiastically, seven days a week, and offer buffet meals "or lamb roast on request."

In 1997 they constructed a new tank room and additional tasting room.

Winemaker: Robert Le Royer

Acreage: 12 (30 more available)

Grape varieties: Cayuga white, St-Pépin, Aurora, Geisenheim 318 and 322, Cabernet Franc, Maréchal Foch, Ste-Croix

Soil: Sandy with a little clay and clay with gravel; Lake Champlain provides a warm microclimate on the valley region

Production: 675 cases

Average tonnage crushed: 9 - 10 tonnes

Winemaking philosophy: "In our procedures the most inventive techniques are used. Also, in the vineyard due to the harsh climate all the vines are buried under 20 inches of earth in the fall. Our pruning system is *gobelet* mixed with double Guyot and a little double Geneva curtain, all on the same vine."

Wines: Own store: *White*—Les Trois Sols, La Dauversière

Red—Terre St-Cyprien, Les Trois Sols Rosé, Le Lambertois

Specialty—Cayuga white/Geisenheim Icewine (trial basis, not available commercially yet)

Store hours: Daily, 10 am — 8 pm

Winery tours: Yes ("anytime")

Public tastings: Yes ("anytime")

Vignoble Les Arpents de Neige

4042 rue Principale
Dunham, Québec
J0E 1M0
Telephone: (450) 295-3383

Just a stone's throw or three up the hill south from the town of Dunham, you'll find the vineyard of Les Arpents de Neige, a name that resonates with French history. "A few acres of snow" were not worth fighting for, according to French King Louis XIV's advisors. Originally planted by Jacques Breault, who once worked for l'Orpailleur, Les Arpents de Neige went into bankruptcy and was bought in 1992 by Gilles Séguin, a restaurateur who, with the help of his French winemaker, Jean-Paul Martin, made a very good Seyval in 1994. In addition, as one would expect, Gilles Séguin offers meals for groups who book ahead.

Winemaker: Jean-Paul Martin
Acreage: 12
Soil: Deep, gravelly
Grape varieties: Seyval, Vidal, Vineland 50201, Pollux, Ortega, Cayuga, Chancellor
Wines: Seyval Blanc, Cuvée Sélectionnée, Cuvée 1er Neige
Store hours: Daily, 9 am—9 pm
Winery tours: Yes
Public tastings: Yes

Vignoble Les Blancs Coteaux

1046 Route 202
Dunham, Québec
J0E 1M0
Telephone/Fax: (450) 295-3503

The youthful Pierre Genesse and his wife Marie-Claude founded their tiny winery in 1989. Pierre learned his winemaking in Burgundy while picking grapes in the Mâconnais. He also studied physical geography in Sherbrooke. The beautiful old wood farmhouse which doubles as the cellar and the couple's home also has a shop where you can buy homemade vinegars, jams, jellies, dried flowers and herbs. Bottling and labelling are done by hand, and the crush is done nearby at a colleague's facility.

Pierre removes leaves to expose the grape clusters to the sun. He vinifies in stainless steel to maintain the perfume of the fruit although he does have ten French and American oak *barriques* and is currently experimenting with Bacchus. He also makes ciders, fortified cider and dry apple wine.

Winemaker: Pierre Genesse
Acreage: 9
Soil: Rocky loam on slate above clay; warm air currents off Lake Champlain moderate spring and early fall frost; situated at the foot of a hill; good drying wind and heat during the day
Grape varieties: Seyval Blanc, Bacchus, Siegerrebe, Seyval Noir, Ste-Croix and "the romantic" Es-219

Production: wine: 1,500 cases, cider: 1,500 cases

Winemaking philosophy: "To maintain very high-quality standards without becoming a large commercial producer. Small is beautiful."

Wines: Own store: Seyval Blanc La Taste, La Taste Élevé en Fûr de Chêne, Vendange de Bacchus

Specialty— Empire (cider and Calvados), Nouaison (cider), Rosé-Gorge (semi-sweet cider)

Store hours: *May to November:* Daily, 10 am — 5 pm; *Winter:* Wednesday to Sunday, 10 am — 5 pm

Public tastings: During store hours

Recommended Wines: Seyval Blanc, La Taste, Empire

Vignoble Les Chants de Vignes

459, chemin de la Rivière
Canton de Magog, Québec
J1X 3W5
Telephone: (819) 847-VINS (8467)
Fax: (819) 847-2940

Situated roughly halfway between Lake Memphremagog and Petit Lac Magog, the new (first harvest 1997) Vignoble les Chants de Vignes is one of the youngest Québec vineyards to be awarded a medal in a national wine championship. Les Chant de Vignes, besides concentrating on making pure, as natural as possible wines, also devotes – with their well-stocked store and catering service — a lot of energy into making any visit to their vineyard a rewarding one. The fact that all the wines are named after musical genres is a cute one, and the play on words of Le Kyrié (a Kir-type beverage) is inspired.

Winemaker: Marc Daniel
Acreage: 10
Soil: Heavy
Grape Varieties: Seyval Blanc, Seyval Noir
Production: 600 cases
Average tonnage crushed: 7 tonnes

Winemaking philosophy: Here, simplicity rules: the theory is that they believe that the best way to let a wine express itself is to limit interventions, corrections and manipulation to the bare minimum. "Let the wine become what is meant to be, all by itself."

Wines: *White*—Le Canon

Red—Le Canon Rouge

Fortified—L'Opéra, a Pineau de Charentes-type wine that is equally good as an apéritif or an after-dinner meditative digéstif. Made with unfermented grape juice, and a specially-selected alcohol that has been macerated with dried fruits

Speciality—Le Kyrié, a pre-mixed Kir made with raspberry syrup

Store: Like all Québec wineries, at the winery only for the moment; eventually at public markets that will sell "produits du terroir"

Store hours: *May to end of September:* Daily, 9 am — 5 pm

Winery tours: *May to end of September:* Daily guided visits, 9 am — 5 pm

Public tastings: Tour and tasting $4 per person; tasting only: $2 per person

Additional features: Reception hall open all year on reservation (musical entertainment or supper theatre available). Restaurant serving fine cuisine open on reservation (Maximum 55 people). Catering service available.

Vignoble les Pervenches

150, chemin Boulais
Rainville-Farnham, Québec
J2N 2P9
Telephone/Fax: (450) 293-8311

The most striking thing about this tiny vineyard is owner/winemaker Yves Monachon's dedication to *vinifera*. Sure, he makes Seyval — and believes it is — for the moment — his best-balanced wine, but, just listening to him talk, his enthusiasm for *vinifera* is infectious.

Growing *vinifera* in Québec is always risky — not because the plants die — but because the *vinifera* plants are only fruitful on a few buds, and if those are the buds that freeze in a late spring frost — presto, no harvest! Yves grows his *vinifera* near the edge of his woods, where the trees act as a natural wind-break, keeping that section of the vineyards some two to three degrees warmer in all seasons. Yves' most striking discovery seems to be that his Pinot Gris (purchased in Ontario — probably an Alsatian clone) is so fruitful that he has to green-harvest some of the bunches in mid-summer to keep the yield down. Yves hills up all his vines, but lays the canes of his Chardonnay and Riesling on the ground to be fully covered by earth, while his Seyval Blanc is grown in goblet fashion and protrudes up out of the hilled-up soil. His next challenge? Riesling.

Winemaker: Yves Monachon

Acreage: 3

Soil: Gravel with pebbles (50%), sandy (50%)

Grape varieties: White: Seyval Blanc, Chardonnay, Geisenheim 318, Pinot Gris; Red: Maréchal Foch

Production: 312 cases

Average tonnage crushed: 4.5 tonnes

Winemaking philosophy: High-grown vines (four feet above ground) with three wire trellis, Yves believes "you've got to get that high for decent exposure to the sun."

Wines: *White*—Varietal naming : Vignoble Les Pervenches Seyval, Vignoble Les Pervenches Chardonnay

Red—Vignoble Les Pervenches Maréchal Foch

Store: Like all Québec wineries, at the winery only for the moment, but is also present at some agricultural fairs, as well

Store hours: Open all *summer*, *winter* call first

Winery tours: Guided, by appointment

Public tastings: Free

Recommended wines: Seyval Blanc, but watch for the
Chardonnay and Pinot Gris

Vignoble Les Trois Clochers

341 Route 202
Dunham, Québec
J0E 1M0
Telephone: (450) 295-2034

Vignoble Les Trois Clochers is just one km or so north east of Les Côtes d'Ardoise on the road into Dunham. Claude Rhéaume and Réal Normandeau created the winery and sold to Robert Brisebois and Nadège Mariam in 1997.

Besides the obligatory Seyval Blanc and a very nice Strawberry wine, the team plans to produce red wine from various varieties. The vineyard was first planted in 1986 in a very enchanting site.

Picnic tables are available during the summer.

Winemaker: Claude Rhéaume

Acreage: 7.5

Soil: Gravelly

Grape varieties: Seyval, Chancellor, Maréchal Foch in production; to come, Vidal, Cliche

Production: 5,000 bottles

Wines: Vin Blanc, Vin de Fraises (a red to come)

Store hours: Daily, 10 am—5 pm (*January to April* by appointment)

Winery tours: Yes (by appointment)

Public tastings: Yes

Vignoble Morou

238 Route 221
Napierville, Québec
J0J 1L0
Telephone/fax: (450) 245-7569
e-mail: morou@sympatico.ca
web site:
www3.sympatico.ca/~morou/

Monique Morin and Etienne Héroux, a chemical engineer, founded Vignoble Morou in 1987 close to the head of Lake Champlain. They planted a range of hybrids to see what was best for their particular microclimate. They use American oak barrels to age their best reds as well as their elegant white, Clos Napierois.

In the sports world, a "Most Improved Player" award is often bestowed. If such an accolade were bestowed on winemakers, it would go to Etienne and Monique for sheer industry and commitment. Etienne rolls all his vats outside for up to a week in -5° Celsius weather to precipitate as much tartaric acid as possible (the small growers in Meursault open their doors to their white wine cellar to achieve the same effect). This is the true mark of a vigneron — not wanting to adulterate his wines with chemical de-acidification.

Picnic facilities are available.

Winemaker: Etienne Héroux

Acreage: 4.5

Soil: Sandy-loam, flattish vineyard with a slight slope

Grape varieties: Seyval, Vidal, Seibel, Geisenheim clones, Cayuga white, De Chaunac, Maréchal Foch, Gamay, Chancellor

Production: 1,000 cases

Winemaking philosophy: "Small family vineyard, wines of superior quality and a warm welcome for visitors."

Wines: Own store: *White*—Morou Blanc Réserve, Clos Napierois (barrel-aged Geisenheim clones), La Closerie (Cayuga and Seyval)

Red—Morou Rouge Réserve, Morou Rosé Réserve

Store hours: *May to October:* Wednesday to Sunday, 10 am — 6 pm (For the rest of the year, call the house for product availability.)

Winery tours: Yes (reservations for groups of 10 or more; group packages for wine and cheese and cold meals)

Public tastings: Yes ($1 per variety)

_____

Recommended wines: Clos Napierois, Morou White Réserve, Morou Rosé,
Morou Red Réserve, unoaked whites

Vignoble St. Pétronille (Île d'Orléans)

1A, Chemin du Bout   Telephone: (418) 828-9554
de l'Île St.-Pétronille, Québec   Fax: (418) 828-1253
G0A 4C0

According to winemaker Jean Larsen, the famous grape researcher J.O. Vandal finally found fulfilment in his middle '80s when visiting the Vignoble St. Pétronille.
Apparently, the famed nurseryman estimated his chance of producing a good hybrid
as one in 40,000 every time he came up with a new vine. St.-Pétronille was the first
commercial vineyard to be planted substantially to one of his crossings, the Cliche.
Larsen bought the rights in 1989 from Mario Cliche (who had continued Vandal's
work) and had to reproduce all the plants himself.

Jean Larsen loves receiving people, whether single or in groups, and says he gets
about 125 buses per year, mostly Montréalers, Ontarians, Americans and French
tourists (surprisingly enough, Québec City really hasn't discovered him yet). His
wines are 90 per cent white and 10 per cent rosé. The winery's location is splendrous
… facing the Montmorency Falls.

Winemaker: Jean Larsen
Acreage: 12.5
Soil: Well-drained, stratified tuffe shist, on gently-sloping hills of various exposi-
tions.
Grape varieties: Vandal Cliche (90%), Ste. Croix (10%)
Production: 20,000 bottles—about 1,500 cases
Average tonnage crushed: 20 tonnes
Winemaking philosophy: Jean aims to keep his wines as natural as possible by
never chaptalising above the ten per cent alcohol level, by never deacidifying
chemically. Jean always waits for the malolactic fermentation to reduce the
acidity in the wines, even though the malo can take two months to start at
these higher acidity levels.
Wines: *White*—Le St. Pétronille Blanc, Le St. Pétronille Rosé
Sparkling—méthode champenoise—1000 bottles will be produced for the milleni-
um; many are already pre-sold
Store: Like all Québec wineries, at the winery only for the moment; eventually at
public markets that will sell *produits du terroir*

Store hours: Open all *summer*, *winter* by appointment
Winery tours: Guided, at any time
Public tastings: Charge in the summer, but not in the winter

Recommended wine: Le St. Pétronille Blanc

Vignoble Sous les Charmilles

3747, chemin Dunant
Rock Forest, Québec
J1N 3B7
Telephone: (819) 346-7189

In 1986, consulting winemaker Alain Bélanger's (Les Arpents de Neiges, Les Blancs Coteaux, La Bauge, Les Trois Clochers) father planted a few vines near Sherbrooke *pour s'amuser*. What was a hobby has become a passion, and the winery opened its doors in late summer 1995.

A year later Alain (a wine agent and former sommelier who had made wine in Beaujolais and Alsace) left for other interests and co-founder Georges Ducharme took over.

Although most Québec vignerons use earth to bury their vines in winter, Georges has found a revolutionary new material — leaves! He has Sherbrooke's wine enthusiasts saving him their lawn rakings all autumn long (up to 10,000 bags of them!), and after the winter passes he takes off the leaves, composts them, and uses them for natural fertilizer!

Winemaker: Georges Ducharme
Acreage: 7
Soil: Rocky, sandy, gravelly
Grape varieties: Seyval Blanc, Vidal, Bacchus, Maréchal Foch
Production: 11,000 - 16,000 bottles
Wines: Vignoble sous les Charmilles Vin Blanc, Cuvée Spéciale, Fût de Chêne
Store: *May to November:* by appointment
Winery tours: Yes (by appointment)
Public tastings: Yes

Recommended wine: Cuvée Spéciale

NOVA SCOTIA

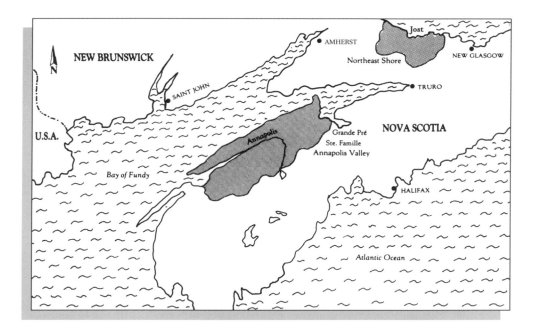

Wine Regions of Nova Scotia

eif Ericsson may have discovered wild grapes in Newfoundland at the beginning of this millennium, but there is harder evidence to support Nova Scotia's claim to be a wine-growing province at least as far back as the beginning of the seventeenth century. In 1611, Louis Hébert, Samuel Champlain's apothecary, loaded his canoe with vines he brought with him from France and paddled up the Bear River between Annapolis and Digby counties to plant a vineyard.

Serious attempts to turn the province into a wine-growing region had to wait until this century. As early as 1913, the Agriculture Canada research station at

Kentville had been planting experimental plots to see what varieties might flourish in the province's short, cool growing season (to date they have evaluated over 200 cultivars). After several decades of trial and error, in 1971 the researchers suggested in a departmental publication that only table varieties seemed viable (even the hardy Concord did not ripen sufficiently). But a decade later, they would be proved mistaken.

Nova Scotia is situated midway between the Equator and the North Pole, and the time between the last spring frost and the first fall frost is much shorter than in Ontario or British Columbia. The average daily temperature during the growing season is also lower than the other two grape-growing provinces.

But happily there are always those healthy sceptics who challenge accepted wisdom and more often than not are proved correct. Roger Dial, a Californian born in 1942, can justifiably claim to be the father of the Nova Scotia wine industry. Although Andrés had a bottling plant in Truro, there were no wine grapes grown on a commercial scale in the province until the late 1970s. Andrés opened its winery in Truro's industrial park in 1965 and purchased Chipman Wines in 1983, an enterprise founded in 1941 that produced fruit wines from apples, cherries, elderberries, blueberries and cranberries.

A political scientist by training, Roger Dial came to lecture at Dalhousie in 1969. During his university days in California, he had worked his way through school as a wine sales representative and had been a partner in the small Davis Bynum winery in Healdsburg. At Dalhousie he met an economist, Norman Morse, who had planted some table grapes on his property at Grand Pré. Roger convinced him to plant wine grapes that he had purchased for his own home winemaking production. In 1978, the two men put in a further three acres of vines — no *vinifera*, since they had been advised against these tender plants, but two hardy Russian varieties from the Amur Valley on the Chinese border, Michurinetz and Severnyi. (This has a certain resonance for Roger Dial since his Ph.D. was in Chinese politics.) The vines had been imported to Canada as a result of a barter deal with the Soviets — Nova Scotian raspberries for Russian vines. The stocks had originally been propagated at the Summerland research station in British Columbia and another barter deal landed them in Kentville. This time the commodity was Nova Scotia blueberries. (The planting of vines must have a domesticating effect because, in 1981, Roger purchased the vineyard and his colleague's house — a splendid 1819 Georgian woodframe building — with the intention of creating a cottage winery.)

Emboldened by the success of the Russian varieties in his basement winemaking activities, Roger Dial convinced Morse to plant more vines and to extend to *vinifera* varieties as well. In 1979, Chardonnay and Gewürztraminer were put into the ground — the first in eastern Canada — but the weather during the following year was so bad that it nearly killed the entire vineyard. Yet 1980 was not without its triumphs. That vintage of Cuvée d'Amur, a Michurinetz-based wine, won a gold medal in New York at the International Wine and Spirit Competition and a silver in Bristol, England. Subsequent harvests proved that wine grapes could flourish in Nova Scotia if they were placed in suitable microclimates. In 1982, Cuvée d'Amur was voted by wine writers as the best Canadian red at a Department of External Affairs tasting to select wines for Canadian embassies and High Commissions around the world. It just may have been coincidence, but that was the year when the Wine Growers' Association of Nova Scotia was founded with Roger Dial as chairman and Hans Jost as vice-chairman, a grape farmer in Malagash, Cumberland County, who would start Nova Scotia's second cottage winery two years later.

In 1983, Roger Dial had planted a 22-acre vineyard 15 miles from his winery at Lakeville and was busy contracting the produce of other local growers to satisfy the demand for his wines at provincial liquor stores. It was not until 1986 that the Nova Scotia government passed the Farm Winery Act enabling him to sell wines at the winery directly to licensees and the visiting public. By 1988, he had 200 acres of vineyards that were either owned outright, bought as joint ventures or contracted in, and had annual sales of $1.2 million. Grand Pré had a healthy six per cent of the provincial wine market. Unfortunately, the combined pressures of the October 1987 stock market crash and the Free Trade Agreement eventually took their toll and forced Roger Dial's winery into receivership. After a couple of years of restructuring, Jim Landry and Karen Avery took over the operation, bringing in the late Bob Claremont as consulting winemaker and wine buyer. But this new effort too was doomed to failure and the partners sold the business in 1994 to Swiss interests.

The Farm Winery Act, though long in coming, helped to consolidate Nova Scotia's nascent wine industry. Under its provisions a winery could sell 350 cases of wine at the farm gate for every acre under vine (minimum ten), even if those newly planted vines had yet to produce a crop. Nor did the wines sold have to be from grapes grown in the province. In order to give incentive to farm wineries to plant grapes, the government allowed them to bottle imported wines, either blended into locally grown grapes or as 100 per cent imports. These are usually sold through the Nova Scotia Liquor Commission (NSLC) and the estate-bottled wines are available at the wineries.

At this time, there are three estate farm wineries in Nova Scotia (Grand Pré is currently inactive) whose grapes are augmented by 15 growers managing 175 acres of vines in seven counties. Production is around nearly 200 tonnes. Suitable grape varieties for winemaking in Nova Scotia are more limited than Ontario and British Columbia. The most widely planted varieties are reds — Michurinetz, Maréchal Foch; whites — Seyval Blanc, New York Muscat, L'Acadie Blanc and a Geisenheim clone, GM.

More early-ripening *vinifera* varieties are now being planted in Nova Scotia. These more sensitive plants are being protected against the cold winters by "hilling" (covering the trunk with earth in the late fall, a technique practised in Québec) or by the use of straw. The vines are grown closer to the ground to benefit from heat retained in the soil. Trellising systems used in Europe with certain modifications have improved the production and survival rate of the vines.

Changes in the Farm Winery Act now require a minimum of 35 per cent Nova Scotia content for a winery start-up and this figure increases by five per cent a year after the second year up to a maximum of 75 per cent local content.

Since the Nova Scotia wine industry is in discussions with VQA Canada to join that organisation they will have to produce 100 per cent Nova Scotia wines.

NOVA SCOTIA WINERIES

Grand Pré Estate Winery

P.O. Box 18
Kings County, Nova
Scotia
B0P 1M0

Grand Pré, the winery
founded by the visionary
Roger Dial in 1980, went
into receivership in 1988.
The estate was taken
over by Jim Landry and
Karen Avery with the
late Bob Claremont as
consulting winemaker.
This new enterprise also
failed and the winery was
purchased in 1993 by a
prominent Swiss banker, Hanspeter W. Stutz.

Hanspeter saw the promise of the historic property, originally built in 1826 and
had a multi-million dollar project designed around the existing winery facility.
The production facilities have been enlarged, a greenhouse for on-site clonal selection constructed as well as a restaurant (and an aroma-therapy salon operated
by Hanspeter's wife) and a viewing gallery overlooking the Minas Basin of the Bay
of Fundy.
Scheduled opening: June, 2000.

Winemaker: Juerg Stutz (Hanspeter's son, currently studying oenology and viticul-
ture in Switzerland)
Grape varieties: L'Acadie (a white cross developed at the Nova Scotia Research
Station), Seyval Blanc, New York Muscat, Vidal, Maréchal Foch, Léon Millot.
Production: (projected) 12,000 cases (100 per cent Nova Scotia grapes)

Habitant Vineyards Ltd.

10318 Highway 221
Canning, Nova Scotia
B0H 1P0
Telephone: (902) 582-7565
Fax: (902) 582-3661
e-mail: wayne@newworldwine.ns.ca
web site: habitant.ca

Peter Jensen and Laura McCain Jensen (who own Creekside in Ontario) are convinced that Chardonnay and Pinot Noir can ripen well enough in Nova Scotia to make sparkling wine of quality. They have plans to open a winery on another vineyard site to do just this. Currently their wines are made mostly from California wine and concentrates or from Ontario wines. The operation is run by Wayne Macdonald, a grower since 1986 and formerly with RCMP intelligence.

Winemaker: Curphy Forestall

Acreage: 28

Soil: Sand, limestone, clay

Grape varieties: Chardonnay, Pinot Noir, L'Acadie Blanc, Seyval, Vidal, Muscat, Baco Noir, Maréchal Foch

Production: 12,000 cases

Average tonnage crushed: 50 tonnes

Average tonnage purchased: 30 tonnes

Winemaking philosophy: "Using the lighter fruit to produce an easy drinking wine, minimal oak usage."

Wines: *White*—Cabot Reserve — Chardonnay, L'Acadie Blanc, Seyval, Cuvée Blanc
Red—Cabot Reserve — Pinot Noir, Merlot, Cabernet Sauvignon, Baco Noir Blush

Store hours: Monday to Friday, 10 am — 5 pm; Saturday, 10 am — 6 pm; Sunday, noon — 5 pm

Winery tours: By appointment

Public tastings: Free

Additional features: Nature walk through the vineyards to the Bay of Fundy tidal basin with its twice daily 30-foot tides

Jost Vineyards

Malagash, Nova Scotia
B0K 1E0
Telephone: (902) 257-2636
Toll free: 1-800-565-4567
Fax: (902) 257-2248

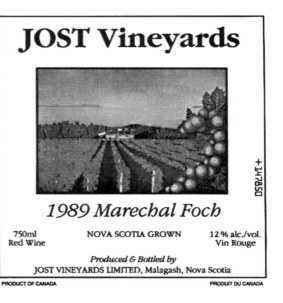

Hans Christian Jost took over the winemaking and management duties of the family business when his father, Hans, died in 1988. The older Jost, who had owned a winery in the Rhine Valley before emigrating to Canada in 1970, was a grape farmer who started Nova Scotia's second cottage winery in 1984. His son went to study winemaking at Geisenheim.

Jost Vineyards is located on the Northumberland Strait along what is called the "Sunshine Coast of Nova Scotia."

Hans buys in grapes from Ontario and Washington State to augment his needs. He still holds the record for Canada's most expensive wine — St. Nicholas Icewine 1985 from Riesling, Kerner and Bacchus grapes. It sold for $60.25 a half bottle.

Winemaker: Hans Christian Jost

Acreage: 65

Soil: Clay loam-loam clay with a reddish hue due to iron content

Grape varieties: Maréchal Foch, De Chaunac, Seyval Blanc, L'Acadie and Geisenheim clone 6493-4, Baco Noir, Vidal, Muscat

Production: 35,000 cases

Winemaking philosophy: "Our goal is to produce crisp, clean wines. The flavour of the wine should come from the fermentation of clean grapes and juice. The long, gentle growing season in Nova Scotia brings forth unique characteristics to our mostly early ripening grape varieties. Minimal movements of the juice and wine in the cellar maintain the full flavours of the wine. The wine is actually made in the vineyard with the cellar work purely assisting in bringing to the forefront the flavours that have been created in the vineyards."

Wines: NSLC: *White*—Riesling Gold Label, Habitant Blanc, Beaver Creek Geisenheim, Chablis, Christinenhof Cabinett, Comtessa, Kellermeister, Icewine

Red—Comtessa Red, Maréchal Foch, Terra Rosa

Rosé—Jost Blush

Winery store: *White*—House wines, Eagle Tree Muscat, Lakeville Muscat, Seyval Blanc, Avondale Blanc, Chardonnay, L'Acadie Blanc, Riesling Vidal, Sonnenhof Vidal

Red—House wine, Premium Oak-Aged Michurinetz, Premium Oak-Aged Maréchal Foch, Severnyi, Leon Millot, Cuvee Rouge, Nouveau Rouge

Speciality—Icewine, Glow Wine (mulled wine)

Fruit—Apple Blossom, Sweet Nectar, Sangria

Store hours: *Summer:* Daily, 7 days a week, 10 am — 6 pm; *Winter:* 10 am — 5 pm, closed Sunday

Winery tours: *Summer:* Daily, noon, 3 pm

Public tastings: During store hours

Recommended wines: Bacchus, Seyval Blanc, Oak-aged Maréchal Foch, Sangria

---

Sainte Famille Wines

Dyke Road (Exit 7 off
  Highway 101)
Falmouth, Nova Scotia
B0P 1L0
Telephone: (902) 798-8311
Toll free: 1-800-565-0993
Fax: (902) 798-9418
e-mail: s.corkum@st-famille@ns.ca
web site: www.st-famille@ns.ca

In 1989, Suzanne and Doug Corkum opened their tiny winery next to their vineyard (planted in 1979) on an old Acadian village site known as "la Paroisse Sainte Famille de Pisquit," a community settled in the 1680s. Today it's known as Falmouth — the gateway to the Annapolis Valley. The square wood building that acts as a winery and gift shop has a California feel to it. The shop promotes local products such as cheese, jams, crafts, etc.

Nevers, Limousin and Allier oak are used in the winemaking. An expansion is planned for 1999 that will include a barrel-ageing cellar, additional cellar space, café and deck. Currently, they have a large, covered gazebo for summer functions and an annual harvest wine festival the first week of October.

Winemaker: Suzanne Corkum

Acreage: 30

Soil: South-facing slope protected by the Avon River from extremes of temperature during the winter months

Grape varieties: Chardonnay, Riesling, Seyval Blanc, Ortega, L'Acadie, German hybrids, Michurinetz, Maréchal Foch, Baco Noir, Cabernet Franc

Production: 4,500 cases

Average tonnage crushed: 65 tonnes

Winemaking philosophy: "I prefer my whites to be clean and crisp with a good balance of fruit. My reds are barrel-aged using Nevers, Limousin and Allier oak. In 1994, we experimented using partial carbonic maceration on the Maréchal Foch which has given us a completely different style of wine for Foch. In future, once our expansion is complete, I plan to start to barrel-ferment some of our whites."

Wines: Own store: *White*—Dry Riesling, Johannisberg Riesling, Estate Seyval, Vidal Blanc, Chardonnay, Premium Chablis, Gold Bell (blended, semi-sweet), L'Acadie Blanc, Rosé

Red—La Paroisse Rouge (a bland of Maréchal Foch and Michurinetz)

Specialty—Acadianna Reserve barrel-aged port-style (Maréchal Foch)

Store hours: *January to March:* Monday to Saturday, 9 am—5 pm; *April to December:* Monday to Saturday, 9 am — 5 pm; Sunday, noon — 5 pm

Winery tours: *May to October:* Daily, 11 am, 2 pm (large groups are requested to book in advance)

Public tastings: During store hours

Recommended wines: Dry Riesling, Chardonnay, La Paroisse Rouge, Seyval

---

Telder-Berry Farm Cottage Winery

1251 Old Enfield Road	Telephone: (902) 883-8433
Nine Mile River, Route 14	Fax: (902) 883-1625
Hants County, Nova Scotia	e-mail: telwines@ns.sympatico.ca
B0N 1M0	web site:www3.ns.sympatico.ca/tel-wines/index.htm

Bob Telder and his son Brian began making fruit wines from raspberries, blueberries and strawberries grown in their 20-acre U-pick farm. The "wines" are fermented in a newly constructed 2,200-sq. ft. facility, which opened on July 1, 1993. The products are made without additives in dry, off-dry and sweet styles. Visitors can see the operation.

Winemaker: Jackie Woodworth

Acreage: 20

Soil: Sandy loam

Fruit wines: Strawberry, Blueberry, Appleberry, Cranberry, Cranberry Apple, Apple-Chablis Style, Pear, Saugnia, Strawberry, Winter Wine, Cherry

PRINCE EDWARD ISLAND WINERY

Rossignol Estate Winery

RR #4
Murray River,
Prince Edward Island,
C0A 1W0
Telephone: (902) 962-4193
Fax: (902) 962-4193

A winery in PEI! John Rossignol is an oenological pioneer. His winery, the first in the province, was established in 1995 in Little Sands along the South Shore of Kings County. You could call it Canada's only salt water farm winery. Rossignol's labels are the work of his neighbour, folk artist Nancy Perkins as well as by John himself. In order to protect tender vinifera vines from the harsh climate John has convinced former tobacco growers to use their greenhouses to grow grape vines.

Winemaker: John Rossignol
Acreage: 7
Soil: sandy loam
Grape varieties: (outdoors) Seyval Blanc, Marechal Foch, Valient; (in greenhouses) Ortega, Chardonnay, Lucy Koleman, Cabernet Franc
Production: 3,000 cases
Average tonnage crushed: approximately 24 tonnes grapes and fruit
Annual tonnage purchased: approximately 16 tonnes
Winemaking philosophy: "We look for clean, stable products with balanced acids and maximum fruit."
Wines: White—Selectionne Blanc, Seyval Blanc, Ortega Chardonnay, Late Harvest Ortega
Red—Selectionne Rouge (Marechal Foch), Pinot Cabernet, Valient
Fruit wines—Strawberry Rhubarb, Raspberry, Cider, Blueberry, Strawberry, Cranberry
Store hours: *June to October:* Monday to Saturday, 1 am – 5 pm; Sunday, 1 pm – 5 pm
Winery tours: self-guided or conducted by appointment
Public tastings: charges donated to charity

Recommended wines: Pinot/Cabernet, Seyval, Strawberry Rhubarb

NEWFOUNDLAND WINERY

Markland Cottage Winery

Bond Road, Box 98
Whitbourne, Newfoundland
A0B 3K0
Telephone: (709) 759-3003
Fax: (709) 759-2086
e-mail:
markland@nf.sympatico.ca
web site: www.netfx.ca/markland

Dr. Rodrigues took over a decommissioned cottage hospital on the Avalon Peninsula, 50 miles west of St. John's, to open his fruit winery in 1994. Wines are made from local wild berries, blueberries, ligonberries and cloudberries. They also make wines from farm grown fruit: strawberries and plums from Newfoundland and raspberries from Nova Scotia. Since summer 1998 the winery has been certified Kosher (COR 530). They are also in the implementation stage of ISO 9002. The winery has a capacity of 25,000 cases per year.

Winemaking philosophy: "We are a proud Newfoundland company dedicated to producing world class exotic wines using primarily Newfoundland berries. We are committed to continuously improving our wines and levels of service by encouraging education, innovation, personal and corporate loyalty, and growth."

Wines: Semi-sweet Blueberry, Dry Blueberry, Ligonberry, Barren's Blend (60 per cent blueberry and 40 per cent ligonberry), Cloudberry, Strawberry, Raspberry, Plum

ICEWINE

$\mathcal{C}$anada is becoming recognized as one of the world's best producers of Icewine. Ontario is the most prolific source of this gift of winter to the wine lover; virtually every winery in the province produces the honeyed nectar on an annual basis.

Inniskillin gave this fact global recognition at Vinexpo 1991 in Bordeaux when it won the Grand Prix d'Honneur for its Vidal Icewine 1989 — one of only 19 such medals out of 4,100 entries. The message was further driven home when Stonechurch won a Grand Gold Award at Vinitaly, Verona, in 1994 for its 1991 Vidal Icewine, and Reif in 1995 for its Vidal Icewine 1993. Since then, Ontario Icewine has regularly won gold at international competitions.

Canada is, in fact, the world's largest producer of this vinous rarity. Ontario alone produces 15,000 to 20,000 cases. (Small amounts are made in British Columbia, Québec and Nova Scotia.)

Icewine, or *Eiswein* as the Germans call it, is the product of frozen grapes. A small portion of the vineyard is left unpicked during the September-October harvest and the bunches are allowed to hang on the vine until the mercury drops to at least -7º Celsius. At this frigid temperature the sugar-rich juice begins to freeze. If the grapes are picked in their frozen state and pressed while they are as hard as marbles, the small amount of juice recovered will be intensely sweet and high in acidity. The wine made from this juice will be an ambrosia fit for Dionysus himself.

Like most gastronomic breakthroughs, the discovery of Icewine was accidental. Producers in Franconia in 1794 made virtue of necessity by pressing juice from frozen grapes. They were amazed by the abnormally high concentration of sugars and acids which hitherto they had achieved only by allowing the grapes to desiccate on straw mats before pressing or by the effects of Botrytis Cinerea. (This disease is known as "noble rot"; it afflicts grapes in autumn usually in regions where there is early morning fog and humid, sunny afternoons. A mushroom-like fungus attaches itself to the berries, puncturing their skins and allowing the juice to evaporate. The world's great dessert wines such as Sauternes, Riesling Trockenbeerenauslese and Tokay Aszu Essence are made from grapes afflicted by this benign disease.)

It was not until the middle of the last century in the Rheingau that German winegrowers made conscious efforts to produce Icewine on a consistent basis. However, they found they could not make it every year since the sub-zero cold spell has to last for several days to ensure that the grapes remain frozen solid during picking and the lengthy pressing process which can take up to three days or longer. Grapes are 80 per cent water, and when this water is frozen and driven off under pressure as shards of ice, the resulting juice will be miraculously sweet. A sudden thaw causes the ice to melt, diluting the sugar in each grape.

This means that temperatures for Icewine are critical. In Germany, the pickers must be out well before dawn to harvest the grapes before the sun comes up. Some German producers even go so far as to rig an outdoor thermostat to their alarm clocks so as not to miss a really cold morning. But in Ontario there is no need for such dramatics. The winemakers can get a good night's sleep secure in the knowledge that sometime between November and February our climate will afford them a stretch of polar temperatures. As a result, Ontario Icewine is an annual event and as predictable as the turning maples. Sometimes the cold comes early, as it did in 1991. On October 29, in British Columbia, Hainle Vineyards, CedarCreek and Gehringer Brothers were able to pick frozen grapes for Icewine when temperatures plunged to -13° Celsius.

Not all grapes can make Icewine. Only the thick-skinned, late-maturing varieties such as Riesling and Vidal can hang in there for the duration against such predators as gray rot, powdery mildew, unseasonal warmth, wind, rain, sugar-crazed starlings — and the occasional Ontario bureaucrat. The very first attempts at producing Icewine in Canada on a commercial basis were sabotaged by bird and man. In 1983, Inniskillin lost its entire crop to the birds the day before picking was scheduled. Walter Strehn at Pelee Island Vineyards had taken the precaution of netting his vines to protect them from the feathered frenzy. Some persistent blue jays, however, managed to break through his nets and were trapped in the mesh. A passing bird-fancier reported this to the Ministry of Natural Resources whose officials descended upon the vineyard and tore off the netting. Strehn not only lost $25,000 worth of Riesling grapes to the rapacious flock but, to add insult to injury, he was charged with trapping birds out of season — using dried grapes as bait! Happily, the case was dropped, and with the grapes that were left Strehn managed to make 50 cases of Riesling Icewine 1983.

Since those days, more and more Ontario wineries have jumped on the Icewine bandwagon. Their wines literally sell out the moment they reach the stores. To avoid disappointment, customers have been encouraged to reserve their bottles while the grapes are still hanging on the vine. In Japan, these wines sell for up to $200 the half bottle (the price in Canada ranges from $29.95 to $50). Note: Many Ontario wineries are making a second pressing of their Icewine grapes to produce a more affordable and less concentrated dessert wine they call Select Late Harvest or Winter Wine.

But whenever you leave grapes on the vine once they have ripened, you are taking an enormous gamble. If birds and animals don't get them, mildew and rot or a sudden storm might. So growers reserve only a small portion of their Vidal or Riesling grapes for Icewine — a couple of acres at most.

A vineyard left for Icewine is really a very sorry sight. The mesh-covered vines are completely denuded of leaves and the grapes are brown and shrivelled, hanging like so many bats from the frozen canes. The wrinkled grapes are ugly but taste wonderfully sweet — like frozen raisins.

The stems that attach the bunches to the vine are dried out and brittle, so a strong wind or an ice storm could easily knock them to the ground. A twist of the wrist is all that is needed to pick them.

Usually there is snow and a high wind which makes picking an experience similar to Scott's trek to Antarctica. When the wind howls through the vineyard, driving the snow before it, the wind-chill factor can make a temperature of -10° Celsius seem like -40°. Harvesting Icewine grapes is a torturous business. Pickers, fortified with tea and brandy, brave the elements for two hours at a time before rushing back to the winery to warm up.

And when the tractor delivers the precious boxes of grapes to the winery, the hard work begins. Since the grapes must remain frozen, the pressing is done *al fresco* or the winery doors are left open. The presses have to be worked slowly, otherwise the bunches will turn to a solid block of ice yielding nothing. Some producers throw rice husks into the press which pierce the skins of the grapes and create channels for the juice to flow through the mass of ice. Sometimes it takes two or three hours before the first drop of juice appears. These drops will be the sweetest since grape sugars have a lower freezing point than water.

Roughly speaking, one kilogram of grapes will produce sufficient juice to ferment into one bottle of wine. The juice from a kilogram of Icewine grapes will produce one-fifth of that amount and less, depending on the degree of dehydration caused by wind and winter sunshine. The longer the grapes hang on the vine, the less juice there will be. So a cold snap in December will yield more Icewine than having to wait for a harvest date in January when there will be a crop weight loss of 60 per cent or more over normal harvest weights.

The oily juice, once extracted from the marble-hard grapes, is allowed to settle for three or four days and then it is clarified of dust and debris by racking from one tank to another. The colourless liquid is cold and will not permit fermenting to start, and a special yeast has to be added to activate that process in stainless steel tanks. Because of the very high sugars, the fermentation is very slow and can take months. But when the amber wine is finally in bottle, it has the capacity to age for a decade or more.

While Germany may be recognized by the world as the home of Icewine, ironically the Germans cannot make it every year. Canadian winemakers can. Klaus Reif, the winemaker at Reif Winery, has produced Icewine in both countries. While studying oenology at the Geisenheim Institute in Germany, he worked at a government winery in Neustadt in the Pfalz. In 1983, he made his first Icewine there from Riesling grapes. Four years later he made Icewine from Vidal grapes grown in his uncle's vineyard at Niagara-on-the-Lake. "The juice comes out like honey here," says Klaus. "In Germany it drops like ordinary wine."

Robert Mielzynski, formerly of Hillebrand Estates, who had also studied winemaking in Germany, agrees: "A lot of the Icewines I tried in Germany were less viscous and more acidic that ours. We get higher sugar levels."

Neustadt is around the 50th latitude; Niagara near the 43rd. Although our winters are more formidable than those of Germany, we enjoy a growing season with more sunshine hours, resembling that of Burgundy. Our continental climate in southern Ontario gives us high peaking temperatures in July, the vine's most active growing month. This means that grapes planted in the Niagara Peninsula can attain higher sugar readings than in Germany, especially late-picked varieties because of dramatic fluctuations of temperature in the fall season. "From September on," says Karl Kaiser, winemaker and co-owner of Inniskillin, "the weather can turn cold and then suddenly warm up again. This warming-freezing effect makes the grapes dehydrate. Loss of water builds up the sugars. In January we have very windy weather that further desiccates the grapes so that when we harvest the Icewine we have very concentrated flavours."

So when the thermometer takes that first plunge of winter, think of the grape pickers down on the Niagara Peninsula, bundling up to harvest the grapes of frost. Bat-brown and shrivelled like the old men of the mountains, those bunches hanging precariously from the vine may look unappetizing but the lusciously sweet wine they produce is worth all the numb fingers and raw cheeks. At least the vintners have machines to press the juice from the frozen berries; they don't have go through the procedure in their bare feet!

The credit for the first Canadian Icewine must go to the late Walter Hainle in B.C. who began making it from Okanagan Riesling in 1973 for family and friends. Tilman Hainle confesses that the family has one bottle of the 1974 vintage left ("in a glamorous Lowenbräu bottle with matching cap and homemade label"). "We have made Icewine every year since then, except in 1977. It is possible to make Icewine every year in B.C., although the picking dates and quantities vary widely. Usually, we have to wait until November or December for the appropriate temperatures."

Up until 1983, the Hainles used Okanagan Riesling to make their Icewine, but since then they have used a number of varieties including Traminer, Pinot Noir and Riesling. "We felt that Riesling is the most successful variety for our Icewine," says Tilman. Over the years their sugar levels have varied from 33 Brix to 57.5 Brix. A range of 35 to 40 Brix is typical at a temperature of -9° Celsius to -12° Celsius.

The quantity of juice the Hainles got from their frozen grapes ranged from as little as 20 litres in 1990 to as much as 580 litres in 1987. "The maximum quantity for us is limited by our mechanical capability — one press will yield from 150 to 300 litres of juice, and we don't have the crop or the time to do more than one press." Tilman Hainle is also reluctant to produce large quantities of Icewine. The wine, he contends, is a curiosity which garners a lot of publicity, chiefly because of its rarity and because it is not sufficiently cost efficient to warrant making it a large part of their portfolio.

REFERENCES

Magazines covering Canadian Wines

Winetidings
Wine Access

Web sites

Canadian Wine:

www.canwine.com/index.html

Ontario:

www.wineroute.com
www.tdg.ca/ontag/grape/

British Columbia:

www.bcwine.com
www.communityinternet.com/obo/winery.html
www.bcbiz.com/okdirect/okwineinfo_main.asp

Quebec:

www.cam.org/~lav-lec/vignes.html

About the Author

Tony Aspler is the most widely read wine writer in Canada. He has been active on the international wine scene since 1964. As a consultant and wine judge, he makes frequent trips to the vineyards and wine fairs of Europe and the new world and is recognized as the leading authority on Canadian wines.

His previous books include *Travels with my Corkscrew, Aligoté to Zinfandel, Tony Aspler's Wine Lover's Companion, Tony Aspler's Dinner Companion* (with Jacques Marie), *Cellar and Silver* (with Rose Murray), *The Wine Lover Cooks* (with Kathleen Sloan) and *Tony Aspler's International Guide to Wine*. He contributed to Jancis Robinson's *Oxford Companion to Wine* and the *Larousse Encyclopedia of Wine*.

He is the editor of *Winetidings Magazine* and has been the *Toronto Star's* wine columnist since 1980. He writes for a variety of wine magazines around the world.

Tony Aspler is a member of the North American Advisory Board of the Institute of Masters of Wine and the organiser of the annual airOntario Wine Awards competition.

He has also created a wine writer detective, Ezra Brant, who has appeared in *Blood Is Thicker Than Beaujolais, The Beast of Barbaresco* and *Death on the Douro*.

Reach Tony at his website www.tonyaspler.com.